The Underground Guide to Teenage Sexuality

The

UNDERGROUND
Guide to
Teenage Sexuality

An Essential Handbook
for Today's Teens and Parents

SECOND EDITION

Michael J. Basso

Fairview Press
Minneapolis

Published by Fairview Press, 2450 Riverside Avenue, Minneapolis, Minnesota 55454. Fairview Press is a division of Fairview Health Services, a community-focused health system affiliated with the University of Minnesota and providing a complete range of services, from the prevention of illness and injury to care for the most complex medical conditions. For a free current catalog of Fairview Press titles, please call toll-free 1-800-544-8207. Or visit our Web site at www.fairviewpress.org.

Library of Congress Cataloging-in-Publication Data
Basso, Michael J., 1964-
   The underground guide to teenage sexuality / Michael J. Basso.— 2nd ed.
         p. cm.
Includes bibliographical references and index.
Summary: Presents facts about human sexuality, including anatomy, sexually transmitted diseases, contraception, homosexuality, and sexual intercourse.
   ISBN 1-57749-131-9 (trade pbk. : alk. paper)
   1. Sex instruction for teenagers. [1. Sex instruction for youth.] I. Title.
   HQ35.B337 2003
   613.9'071—dc21

                                                                2003002490

First edition: 1997
Second edition: 2003
Printed in the United States of America
07   8 7 6 5

Cover by Laurie Ingram Design (www.laurieingramdesign.com)
Interior by Dorie McClelland, Spring Book Design

TO MY TEACHERS:

Signora Teresa Latorre—who showed me there is more to education than reading, writing, and arithmetic.

Dr. Michael Perlin—who supported my idealism and guided me toward the path of living life as a limitless individual.

TO MY STUDENTS:

You are my inspiration and the reason for my perspiration. Thanks for all the laughs, experiences, and all the lessons you have taught me. Most of all, thank you for letting me into your lives.

This book is dedicated to you.

THANKS TO:

My illustrators, Abraham Jauregui and Clayton Henry, for their special talents, hard work, and patience throughout this entire production. You made the difference.

SPECIAL THANKS TO:

Pop—for his wisdom and support.

Gram—for making me her special prince from day one.

Mom and Dad—for providing me with endless opportunities to learn from their lives; although sometimes painful, always valuable and necessary.

Frank—for being a bro and helping me survive through the not-always-dishwasher-safe plastic fork days.

Marisa dolly—for being my favorite person in the whole wide world.

Leslie, mi amore—for giving me the strength to endure and a love I have never known before. You truly are beautiful. Te amo.

Contents

Sexual Anatomy

I love driving my car. I'm a good driver too, contrary to what my mother thinks. I can still remember the first time I got behind the wheel of a car. I was going to drive—yes!

My driving teacher was by my side going through what seemed to be a long and unnecessary delay of my driving time. "Michael, this is the brake. When you step on the brake, it slows the car. This is the accelerator. When you step on this, it makes the car go into motion."

So it went for the ignition, the turn signal, lights, windshield wipers, horn, and mirrors. I thought, "Argh! Let's go already!" But let's not forget the safety belt. After what seemed to be the entire afternoon, we finally got down to business. I couldn't believe that I was the one cruising the streets.

My driving teacher had an odd way of letting me know when I was driving a bit too fast: he would stick his head out the window and scream to my friends, "Where's the fire?" Other than that it was a great experience.

Could you imagine driving a car without knowing and understanding the basic equipment that operates it? Could you drive without knowing what causes the car to go, stop, or turn? In driver's education we learn some basic parts of car anatomy that allow us to drive. Brakes, accelerator, steering wheel, turn signal, speedometer, and the fuel gauge, to name a few, become part of our working car anatomy vocabulary.

Cars are similar to our bodies, except we are far more complex and get much better mileage. Before we can go any further into this "sexual operating manual," we need to understand the basics. Just like your first driving experience, the sexual basics may at first appear to be unnecessary, but you will soon discover that we cannot discuss sexuality without knowing these basics.

I will keep it brief and to the point. Realize that this could be presented in a very detailed manner, but for your purposes, this will put you ahead of the pack without making you crazy with a lot of information that you probably don't need right now. By understanding the basics, you will be able to understand the more complex topics of sexuality.

The Male Reproductive System

PENIS: The external (outside the body) organ that the male urinates (pees) with. This is also the part, when it is hard and erect (stiff), that goes into a partner's body during vaginal, oral, and anal intercourse. The long cylinder part is the shaft. The cone-shaped end is the glans.

SCROTUM: A pouch of skin that holds the testes.

TESTES: (Sometimes called the testicles, "balls," or "nuts.") These look like two separate, oval-shaped eggs. They produce sperm (the male egg).

EPIDIDYMIS: The comma-shaped part that sits on top of each testicle. The epididymis receives sperm (the male egg) from the testicle and helps the sperm grow and develop.

VAS DEFERENS: The tube that carries the sperm to the urethra. The vas deferens starts at the epididymis and ends at the ampulla.

AMPULLA: The enlarged end of the vas deferens. This is where the sperm are mixed with different fluids to make semen.

SEMINAL VESICLE: A baglike structure that produces a mucuslike fluid. Seminal vesicle fluid mixes with sperm and helps keep the sperm healthy.

PROSTATE GLAND: The gland located below the urinary bladder. The prostate gland produces a thin, milky fluid that also mixes with the sperm to help protect them.

COWPER'S GLANDS: Two small, round glands below the prostate gland. The Cowper's glands produce a mucuslike fluid that lubricates the end of the penis before intercourse. This fluid also helps protect the sperm.

URETHRA: The tube that carries urine (pee) or semen to the outside of the body. The urethra leads from the urinary bladder to the urinary opening at the tip of the penis.

URINARY OPENING: The slit at the end of the glans penis where urine (or semen) comes out of the body.

ANUS: The opening between the buttocks (butt) where feces (poop) comes out.

SPERM: The male egg. Technically, sperm is short for spermatozoa. This is a cell that joins with the female's ovum to make a baby. A healthy sperm looks like a tiny tadpole.

SEMEN: The fluid that comes out of the penis when the male ejaculates. Semen is made of sperm, seminal vesicle fluid, prostate gland fluid, and a small amount of Cowper's gland fluid.

The Male's Sexual Anatomy
(Inside View)

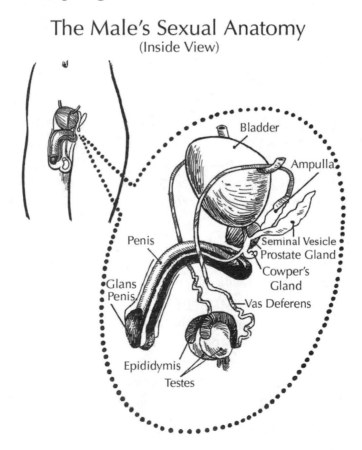

EJACULATION: Semen coming out of the penis.

ERECTION: When the penis becomes harder and larger.

FORESKIN: The loose skin around the glans penis and the upper shaft of the penis. In uncircumcised males, this skin also covers the glans penis.

How big should the penis be? (How do I compare?)

I can't think of a time when the human male did not constantly worry about the size of his penis. Your dad asked this question; your grandfather, great-grandfather, and just about every male in history probably did, too. In fact, you probably wonder how you compare to other guys in the size department. Regardless of how old you are, when given the chance you might check out the size of another guy's penis. No, this doesn't mean you're homosexual (gay); you just want to know how you measure up. Let's see if this sounds familiar.

SCENE #1: After gym class or practice, you're hot, sweaty, and dirty. It's time to hit the showers. You're with the guys and one of two things will happen:

1. Without anyone noticing, you quickly glance down at another guy's penis for a quick comparison.

2. You want to see if the other guy's penis is bigger than yours, but force yourself not to look and keep your head straight up or down. You don't want anyone to catch you looking around because they might think you're a little weird. Right?

SCENE #2: Another "showering with the guys" phenomenon is the "quick shower" or the "corner shower."

While resisting the urge to compare, you may also be embarrassed about one of the other guys noticing that your penis is not quite as large as his. Having that news hit the front page of the school newspaper is not what you were hoping for in school popularity.

So, what do you do? Like the Flash—rinse, suds, rinse, and you're out of there. Or you stand in the corner, slightly bent at an angle to block any clear view of what you own. Fairly effective, I might add.

Do you think that older men are much different? No, no.

SCENE #3: Next time you are in a public bathroom at a restaurant or ball game, notice where the grown men are looking: straight ahead or straight down. They don't want to get caught looking around, either. People might think they're weird.

Let me reassure you that looking at another guy's penis does not mean you are gay. It's almost like looking through bodybuilding magazines. If you look at bulging biceps, triceps, or any other muscle, this does not mean that you're gay.

To put your mind at ease, the average size of the adult erect penis is about six and a half inches. The size of the penis when it is flaccid (soft) makes no difference in how big it will be when it becomes erect.

Although the average adult erect penis is about six and a half inches, penises do come in different sizes and lengths. I honestly don't know what the *Guinness Book of World Records* has as the longest penis, but penis size can vary from a few inches less or more than six inches. A guy's body (including his penis size) will continue to grow and develop until about the age of twenty-one. Regardless of whether you have a three-inch or nine-inch penis, the good news is that when it comes to sex (intercourse) it doesn't matter what size your penis is, contrary to what guys joke about.

The reason why the size of the penis makes very little difference when it comes to "satisfying" a female sexual partner during intercourse is that only the first two inches or so of the vagina are sensitive. (The vagina is about five inches long.) The back few inches of the female vagina are not very sensitive. So even if the male has a three-inch penis, the female will only feel the penis with the first two or so inches of her vagina.

What is a circumcised penis?

When the male is born, there is a loose fold of skin covering the glans penis. This fold of skin is called the foreskin. Within the first few days after birth, the parents may have a circumcision performed. The circumcision cuts away the foreskin that covers the glans penis.

Gentlemen, if you look at your penis and there is no foreskin covering your glans penis and you see a cone-shaped end—guess what? You've been circumcised!

What type of penis do you have?

Uncircumcised

An uncircumcised penis has the foreskin covering the glans penis.

Circumcised

A circumcised penis has had the foreskin removed, exposing the glans penis.

Why would someone want to do that to the little guy? Originally it was done for religious reasons if you were Jewish or Muslim. Today, doctors encourage circumcision to prevent infections that sometimes occur in uncircumcised males. When the foreskin is not removed by circumcision, a thick secretion called smegma may accumulate under the foreskin. If the smegma is not washed away when the male takes a shower, it will begin to smell and may even develop into an infection on the glans penis. However, as long as the male pulls back the foreskin and washes the glans penis, he shouldn't have any more problems than a circumcised male. Whether you are circumcised or not, the penis works the same way.

What is an erection?

For those of you gentlemen who have not had the experience of finding yourself sitting in class, at the dinner table, on a date, or at the beach with an erection for no apparent reason at all, you can consider yourselves lucky. However, some of you have already discovered that erections can occur at just about any time, anywhere, and particularly when you would least like them to. Those are the breaks, fellas.

An erection, of course, is when the penis becomes hard and larger than when it was flaccid (soft). The penis is not made of bone and does not have any bone inside of it. It becomes erect when blood rushes into it, causing it to swell.

How an Erection Happens

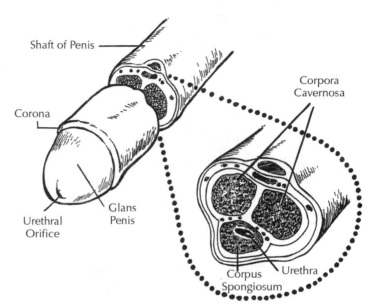

Shaft of Penis

Corona

Urethral Orifice

Glans Penis

Corpora Cavernosa

Corpus Spongiosum

Urethra

Blood rushes into the spongy tissue of the penis (the corpora cavernosa and the corpus spongiosm) and causes the penis to become hard and erect.

Think about it this way: A dried-out sponge looks a bit shriveled up. Watch what happens to the size of the sponge if you put it under running water. As water fills the sponge, it will swell and become larger.

Your penis is filled with erectile tissue. This tissue works a lot like a sponge. When blood rushes into the penis, it fills all the tiny spaces in the erectile tissue (just like water in a sponge), and the penis becomes erect.

While the blood is filling the erectile tissue, blood flow away from the penis slows down. This also causes an erection. Why is this important? Have you ever woken up with an erection or found yourself with a potentially embarrassing bulge as you sat in history class? If your urinary bladder is full (if you need to use the bathroom), this will put pressure at the base (or bottom) of the penis and slow the blood flow away from the penis. If blood isn't leaving the penis, guess where it stays? That's right! The penis fills with blood and becomes erect. The way you sit in class may also put pressure at the base of the penis and cause an erection.

There are other reasons why erections occur besides needing to use the bathroom or sitting incorrectly. In case you haven't already guessed, sexual stimulation also causes erections. Males can get erections from being touched, seeing something sexually exciting, or fantasizing. Sometimes it doesn't take much.

It is normal to have erections. Erections can occur quickly (in seconds) or slowly (in minutes) and many times a day. If you have many erections a day, there is little for you to worry about. There is no damage done by having repeated erections. Erections are normal bodily functions.

What are sperm?

Sperm, more appropriately known as spermatozoa, look like little microscopic tadpoles. Sperm are the male cells that unite with the female egg (ovum) to cause a pregnancy (start the development of a baby). The sperm carry the father's genetic material, which will help decide the baby's hair and eye color and what the baby will look like. The mother's ovum carries her genetic material, which also helps determine what the baby will look like.

Sperm production starts when the male begins puberty (about ages ten to sixteen) and may continue for the remainder of his life. Males produce millions of sperm every day. Sperm are so small that you can fit more than 100 million in just one drop of fluid.

Once the sperm are part of semen, they begin to move around or "swim" by moving their tails back and forth, just like tadpoles.

The male body produces millions of sperm because sperm are kind of wimpy. They are sensitive to temperature changes in the testes, acid in the urethra, and the not-so-friendly environment in the female's vagina. (The vagina is also very acidic.) So many sperm are produced because so many are destroyed. In fact, when the male ejaculates, his semen may have as many as 600 million sperm in it. Only about fifty sperm may actually ever reach the female's ovum.

The scrotum is very important in determining the health and number of sperm. Have you ever gotten out of a cold pool and noticed that your scrotum

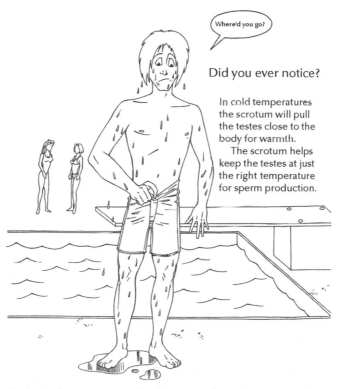

was shriveled up and your testes had somewhat disappeared? Have you ever taken a hot shower and noticed that your scrotum was loose and your testicles hung lower than usual? Well, your scrotum is a type of thermostat. It regulates the temperature of your testes. To produce healthy sperm, your testes must be about five degrees cooler than your body temperature. This is why your testes hang outside your body instead of being inside your body like the female's ovaries. If your testes are too cold, the scrotum will tighten and pull the testes closer into the body where it is warmer. If your testes are too warm, the scrotum will loosen and bring the testes further away from the body, where it is cooler. This really is a super system.

Wearing tight underwear or pants could cause the male to have low numbers of sperm in his semen. With tight pants, the scrotum cannot move the testes to cooler temperatures because the pants are pressing the testes too close to the body. The result may be a lower number of sperm. To avoid this, wear comfortable underwear and pants and avoid wearing anything too tight for long periods of time.

What is semen?

Semen is the fluid that comes out of the penis when the male ejaculates. It may look cloudy, milky, or yellowish and may be slippery or sticky.

Semen is made up of sperm, prostate gland fluid, seminal vesicle fluid, and Cowper's gland fluid. It is important to remember that the male does not ejaculate just sperm; he ejaculates semen. Semen is more than sperm, and sperm is only a part of semen. Semen contains sperm, and sperm are in semen. So next time you hear someone say that the male ejaculates sperm, you can tell them that the male ejaculates semen that contains sperm.

Should I do anything to make sure my sexual organs stay healthy?

Yes! Guys, pay attention here: There is something called testicular cancer, which is a type of cancer that develops and spreads on the testes.

If a male develops testicular cancer, he may need to have part of one testicle, an entire testicle, or both testes removed. If the cancer is not caught in time, it may spread to other parts of the body and even cause death. The tricky part about testicular cancer is that it doesn't cause any pain and often the male feels fine and doesn't know he has it. It may appear while you're in your twenties, thirties, or older, so you need to check for it each and every month, just in case.

Girls have a breast self-exam that they need to do each month to check for cancer, and guys have a testicular self-exam that they need to do each month. A testicular exam is simple, painless, and quick.

Once a month, while you're taking a hot shower and your testes are hanging lower and away from your body, gently feel around each testicle for small lumps. Use your fingertips and thumb and feel all the way around each testicle. Once you've checked each testicle, you're done!

This testicular self-exam is so simple that in less than a minute a month you can help protect your testes and your life.

Warning! Each semester when we go over this in class, at least one guy will be waiting in my parking space the next morning as I drive into the teacher's parking lot. With sweat pouring from his body, feeling certain that he'll need to have his testes removed, he explains how he felt a lump on each of his testes.

Guys, before you go crazy, if you look at a picture of the testes, you will see a comma-shaped part on top of each testicle. This is the epididymis. When you feel behind the top part of each testicle, you may actually feel the spongy epididymis. In fact, if you take your time, you may even feel something like a vein in that area. That finlike object is probably your vas deferens. (Pretty good, eh?) These things are supposed to be there.

What you are looking for is something like

Monthly Testicular Exam

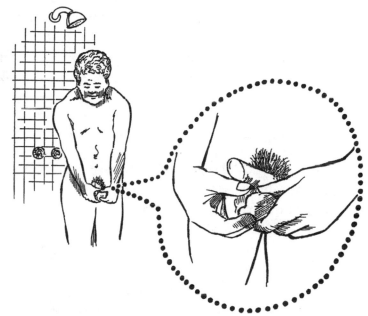

After a warm shower, each testicle should be checked for lumps that may be cancerous

a tiny, smooth bump on each testicle. If you have ever banged your head, a few minutes later you can feel a hard lump on your head. A cancer lump on your testicle feels the same way, except it is much smaller.

If you do feel something like that on either testicle, see a doctor. The problem won't go away by itself. Even though it is unlikely that you will develop testicular cancer during your teen years, why take a chance? Remember what you have to lose!

You can have the doctor do a testicular exam for you, but it seems like a lot of time and money each month for something you can check yourself.

Guys, listen up. This is something you need to do. Just like brushing your teeth and taking showers, testicular exams are another way of taking care of your body.

If you had your dream car, you would probably put a lot of time into tuning it up and doing the things that need to be done to keep it running smoothly. Well, your body is a much more complex and important machine. Take care of it!

A tip for the brave guy who cares: If you have the guts, remind your dad, uncle, and brothers (in their teens or older) to make sure that they are taking care of themselves, too. Educate them if necessary.

Should males do breast exams?

No and yes. Males don't usually have fatty breast tissue, but many young guys in their early teens develop something called gynecomastia, which is a big word for breast development in males. Gynecomastia in males is just a buildup of fatty tissue in the nipple area. This is normal and almost always goes away as you get older. Gynecomastia is just one of those "growing up" things that seem to happen just to drive you crazy.

Sometimes, in both males and females (usually in the early teens), a small lump develops underneath the nipple. This happens frequently and is rarely a problem. If you feel this lump, you shouldn't worry, but see a doctor and get it checked out just to be sure. Like gynecomastia, this lump during the teen years usually fades away as you get older.

For more information on breast or testicular cancer, call the Cancer Information Service (1-800-422-6237). This organization will be able to send you more information about cancer or answer any questions you may have.

Male Sexual Anatomy: Putting It All Together

To get an idea of how these parts work together, we should probably start with the testes and move up from there.

The male has two testes that are shaped like small eggs. The testes are held outside of the body in a pouch of skin called the scrotum. In most males the left testicle hangs a little lower than the right one, but if that is not the case with you there is no need to worry. The testes produce the male eggs or cells called sperm, which can fertilize the female's egg, called the ovum.

After the sperm are produced in the testes, they will move into the epididymis so they can mature and grow stronger. If the male is becoming sexually excited, the mature sperm will leave the epididymis and travel up the vas deferens to the ampulla, which is like a mixing room. While the sperm are in the ampulla, the seminal vesicles produce a fluid and send it into the ampulla to be mixed with the sperm. The prostate gland will also secrete a fluid that will be mixed with the sperm and seminal vesicle fluid.

Meanwhile, the Cowper's glands have made a fluid to coat the urethra and protect the sperm as they travel by. Semen will travel through the urethra and out the urinary opening when the male ejaculates.

The Female Reproductive System

The female's sexual anatomy can be a bit more complex and confusing, not only to males but to the owners themselves—yes, females, too. And understandably, I might add. With the male, his external parts are right out in the open where he and everyone else can see them. The female, however, has all of her genitalia (external sexual parts) covered with hair and at an angle so they are difficult to see. In fact, the young ladies in class (the guys, as well) usually get very quiet when we start talking about their genitals. I can see in their faces, they are saying to themselves, "I didn't know that." The truth is, ladies, unless you have sat up while you were lying down and placed a mirror between your legs, you have probably never seen what is down there. If you have not done this yet, the diagram on page 14 will show you exactly what I mean so you can check for yourself.

If you were to place the mirror between your legs, you would see something that resembles the diagram. I say resembles because each vulva (vulva is the term we use to describe the female's genital area) is different.

Your face has two eyes, a nose, mouth, and eyebrows, yet your face is different than everyone else's. Everyone has the same parts on their face, yet everyone looks different. Each vulva has the same parts as every other vulva, but each vulva looks different. My point is that if you see something in the mirror that looks different than what is in the diagram, don't worry; you are not a teenage mutant.

Here is a description of the female reproductive system:

MONS VENERIS: The hairy part on top. The mons veneris is the layer of fatty tissue that covers the pubic bone.

CLITORAL HOOD: A piece of skin that covers the clitoris. The clitoral hood may cover all of the clitoris or just part of it.

CLITORIS: A small, very sensitive piece of skin. The clitoris does not seem to have any real purpose except to tingle and feel good when it is touched.

URETHRAL OPENING: The opening where the female urinates (pees) from. When the female urinates, the urine comes from this opening, not from the vagina.

VAGINAL OPENING: This is the opening to the vagina. This is the place where the erect penis goes during intercourse and where the female's menstrual flow (period) comes out. This is also where the baby comes out during birth.

Each female has a different looking vulva.

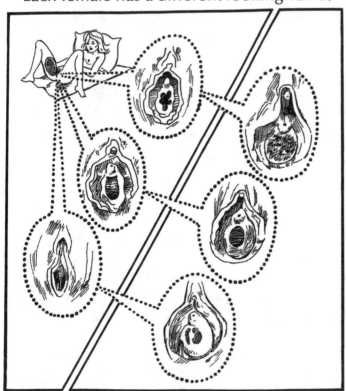

HYMEN: A piece of skin that may partially or totally cover the vaginal opening. The hymen is sometimes referred to as the "cherry" in slang terms. The common myth is that if the female's "cherry is broken," it means that she has had intercourse and is no longer a "virgin." This is not true. In reality, a separated hymen has nothing to do with virginity. Usually the hymen is separated while the female is growing as she exercises or plays. Nobody can tell if a female has had sex based on whether her hymen is separated or not. Unless the female is pregnant or has an STD (sexually transmitted disease), even a doctor cannot tell if the female has had sex. Sometimes a parent will tell his/her daughter that the doctor will see if she has had sex by looking to see if the hymen has been separated, but this is just a scare tactic.

BARTHOLIN'S GLAND OPENING: Creates a small amount of fluid that may help moisten the vagina.

ANUS: The place between the buttocks (butt) where feces (poop) comes out.

LABIA MINORA: Small, inner lips around the opening to the vagina.

LABIA MAJORA: Large, outer lips around the labia minora.

The female has even more parts on the inside of her body. These are the parts that make up the internal reproductive system of the female:

OVARIES: Two oval-shaped objects that hold the female's ova (eggs).

OVUM: The tiny female egg that joins with the male sperm

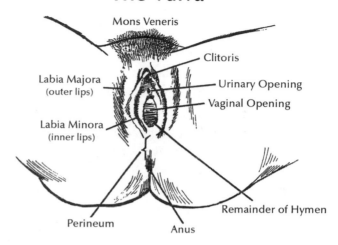

The Female Reproductive System
The Vulva

Mons Veneris

Clitoris

Labia Majora (outer lips)

Urinary Opening

Vaginal Opening

Labia Minora (inner lips)

Remainder of Hymen

Perineum

Anus

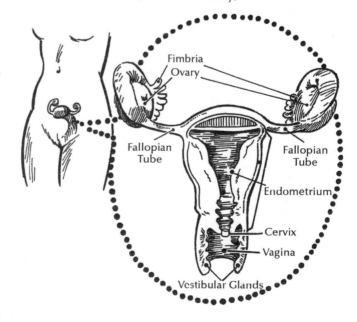

The Female Reproductive System
(inside the body)

Fimbria

Ovary

Fallopian Tube

Fallopian Tube

Endometrium

Cervix

Vagina

Vestibular Glands

to cause a pregnancy. The ovum carries all of the female's genetic material, which, along with the male's sperm, will help determine what the baby looks like.

OVARIAN FOLLICLES: Small compartments that make up the ovaries and hold each individual ovum until it is ripe and ready to be released.

FALLOPIAN TUBES: Thin tubes (about as thick as a single piece of hair) that carry the ova (ova is plural for ovum) to the uterus.

FIMBRIA: Small fingerlike extensions on the ends of the Fallopian tubes.

UTERUS: A hollow, pear-shaped, muscular organ where a fetus develops. The uterus sheds a layer of tissue that comes out about once a month in the form of a menstrual period.

ENDOMETRIUM: The first layer of tissue in the uterus that gets thick and falls off during menstruation.

CERVIX: A small opening between the uterus and the vagina.

VAGINA: The passageway leading from the uterus to outside the body.

BARTHOLIN'S GLANDS: Two small glands located within the walls of the vagina that secrete a small amount fluid.

Female Sexual Anatomy: Putting It All Together

Now that you have a basic idea of what the female's parts are, let's see how they work together.

The female's ovaries are made of tiny sacs or compartments called ovarian follicles. Inside each ovarian follicle is an ovum. Each month when the female is menstruating, she will secrete hormones that will cause one of the ovarian follicles to break open and release the ovum inside of it. The ovum will be gently pulled into the Fallopian tube by the fimbria. The tiny ovum will continue to travel up the Fallopian tube toward the uterus.

In a few days, if the ovum is not fertilized by the male sperm, it will break apart, along with the first lining of the uterus (the endometrium), and will begin to come out of the female's body. The dissolved endometrium and ovum will travel through the cervix and out of the vagina, and the female will see this come out as her "period" or "menstrual bleeding."

What About Breasts?

The breast is made of milk glands (also called mammary glands) surrounded by fatty tissue. Each breast has a larger darkened area of skin called the areola, which is sensitive to touch and temperature. Toward the center of the areola is a round nipple, which is also sensitive to touch and temperature.

The main purpose of the female's breasts is to provide her newborn baby with nourishment after birth, but in the United States, breasts have become an obsession. We have glorified the breast and turned it into a sexual object for people to stare at, admire, desire, and use as a way of measuring how attractive a female is. In all fairness to guys, it should be mentioned that not all people in America feel this way and certainly not the majority of people from other countries. When you watch TV, look through magazines, or stroll through the halls at school, however, it seems that females with bigger breasts seem to get the most attention. This is not always true, but unfortunately it often seems that way.

Girls and guys all have certain parts of the body that they are attracted to. It might be the legs, butt, broad shoulders, muscles, washboard stomach, hips, hands, eyes, hair, and face, to name just a few of the more popular areas. But it seems that in the United States, the female breast holds some special value.

In most other countries, the breast does not have the same degree of importance as it does in the United States. For example, in some parts of Europe, females often go to the beach topless, exposing their breasts for everyone to see. In these areas, a topless female is as shocking as a topless male is in the United States—it's no big deal.

The Breast

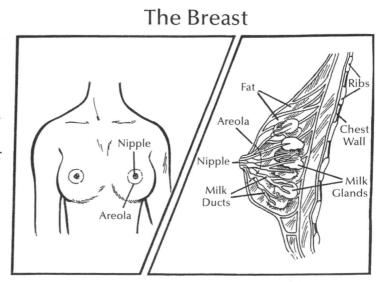

When European women come to the United States' beaches to vacation and take their tops off, they quickly discover that they are as popular as movie stars. Men stop to stare and smile, point fingers, and make all kinds of silly comments. Usually at this point, females will put their tops back on because they're not used to this kind of treatment.

Even many of today's most popular movie, TV, and singing performers have gained fame and fortune not necessarily through any special talents, but by exposing their breasts and bodies to get the attention of the American public. Can you think of anyone who has done this?

Now, this can sometimes present a problem. If you're growing up in the United States and people are placing such importance on the "bigger is better" breast theory, how would females with smaller breasts feel? Many times my female students will come to me feeling embarrassed and frustrated because they are not developing as fast or as much as they would like.

Breasts come in all sizes and shapes. Just like every other part of the body, breasts can be small, medium, large, flat, oval, round, pointy, perky, droopy, with small or large areolae, and on and on. Regardless of the size and shape of the breasts, they work the same way. As far as sensitivity, whether the breasts are big or small, they are equally sensitive to touch and excitement.

Breast size and shape change all the time. You will soon discover this on your own, but because you are in your teens, you may think that the breasts you see in the mirror will stay the same forever. No ma'am! Breast shape and size change during different stages in your life. As a teen, you may have growth spurts every few years. Many of my fourteen- to seventeen-year-old girls worry that they have stopped developing. But you don't ever stop changing. Here are some examples:

MONTHLY: Depending on the female's menstrual cycle, there will be slight changes in the shape and sensitivity of the breasts. Edema (water retention/ bloating) may also cause some changes in the size and shape of the breast.

TEEN YEARS: During the teen years, the breasts are often firmer and smaller than they will be in the adult years.

ADULT YEARS (AGES TWENTY TO FIFTY): During the adult years, the breasts may change in shape and size depending on weight loss or weight gain. Because the breast is made up mostly of fat, when the female gains weight, some excess fat will be stored in the breasts, changing their shape. The opposite happens if the female loses weight.

DURING PREGNANCY: The female's breasts will usually grow much larger during pregnancy. The mammary glands are starting to fill with fluid in preparation for breastfeeding, and additional fat is being stored, making the breasts look almost swollen. After pregnancy and breastfeeding, the breasts will return to about the same size and shape as they were before the pregnancy, although sometimes they may have a little different shape.

OLDER YEARS (OVER AGE FIFTY): During this time of life, the breasts and skin in general may start to lose elasticity. If you've ever had a pair of socks with worn-out elastic bands, you've

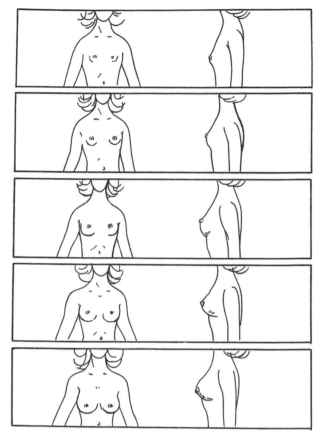

The size and shape of the breasts can change as the female grows up.

noticed that they stay stretched out and have a different shape than they had originally. Skin and breasts tend to do the same thing. Sometimes the breasts may droop or hang.

Breast pills/creams/exercises don't work. Sales people have been selling special pills and creams for years. Remember that people trying to make money will say and do almost anything to sell their products. Breast pills, vitamins, minerals, creams, massagers, and exercisers don't work. If they did, everyone would be using them to get the kind of breasts they want. It doesn't matter if it's a special blend of herbs, vitamins, and minerals; amino acids; liquids from deep underground; or movie-star endorsed growth enhancers taken from the breasts of 44D-cup women, please realize that this is a sales game. Salespeople will often say anything to get the money from your pocket and into their bank accounts. Save your money and your time. Don't buy these things, regardless of how tempting they may appear.

Your breast size has already been determined for you by your parents' genetics. Although this is not always true all the time, you can expect to have breasts about the same size as your mom's or grandmother's. This will, of course, vary with how much body fat you have compared to Mom or Grandma and the different stages of life that each of you are in. Try to remember that your body, including your breasts, will continue to grow and develop until about age twenty-one.

What are stretch marks and how can I get rid of them?

Stretch marks are small lines that sometimes appear on different parts of the body, often the breasts. They are harmless and usually go away on their own.

Stretch marks appear when a particular body part, like the breast, grows larger and the surrounding skin stretches to accommodate the increase in size.

Some females feel that putting special creams, lotions, or oils on the stretch marks will make them disappear faster, but there isn't any proof that this is true.

Is there something wrong if my breasts are not the same size?

Many times the left breast is a bit larger than the right one. If one breast is bigger than the other, don't worry. In fact, sometimes one leg is longer than the other, one foot can be bigger than the other, and the same is true for arms and hands. Nobody will notice this except you, so relax.

What is a breast self-exam?

A breast self-exam checks the breasts for lumps that might be an early sign of breast cancer. Breast cancer is painless as it develops. Many thousands of women die each year of breast cancer.

Many of these lives could be saved if more women performed a breast self-exam each month. The good news is that more women are starting to perform breast self-exams each month, and fewer women are dying from breast cancer each year.

The Monthly Breast Self-Examination

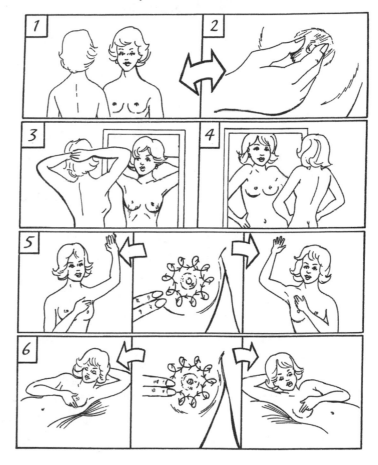

At what age should I start doing a breast self-exam?

Most doctors recommend that females start doing breast self-exams once menstruation starts. Even though breast cancer is extremely rare before the age of thirty, you should begin doing a breast self-exam now to get into a lifelong habit. It is also important that you become as familiar with your breasts as possible. If you are familiar with your breasts, you will know what is normal for you and what is not.

When should I do a breast self-exam?

You should do a breast self-exam once a month, right after your period has stopped. If you perform a breast self-exam just before or during your period, you may notice little lumps or hard areas that are caused by your menstrual cycle and think that these might be signs of cancer.

The best time to do your breast self-exam is a day or so after your period has stopped and your breasts are more likely to be back to normal.

How do you do a breast self-exam?

It's easy! What you are basically doing is looking for any strange changes in the shape of your breasts and feeling for any lumps or other changes.

Before you begin, relax. Here's your big chance to be your own doctor. Take your time during your breast exam. You should do your breast exam in a room with a mirror and have a pillow or folded towel with you (like in your bedroom or bathroom).

STEP 1: Stand in front of a mirror with your arms at your sides. Look at each breast for any dimples (like little dents in a car, or dimples when some-body smiles), bumps, rough skin, or sores.

STEP 2: Gently squeeze each nipple and look for any discharge or fluid coming out.

STEP 3: Continue to stand in front of the mirror and put your hands behind your head. Once again, look at your breasts for any dimples (dents), bumps, swelling, or other changes in the shape of your breasts that look different from the month before.

STEP 4: Still standing in front of the mirror, put your hands on your hips. Bring your shoulders and elbows forward, and, at the same time, press your hands into your hips. While you're doing this, you should again look for any dimples, bumps, swelling, or changes in the shape of your breasts since the previous month.

STEP 5: Raise your left arm above your head. With your right hand, begin to feel your left breast for any lumps underneath the skin or inside the breast tissue. A lump will probably feel very small, hard, or thick. If you imagine feeling for a small jellybean inside of a plastic bag filled with Jell-O, you can get an idea of what you're supposed to be feeling for. Use the soft, cushiony part of your fingertips and press softly into the breast. Make little circles around the entire breast with your fingertips. Start at the top of the breast and move along the outer sides of the breast, slowly working your way toward the areola and nipple. Be sure to check the entire breast. This includes the area between the breast and the armpit, underneath the breast (if you have larger breasts), and the areola and nipple. Once you have completely checked your left breast, raise your right arm above your head, take your left hand, and do the same thing to your right breast.

STEP 6: Lie down on your back and place a pillow or folded towel underneath your left shoulder. Raise your left arm over your head again. Just like in the previous step, softly press your fingertips into your left breast and make small circles around the entire breast, working your way around to the areola and nipple. Once you have completely checked the left breast for lumps, switch the pillow or folded towel to your right shoulder, raise your right arm above your head, and examine your right breast.

You check the breast when you are lying down because the breast tissue is put in a different position, which may expose a lump.

Ta-da! That's a breast self-exam. There are slightly different ways of doing breast exams, but they are all very similar.

What should I do if I find a lump?

Don't panic. Once again, it is extremely rare for females under age thirty to have breast cancer.

Each breast has its own "feel," which may be lumpy or hard in certain parts. Quite often you will feel ligaments (tough strands of tissue), swollen tissue inside the breast, ribs, or the muscle underneath the breast. Don't freak out every time you feel something in your breast. When you feel something new in your breast that wasn't there the month before, that's when there may be some cause for concern. When in doubt, check it out. See your doctor and have her/him check you out to be sure.

The most difficult part of a breast self-exam is wondering about cancer every time you feel something. This is normal, but you should only become concerned when you find a new lump. This is why it is a good idea to start doing breast exams every month: so you can become familiar with how your breast normally feels. After many months of practice doing breast exams, you will be able to tell the difference between "normal" lumps and "strange" lumps.

If you do find a lump in your breast, it does not mean you have cancer. Most lumps are not cancer. If you do feel a new lump; see dimpling, bumps, swelling, rough skin, or sores on your breasts, areolea, or nipples; or have a fluid come out of your nipples when you are not pregnant or breastfeeding, then a quick trip to your doctor will answer any concerns you might have.

What if fluid is coming out of my nipples?

Fluid or discharge should not come out of your nipples. The only time that fluid should come out of a female's nipples is in the last few months of pregnancy or when she is breastfeeding.

If fluid does come out of your nipples, you should see your doctor. It might be caused by a hormone imbalance, but see your doctor to find out for sure.

The Vagina (An Owner's Manual)

The vagina is a passageway leading from the uterus to the outside of the body. It allows menstrual flow to leave the body, receives the erect penis during intercourse, and is known as the birth canal because the baby travels through it during birth.

One way that you can think of the vagina is to picture a balloon. If you can imagine a deflated, flat balloon (with no air in it), you can see that it has an open end, which allows air to go in or out. When there is no air inside the balloon, the inside walls of the balloon touch each other. When you blow air into the balloon, it stretches and expands to hold the air. When you let the air out, the balloon returns back to normal.

The vagina is a lot like the balloon. At one end is an opening (the vaginal opening) that can allow things to go in or out. The vagina is normally flat like a deflated balloon, which allows the inside walls to touch. Like the balloon, the vagina also stretches and expands to fit around whatever goes into it or leaves it. The vagina can expand and stretch to fit around a tampon, the erect penis during intercourse, and even a baby's head and body during childbirth. Once again, like the balloon, the vagina will go back to its normal size when there is nothing inside it. It will not stay stretched.

There is one big difference between the balloon and the vagina, however. The vagina has another small opening at the other end (just like a tunnel). It is much smaller than the vaginal opening and is about the size of a pencil (the thickness or diameter, not the length). This opening is called the cervix. The cervix is the opening that leads to the uterus. The cervix lets the menstrual flow (period) come out of the uterus. The cervix also allows the male's sperm to leave the vagina and enter the uterus after he ejaculates.

Other things you might like to know about the vagina: it is about five and a

The Functions of the Vagina

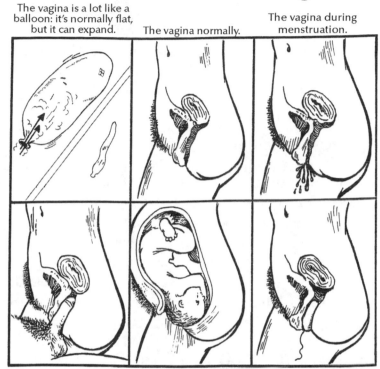

The vagina is a lot like a balloon: it's normally flat, but it can expand.

The vagina normally.

The vagina during menstruation.

The vagina receives the erect penis during intercourse.

The baby will pass through the vagina during birth.

The vagina with a tampon inserted.

half inches long and feels like the inside of your mouth. The inside walls of both the vagina and the mouth are covered with a soft skin called the mucosa lining. During intercourse, the lining in the vagina (along with the Bartholin's glands) produces a moist fluid that is used as lubrication. This lubrication makes insertion of the penis into the vagina during intercourse easier and smoother. The vagina does this all on its own. Ladies, you may notice this lubrication as a wetness when you are stimulated or aroused.

Vaginal lubrication does not flow or "ejaculate" out of the vagina. It feels like drops of slippery fluid on the vagina.

Can the male's penis fit through the cervix during sex?

No, the cervix is too small and doesn't stretch like the vagina. The only time the cervix stretches on its own is when a baby is being born. Then it stretches to allow the baby to enter into the vagina.

Does the female urinate from her vagina?

No. Most guys (and many girls) think that urine (pee) comes out of the vagina. Close, but not quite. In the diagram on page 15, you can see a small slit above the vaginal opening. This is the urinary opening. This is where the female urinates from—not the vagina. Remember, the female urinates from the urinary opening and menstruates (has her period) from her vaginal opening. These are two different places.

To put your mind at ease, the male cannot make a mistake during intercourse and put his erect penis into the urinary opening instead of the vaginal opening. The urinary opening is just a small slit and will not allow the penis to enter it. You might not be able to see the urinary opening even if you hunted for it.

Should the vulva have a smell?

Sometimes the vulva has a slight odor or "fragrance," which is quite normal and natural. This natural odor cannot be detected by anyone other than maybe the female herself.

If there is a strong odor along with a discharge (fluid coming out) from the vagina, this may mean that the female has a yeast infection. Yeast infections are quite common and are usually easy to treat. For further information on yeast infections, you can read more about them in the STD (Sexually Transmitted Diseases) chapter, or talk to your parents, a trusted adult, a drugstore pharmacist, or your doctor.

Does the vagina need any type of special care?

Most vaginas are pretty much low maintenance. What this means is that if you do a few simple things regularly, there isn't much that can go wrong.

WASHING: This sounds simple to most of us, but believe it or not, some people just do not like to wash. There are no special tricks here. The vulva, just like every other part of the body, sweats during the day. There are harmful bacteria that would love to grow around and into the vagina if given the chance. So, at least once a day, make sure that you shower or take a bath. Washing the whole outer vulva area with warm water and mild soap will do nicely. You do not need to clean inside the vagina. The inside of the vagina has its own natural cleaning system that pushes out any fluids and bacteria. One last point: keep the soap as plain as possible. Perfumed soaps may irritate the vulva. After you wash, be sure to dry the vulva area well. And yes, it is okay to shower when you are having your period!

FRONT TO BACK: What this means is each time you finish going to the bathroom (#1 or #2, pee or poop, whatever you know it as), clean yourself with toilet tissue from the front to the back. You want to keep the vaginal opening as clean as possible. If you do not clean yourself from front to back, you may find yourself with an infection.

DRY, DRY, DRY: Sometimes, much to your horror, the vulva develops an odor. This is caused by bacteria. When bacteria grow in wet or moist areas and react with air, they give off an odor, just like on other body parts. Relax; no one can smell this odor except maybe you when you get undressed, or if for some strange reason someone were to put their nose down there and try to smell you when you were undressing. So, before you even think of it and run off to the store, there is no need for any special vulva deodorant or perfume, even though many people (companies and salespeople) will try to make some money selling you that stuff. What you should do is keep the vulva as dry as possible throughout the day. After gym class, even if you don't have showers at your school, clean the vulva with water and then dry, dry, dry. If for some reason you are not able to clean the vulva, or even if you are, put on a fresh pair of underwear. Any time your underwear is sweaty or moist, like after gym class, athletic practice, or just after school, you should put on a fresh pair of underwear. The nice thing about underwear is that you can put a pair in a school bag/knapsack/purse and it doesn't take up too much room. (If you're easily embarrassed, be careful not to put them in a place where they might pop out!)

NO NEED TO DOUCHE: For you guys reading this, and you young ladies who have heard of douching but don't have the slightest idea of what a douche is or does (other than it appears to make women run through open grassy fields in commercials), let me explain.

When a female douches, she uses a fluid and tries to "clean" or "flush out" her vagina. Imagine going in the backyard with a bucket. If you held the bucket upside down and tried to clean the inside of it with water from a garden hose, you can see what douching is like. The female takes a plastic bottle and "squirts" sterile fluid into her vagina. In the "old days," women used to use water, sometimes mixed with a spoonful of vinegar. Today, women go to the store and buy specially shaped bottles filled with water mixed with perfumes and other chemicals. There is a problem with this age-old practice, though: Even though some bacteria can cause infection, believe it or not, other bacteria are good. In fact, females have normal, healthy bacteria in the vagina that help to destroy other germs that can cause vaginal infections. When a female douches frequently (more than twice a month), she runs the risk of "flushing out" and destroying these beneficial bacteria. When the good bacteria are destroyed, other germs can grow and multiply and cause an infection. The bottom line is that even though douching is an old practice, unless a doctor recommends that you douche, it isn't necessary and is possibly harmful.

What is a pelvic exam?

A pelvic exam is a checkup of the female's reproductive organs that can detect any number of problems from minor infections to cervical cancer.

Your regular medical doctor or a gynecologist can perform a pelvic exam. (A gynecologist is a doctor who specializes in the health of the female's reproductive organs.) Whatever type of doctor you choose, she/he should be someone that you are comfortable with. She/He should explain beforehand everything that will happen during the exam and answer every question you may have.

When should a female begin getting pelvic exams?

Most doctors recommend pelvic exams for females who are sexually active; over eighteen years old; experiencing pain in their pelvic area; or having menstrual problems, itching, or a strong-smelling vaginal discharge.

If you don't fall into one of these groups, then you probably don't need a pelvic exam. But if you do fit into one of these groups, you should have a pelvic exam.

What happens during a pelvic exam?

The first thing the doctor will do is talk with you and get to know you a little bit. For simplicity's sake, let's assume that your doctor will be a woman. She will start to ask you questions about your health and then explain everything that she will be doing.

You will be asked to go to the bathroom and urinate (pee) to empty your urinary bladder. After that, you will change out of your clothes and into a not-so-sporty cloth or paper gown/robe. Most doctors will perform a breast exam to check for any lumps that might be a problem. If you are unsure of what you are looking for when you do your breast self-exam, or if you have felt something that you weren't sure about, now would be a good time to ask the doctor some questions.

Once the breast exam is finished, she will ask you to lie down on your back on the table and put your knees up. There may be something called stirrups that the doctor will ask you to put your feet into. Stirrups just help keep the legs apart.

At this point you might start to feel a bit shy or weird. This is normal and understandable. This is certainly not an everyday event for most females. Try to remember that for the doctor this is as normal as asking people to open their mouths and say "aaah." She has done hundreds of pelvic exams and she just wants to make sure that you are healthy.

The doctor will put on some thin gloves and check your vulva for any signs of irritation or other problems. The doctor should tell you what she is doing and seeing as she checks you, but if she doesn't, ask! Asking questions usually helps ease the tension.

The doctor will put a lubricant on her glove and insert one or two of her fingers into your vagina. At the same time, she will gently push down on your abdomen and pelvic region with the other hand. The doctor is feeling the outline of your uterus, ovaries, and vagina with her fingers. This shouldn't hurt, but it may feel uncomfortable. If for some reason there is pain or you want to take a break, tell the doctor to stop. She will understand. Remember, she has to go through this every year, too.

The doctor may also want to check your organs from another angle and will remove one of her fingers and place it into the rectum (butt). It will feel like you need to go to the bathroom, but that feeling will stop as soon as she removes her finger. Now would be a good time to remind yourself that pelvic exams are necessary and that the doctor really is there to help you. Sometimes a little humor helps.

The doctor will remove her fingers and then tell you that she is about to insert the speculum. The doctor should show you what a speculum is and how it works before the examination begins. A speculum is a piece of plastic that holds open the walls of the vagina so the doctor can see your cervix and perform a Pap test (also called a Pap smear).

In a Pap test, the doctor takes cells from your cervix and looks at them under a microscope to see if any of them are cancerous. To do this, the doctor will take a long cotton swab or spatula and, as the speculum holds open your vagina, she will gently brush against your cervix with the swab. She will put the cells on a glass slide and send it to a laboratory to be examined. The doctor will then remove the speculum.

There shouldn't be any pain involved during this exam, but if you are feeling uncomfortable, speak up.

How much does a pelvic exam cost?

The cost varies. You might be able to find a clinic that charges you just a few dollars, but for something like a pelvic exam, your first priority should be to find a doctor with whom you feel comfortable. The cost can range from just a few dollars to more than one hundred dollars.

Do you need a parent's consent to have a pelvic exam done?

This varies from state to state. If you find a doctor you like, ask what her/his policy is regarding pelvic exams. Pelvic exams are not usually a big deal. If you feel you would rather not have your mom or dad know, that is entirely up to you, but often your mom might be able to suggest a good doctor.

Is there something wrong if it hurts when I urinate and I need to urinate all the time?

If you have painful and frequent urination, there could be any number of causes. If you have engaged in sexual intercourse, this could be a sign that you have been infected with a sexually transmitted germ, or you could have a urinary tract infection. You should see a doctor soon to find out what the problem is for sure.

What is a urinary tract infection?

A urinary tract infection (also called cystitis) is an inflammation or swelling of the urethra and urinary bladder. Certain bacteria find their way into the urethra and start to multiply. The bacteria will spread to the urinary bladder, where the female may feel discomfort or pain. Unfortunately, urinary tract infections are common in females.

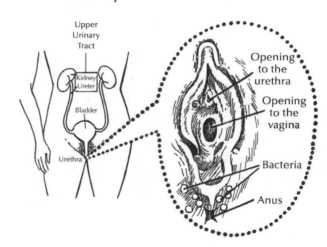

Urinary Tract Infections

Painful urination may be caused by a urinary tract infection. Bacteria from the anus can find their way into the urinary opening and cause a urinary tract infection.

How can I avoid urinary tract infections?

Any activity that brings these bacteria close to the urinary opening should be avoided. One common cause of urinary tract infections is cleaning your vaginal area the wrong way. If you wipe yourself after you defecate (poop) from back to front, instead of front to back, you bring these bacteria up from the anus close to the urinary opening, where they may find their way in.

Intercourse may not necessarily cause the bacteria to get close to the urinary opening, but if bacteria are already there, sex seems to help "push" these bacteria into the urinary bladder. The risk of getting a urinary tract infection increases greatly when a female engages in intercourse.

Remember, to help prevent urinary tract infections, clean yourself from front to back, urinate before and after intercourse (if you are sexually active), and drink plenty of water.

Are urinary tract infections curable?

Yes. You can try to solve the problem yourself by drinking water or cranberry juice, and often the infection will clear itself. If the situation does not improve or worsens, then you may need a trip to the doctor, or at least a telephone call if this happens often. Once the doctor has determined that you have a urinary tract infection, she/he will probably prescribe a few days' worth of antibiotic pills.

Who's the boss when I go see the doctor?

YOU ARE! You (or your insurance) is paying the doctor for her/his professional advice and treatment, so she/he works for you. Ask questions and be sure that your doctor treats you courteously and with sensitivity. If she/he doesn't, then you can file a complaint with her/his boss, with the insurance company, or state medical board. There are a number of search engines on the Internet that you can use to find agencies with which to file a complaint. Most important, if a doctor, nurse, or any member of the medical staff is doing something that you feel is wrong or inappropriate, tell him/her to stop, and leave if you need to.

Menstruation: It's That Time of Life!

It's that time of life! First the breasts start to appear and then hair on the vulva (pubic area) begins to appear. The hips may get a bit wider and rounder, and then, one day, menarche—otherwise known as your first period—appears. Welcome to the club, young ladies. If you're not a member yet, not to worry, there's no rush. Menstruation is surely not too far away. In fact, each female between the ages of nine and sixteen will begin to experience what her mother, grandmother, great-grandmother, and every female since the beginning of time has experienced.

I hope, though, you won't be as scared about what is happening to your body as your mom or other females may have been. I'll tell you what's true and what isn't, and I'll try to keep it simple.

Menstruation has many different names. When a female says, "I've got my period," it means that there is a small amount of blood trickling from her vagina. Don't worry; this is supposed to happen. In fact, this will usually happen about once a month.

Menstruation is a sign that the female is physically capable of becoming pregnant and possibly having a baby. When the female begins menstruating, her reproductive system is going through many changes. When a female has her period (that trickling of blood from her vagina), that is just one of the many things that happens during her menstruation or menstrual cycle. The female doesn't see what happens during her menstrual cycle, except for her period.

The menstrual cycle is actually a series of things that happen. Just like the numbers 1, 2, 3, 4 are a series of numbers, the menstrual cycle is a series of changes in the female's body, one of them being her period. There is more to the menstrual cycle than having a period, though. Let's go through the series of changes as they occur in the female.

STAGE I: During this stage, blood begins to trickle from the female's vagina. What is actually happening is that the uterine lining (a thin layer of skin on the uterus) begins to fall off and come out of the vagina in the form of blood. Yes, that blood you see is actually skin from your uterus that has fallen off and is coming out through your vagina. Don't worry, though; the

The endometrium begins to trickle out of the vagina

The endometrium begins to grow back. At the same time, the ovum starts to ripen in the ovary.

The ovum bursts out of the ovary and travels into the Fallopian tube. The endometrium is thick again.

The ovum travels toward the uterus. The endometrium is thick in case the ovum becomes fertilized by the male sperm. If the ovum is not fertilized, the endometrium begins to fall off and the menstrual cycle starts again.

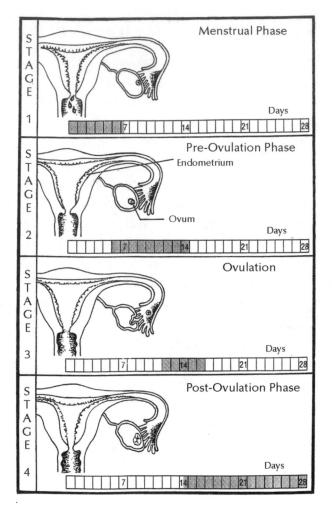

endometrium (skin on the uterus) grows back each month and is part of what normally happens during the menstrual cycle. This stage is known as the menstrual phase.

STAGE 2: During this stage, the uterine lining begins to grow back, and an ovum (the female's egg) is beginning to be released from the female's ovary. This stage is known as the preovulation phase.

STAGE 3: This is when the ovum (female egg) bursts out of the ovary and begins its journey into the Fallopian tube toward the uterus. Also by this time, the endometrium (uterine lining) has grown back and is beginning to get thick. This stage is known as the ovulation phase.

STAGE 4: During this stage, the ovum is traveling toward the uterus. The endometrium is thick, just in case the ovum becomes fertilized by the sperm (the male egg). This stage is known as the postovulation phase.

If the female engages in intercourse (sex) with a male, and the male ejaculates his semen into her vagina, his sperm may fertilize (join with) her ovum. If this happens, the female will be pregnant. The fertilized ovum will attach itself to the nutrient-rich endometrium where it will grow.

If the ovum is not fertilized (joined) with a sperm, then there is no use for the endometrium (uterine lining), so it will begin to fall off again, and the female will have her period—bringing us back to stage 1 and the beginning of a new menstrual cycle. (By the way: the unfertilized ovum simply breaks apart and trickles out with the uterine lining.)

That is the menstrual cycle in its most basic form. Each month, that series of stages takes place inside the female. It can take anywhere from twenty days to thirty-five days for this cycle to be completed. The average menstrual cycle takes about twenty-eight days. This means that every twenty-eight days, the female will have her period again. Keep in mind, though, that the length of time for each cycle can vary from person to person and from month to month. Anywhere from twenty to thirty-five days is normal.

If you understood these basics of what happens during the menstrual cycle, congratulations! You know more than most people. Here are a few common facts and myths about menstruation that should be simpler to understand.

Facts and Fiction about Menstruation

Since the beginning of time, misinformation about menstruation has been passed on from generation to generation. Unfortunately, these untruths often cause confusion or fear.

Listed here are a few of the questions that are often asked about menstruation.

What happens each month when a girl has her period (menstruates)?

The lining of the uterus comes off and comes out in the form of blood.

Every month the lining of the uterus prepares to receive a fertilized egg and help it develop into a baby. When pregnancy does not occur, the uterine lining (endometrium) is not needed, so it is shed (comes out) from the uterus and the vagina. This is called menstruation.

At what age should a girl begin to menstruate?

A girl can begin menstruating anytime from about the age of nine to sixteen years old. Many girls begin menstruating around age twelve or thirteen. If the female has not started menstruating by age sixteen, she should get a checkup from her doctor.

Do males menstruate?

No, males do not menstruate. Only females menstruate.

Sometimes there is a small amount of whitish stuff on my underwear. What is that?

Sometimes there may be a small amount of whitish discharge that either the vagina or cervix produces and pushes out of the body. The vagina or cervix produces this discharge to keep itself healthy. If you find that you sometimes have this discharge, don't be alarmed. This is normal. If you don't find this whitish discharge on occasion, this is all right, too. The only time that you should be concerned is if there seems to be quite a bit of this discharge, it is yellowish in color, it has an unpleasant odor, and it is itchy. This may indicate that you have a yeast infection or, if you have engaged in unprotected intercourse, that you have become infected with a sexually transmitted disease (STD). You should get help from your doctor.

What causes irregular periods?

Menstruation is caused by hormones. A great deal of stress, emotional ups and downs, extremely low body fat, or a change in lifestyle can all create hormone imbalances, which may cause the female to skip her period for months at a time. Usually as a female gets older, her menstrual cycle becomes more regular. If you have missed a period and are usually very regular, consult your doctor to determine if there is a problem and put your mind at ease.

Is there a way I can get my periods to become more regular?

Yes. If you visit a doctor, she/he may prescribe birth control pills. One of the side effects of birth control pills is regular menstrual cycles and periods.

How long should a period last?

Two to seven days is normal. If a female has her menstrual bleeding for more than seven days, she should visit her doctor for a checkup.

How much blood should I lose during my period?

The average is about two ounces, or four to five tablespoons over the entire period. If you ask some females how much blood they lose during their period, you may hear answers that make it seem like it's by the quart. This is not true. No one on record has died from menstruating too much. The human body has about eight pints of blood in it. You don't need to worry about losing too much blood. If your menstruation is heavy, you should make sure that you are eating foods that are high in iron or are taking an iron supplement to prevent anemia.

What is PMS?

PMS stands for premenstrual syndrome. PMS is estimated to affect about 20 to 40 percent of all menstruating females. Females who suffer from PMS may have sore breasts, cravings for sweet or salty foods, headaches, tiredness, depression, and water retention (bloating). The female may feel these symptoms for seven to ten days before she has her period. Usually females between the ages of twenty-five and forty-five experience PMS. What causes PMS is unknown, therefore ways of preventing PMS are also unknown. Treatments for the symptoms are listed in the following pages.

Why do you feel cramps during your period?

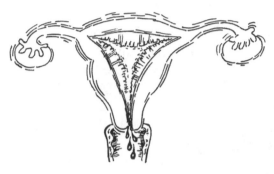

The uterus contracts like any other muscle. Soon it becomes tired and begins to cramp.

Why do I feel cramps before or during my period?

Menstrual cramps are just like other muscle cramps. When a muscle contracts too long or too hard, it tightens and causes discomfort or pain. Menstrual cramps occur because the uterus contracts as it sheds the uterine lining (the endometrium). Eventually, the uterus grows tired and begins to tighten and cramp, causing some pain and discomfort. To relieve some of this discomfort, a pain reliever with ibuprofen may help relax the cramp. (Be sure you don't have bad reactions to ibuprofen or any product you take.) Another way of possibly helping to reduce this discomfort is to participate in a regular exercise program throughout the month. Heating pads and warm baths might also be soothing.

What can I do to relieve the backaches that I sometimes have before or during my period?

Usually ibuprofen and exercising at least three to five times per week, every week (not just during your period), will help relieve some of this discomfort. Again, heating pads and warm baths might be helpful.

Is there anything I can do if I experience breast tenderness and bloating?

Here is where diet plays a major role. A diet low in salt will usually minimize water retention and breast tenderness. Keep in mind that even with a low-salt diet, there may still be a small amount of bloating and breast tenderness.

What if I don't ever menstruate?

Some girls may not menstruate until about sixteen years. If you reach your sixteenth birthday and have not menstruated yet, you may have a condition called primary amenorrhea. A visit to your doctor will help ease your concerns. The doctor will give you a few simple tests and let you know what should be done.

Should I bleed from my vagina at any other time than during my period?

You shouldn't really be bleeding from your vagina at any time except during your period. If you do "spot" or bleed at other times, even though there is little reason to be alarmed, you should see your doctor to make sure everything is okay.

At what age will I stop menstruating?

The age a female stops menstruating varies just as much as when she starts menstruating. Some females may stop menstruating as early as thirty-five. Most women, though, begin what is called menopause sometime in their late forties to early fifties. Menopause is the term that is used to describe the time when the female's menstrual cycle and period begin the process of completely stopping. This is a gradual process that may take months to complete. Of course, when the female's menstrual cycle no longer takes place, she is not able to have any more children.

Pads or tampons—which are right for me?

Just before you have your period, you will want to use some type of menstrual protection so that your underwear or clothing does not get stained when your flow begins. Fortunately there are convenient, effective ways for a female to do this.

PADS: Pads (sometimes called "wings" or "rags") are thin and highly absorbent pieces of cottonlike material that soak up any menstrual fluid. They are placed on the inside of the female's underwear. There is a sticky side on the pad that adheres to the underwear. When she puts her underwear on, the smooth side of the pad covers the vulva. When the female's period begins, the trickles of blood will be absorbed into the pad.

Pads come in different thicknesses for different types of menstrual flow. Usually, "Regular" pads are for medium to heavy flow days, and "Super" pads are for very heavy flow days. With so many brands and types to choose from at the store, look at the drawings on the back of the box for what will work best for you.

Pads should be changed every few hours, so when you are at school, make sure you bring a few extra. Of course, it is certainly okay to shower or bathe each day while you are having your period.

An important note to remember about pads is that they are disposable but cannot be flushed down the toilet. Simply fold the pad and, if you have the original bag that it came in, put the pad back into the bag. Dispose of it in the trash. If you don't have the original bag, you can wrap the used pad in a few sheets of toilet paper and then dispose of it in the trash basket. If you flush the used pad down the toilet, it will block up the plumbing, which will probably get someone very upset!

Pads are easy to use and are quite effective; however, there are a few drawbacks. Pads may develop a slight odor if you don't change them throughout the day. (If you change them every few hours, you shouldn't have any problems.) Also, because pads are used on the outside of the body, the female cannot go swimming while using a pad. The pad will soak up water and become heavy, which could cause an embarrassing situation. If you find yourself at the pool or beach often, you may want to consider using a tampon.

Menstrual Pads

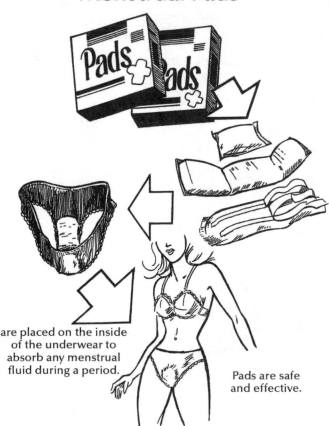

are placed on the inside of the underwear to absorb any menstrual fluid during a period.

Pads are safe and effective.

TAMPONS: Before tampons are explained, it should be mentioned that some people believe that if you use a tampon you are no longer a "virgin." This is one of those myths floating through our culture with no truth to it. A virgin is someone who has not engaged in sexual intercourse. Tampon use does not affect virginity. The only way a female can "lose her virginity" is by engaging in sexual intercourse.

Tampons are small tubes of cotton that are gently inserted into the vagina to absorb the menstrual flow. Just like pads, they are highly absorbent and effective. Also like pads, tampons come in different thicknesses and absorbencies. "Slender" tampons are for light to medium flow for younger females who may have a smaller vaginal opening. "Regular" tampons are also used for light to medium flow days, but are usually used by older females. "Super" tampons are used for medium to heavy flow days, while "Super Plus" tampons are used for very heavy flow. As with pads, there are many brands to choose from. While you are at the store, check each box to find a tampon that may work best for you.

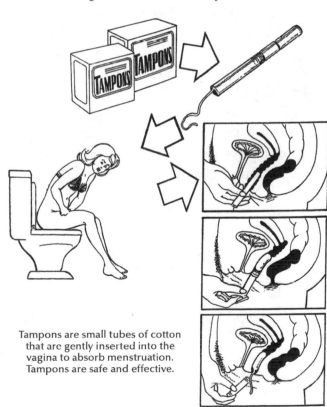

Using a tampon may be a bit more complicated than using a pad for some females. Some females feel uncomfortable or embarrassed about inserting tampons into their vaginas. If you are, don't feel bad; just use pads. Believe it or not, many females who are uncomfortable with tampons at first try them again months or years later and find that they fit more comfortably.

On each tampon box are directions that explain how to use and insert tampons. You

Tampons are small tubes of cotton that are gently inserted into the vagina to absorb menstruation. Tampons are safe and effective.

may use tampons with or without an applicator. One kind is not better than the other. Tampons without an applicator are simply inserted with your fingers. If your tampons come with an applicator, follow the directions on the box. You will probably want to see how the applicator works before you insert it into the vagina, so investigate! Push the end with the string in it into the larger tube. You will see a short, cotton tampon come out the other end. That is the part that will be placed into the vagina to absorb the menstrual flow. What is the string for? Just like pads, after a few hours the tampon will absorb all the menstrual flow it can hold and will need to be changed. Gently pull on the string and the tampon will slide out. Practice using the tampon until you know how it works.

When you use a tampon, most instructions on the box will tell you to get into a squatting position and gently insert the tip of the applicator or tampon into the vagina. It is important that the applicator or tampon be pushed in at an angle toward your lower back and not straight up (the vaginal canal is at an angle, not straight up). Probably the biggest boo-boo that females make at first is not inserting the tampon far enough into the vagina. The tampon should be pushed past the muscles of the outer vagina. When will you know that you have inserted the tampon far enough? You should feel almost nothing! The string will hang outside the vagina, and you should not really feel the tampon inside the vagina. One of the nice things about using a tampon is that it is comfortable. If the tampon is inserted and it feels uncomfortable, it means that you have probably not inserted it far enough.

Advantages to using tampons over pads are that the female can go swimming; she need not be concerned about possible odor; and she will not experience the bulky, diaperlike feeling that she gets with pads.

Tampons should be changed as needed, or at least every four to six hours. Simply pull on the string attached to the tampon and the tampon should slide out. If you find some resistance when you try to remove the tampon, leave the tampon in a little longer. Most likely the tampon has not absorbed enough menstrual flow to make it soft and easy to remove.

After the tampon has been removed, you can flush it down the toilet or roll it in tissue and throw it in the trash like a pad. You should not flush the applicator down the toilet, though.

Are tampons or pads better?

Both are safe and effective. It is a matter of personal preference. Pads are easy to use and do not need to be inserted into the vagina. However, you can't go swimming with them, and some females say that pads can be bulky and a bit uncomfortable. Tampons allow the female to participate in all the activities that she normally does, including swimming, but some females feel uncomfortable inserting the tampon into the vagina and removing it. Some females use both tampons and pads. Your choice should be whatever makes you feel most comfortable.

Can a tampon get lost or stuck inside you?

No. When a tampon is inserted into the vagina, the removal string should remain outside of the body. If for some strange reason the cord gets pushed into the vagina with the tampon, both the string and tampon can be reached with your fingers. The vagina is like a small tube or canal. There is nowhere for the tampon to go.

Can the tampon fit through the cervix? No. The cervix is far too small for a tampon to fit through. It would be like trying to squeeze your thumb through a soda straw; it just won't fit.

Can the string on the tampon break?

Is it possible? Yes. Is it likely? No. The string breaking is very unusual. Even if it does, there is no need for you to worry. The tampon and string cannot get lost inside you. Use a squatting position and insert the tip of your finger to pull the tampon out. Doing this does not hurt at all and is not dangerous.

Can I go to the bathroom if I am using a tampon?

Absolutely. Ladies, you have three separate openings in your genital area. First is your urinary opening where you urinate from (a very tiny opening); second is your vagina where the tampon is inserted (larger opening); and third (a few inches farther back) is your anus where you defecate (poop) from. Having a tampon in the vagina will not affect your using the bathroom. Before you ask: no, you cannot make a mistake and put a tampon in the urinary opening instead of your vagina—it won't fit.

Do tampons cause cancer?

No. There has not been any evidence that shows using tampons will cause cancer.

What is TSS (toxic shock syndrome)?

Toxic shock syndrome is a type of bacterial infection that can lead to death if not treated. Some warning signs of TSS include a sudden high fever (usually 102 °F or higher), diarrhea, vomiting, dizziness, fainting or near fainting, and a rash that looks like a sunburn.

What does TSS have to do with menstruation?

Not much, but TSS cases are reported every so often. Some of these cases involve females who use tampons, and some don't. Before you become scared away from tampons, it should also be mentioned that only about six to seventeen menstruating females per year out of every 100,000 will ever develop TSS, so the chances of infection are low. Even females who don't use tampons can develop TSS. It is not recommended to use super absorbency tampons unless it is absolutely necessary. It seems those females who use tampons that have a higher absorbency than needed are more prone to develop TSS. Use the lowest absorbency that meets your needs.

What is a panty shield for?

A panty shield is a very thin pad that is used just before you think your period is due or at the very end of your period when there is very little bleeding. Some females may use panty shields between periods if they frequently have a heavy vaginal discharge.

If you have more questions about your body, menstruation, or any other sexuality related issue, you can find additional information at Youth Embassy (www.YouthEmbassy.com).

2

Things to Expect During the Teen Years

Right now you're going through an amazing growth process. You are at an exciting, frightening, and often confusing time in your life. Whatever you may be feeling at the moment, you should realize that you're not alone. Even though it doesn't seem so, your friends and classmates are all experiencing the same thing or something similar to what you are experiencing. Your parents, grandparents, and every other adult has gone through what you are going through right now. There's no escaping these changes in your body or the thoughts and feelings that come along with these changes.

Remember that what you're feeling is normal and nothing to be afraid or ashamed of. Here are just a few of the things that go through a young person's mind while he/she is growing up.

Will my looks ever change?

Yes. Your looks will continue to change for the rest of your life, but during the teen years, your body will change and grow so quickly that you will probably look very different from year to year.

During the teen years our bodies can play all kinds of jokes on us, including pimples, changing voices, hair growing in places we don't want it to, breasts that are too big or too small, funny-shaped noses/chins/mouths/ears/faces, long arms or legs, big butts or little butts, bodies that are too skinny or too fat, and on and on.

Your body will eventually settle down and stop growing in your early twenties. Until then, your looks will change without you noticing it most of the time. Take a look at pictures of yourself from when you were two years old, five years old, ten years old, and now. You look different in each picture, don't you? When you are a senior in high school, compare pictures of yourself to when you were a sophomore. You will probably see two different-looking people.

If you are in your teens now and are feeling a little crazy about how you look, relax and be assured that you will look much different when you get older. You're just not finished growing.

Growing up is a lot like baking a cake; if you pull the cake out of the oven to peek at it every two minutes, you will probably worry because it doesn't look the way a finished cake is supposed to. If you leave the cake in the oven for the full baking time, when you pull it out, it will have finished baking and appear exactly the way it is supposed to.

You can look at yourself in the mirror every day. You may not like the way you look, but remember, you're not finished baking. You have a good twenty or twenty-one years of growing before you're finally done; and even then you will continue to change.

What should I do to help get rid of pimples or acne?

Everyone has grown up having to deal with pimples. It helps to think of pimples as your body's way of testing your sense of humor. You will probably notice that when you want to look your best, your body will produce a huge, volcanic formation of a pimple that can be seen by people in the next state. Probably the best thing to do at this point is scream. When you're finished, laughing usually helps a little. This happens to everyone.

Should you pop your pimples?

See what works best for you. Usually tiny pimples just on the surface of the skin can be popped without infecting them and making them worse. If a pimple is large or deep under the skin, you're probably better off leaving it alone. Popping a pimple can infect the area and make it a giant mess. Most dermatologists (skin doctors) say that it is best to leave pimples alone and let them disappear on their own. See what works best for you or consult a dermatologist. If you develop acne (red, swelling pimples underneath the skin), you may want to visit a dermatologist. Dermatologists are popular with teens because a good dermatologist can make a big difference in the war against zits.

As far as buying zit creams to get rid of pimples, you would probably be better off getting some good advice or medication from a dermatologist. Many of the products on the market today don't really produce the results they say they do.

Pimples are just one of those things you have to put up with while you're growing up and your body's hormone levels are fluctuating. The good news is that once you get older, you don't have to deal with pimples as much. Until then, clean excess oil from your face as often as possible during the day. The best times are when you wake up in the morning, after gym class or exercising, after school, and before bed. A good sense of humor will help you through "the pimple years."

For more information on skin care and acne call the American Academy of Dermatology (1-888-462-3376). This is a toll-free telephone call. This organization will have a specialist who will be able to answer your questions, send an information packet, or give you advice on skin care.

Is it normal to think about another person a lot?

Yes. It is normal to think about a certain guy or girl a lot. He/She could be someone from school, the neighborhood, a movie, a TV show, the radio, or just about anywhere. In fact, it is also normal to think about more than one person at a time. Maybe there are two, three, or four people at a time who you think about seeing, meeting, dating, kissing, holding, marrying, and living happily ever after with. This is normal. You may even create little stories, scenes, or ways of being with this person in your dreams.

If you think about someone (or even a few people) a lot, don't worry about it. Turn on some music and enjoy. But try not to get too wrapped up in fantasizing, especially when you are supposed to be concentrating on something else, like your classwork, homework, chores, or your job. Meeting and talking to people can be fun, too. So, enjoy the fantasizing, but don't let it keep you from fulfilling your responsibilities or developing relationships.

If you don't find yourself thinking about another person a lot in a romantic way, this is normal, too. Some people do; some people don't. Either way, there's no harm done.

Is it normal to dream about sex?

Yes. Once again, some people will dream about having sex a lot, some people very little, and others not at all. If you dream about having sex with someone (or a few different people) frequently, this is normal. You're not a pervert or a sex maniac, nor will you be.

If you don't dream about having sex with someone, it doesn't mean there is something wrong with you. Some people do; some people don't. There is no harm done either way.

Are you gay (homosexual) if you have a dream about having sex with another person of the same sex?

No. You don't have any control over what pops into your head while you sleep. Some dreams will appeal to you; some will not. No one is exactly sure why we dream what we do, but either way, dreams and nightmares don't determine who you are or what you want. If you have dreams where you are hugging, kissing, or touching someone, it doesn't say anything about whether you're gay, straight, or bisexual.

What is a "wet dream?"

From around the age of ten through the teen years, a male or female may experience something called a nocturnal emission, or as it is more commonly known, a "wet dream."

When you're sleeping, you may dream about someone who you find very attractive. If you're a male, you may get an erection, have a fluid come out of your penis (this is prelubricating fluid), or even orgasm and ejaculate (have semen come out of your penis). You've just had a wet dream. Although this might be a little embarrassing when you wake up, this is very natural and normal. Your father, grandfather, and uncle may have experienced wet dreams when they were your age; don't worry about it.

Ladies, wet dreams for you are also normal, but they don't seem to happen as frequently as they do with males. You may also have an exciting dream about someone you find attractive. This may cause you to become so sexually stimulated that your vagina may produce a little, or quite a bit of, vaginal lubrication. This will cause you to be a little surprised the next morning when your underwear or pajama pants are moist. Just as with the guys, this is normal and natural.

Not everyone experiences wet dreams, but if you do, remember that this is just another one of the many surprises to expect during the teen years.

What is masturbation? Is it normal to touch your genitals?

Touching or stimulating your genitals in a way that makes you feel good or causes an orgasm is known as masturbation. You will probably hear a lot of jokes made about this topic, but masturbation has been around for a long time.

Even though masturbation can begin in childhood and continue throughout adulthood, people still make jokes about it. Masturbation is just socially unacceptable for some people. This means that many people do it, but it is just not something people like to talk about or admit to. Not to be gross, but masturbation is a little like picking your nose. Many people do it, but it's just not cool to do it in front of other people or talk about it in public. Masturbation is not dangerous or harmful unless it keeps you from meeting your responsibilities or going out and meeting people; otherwise, it is normal.

Some people may never masturbate. Other people may masturbate only once. Some people may masturbate many times a day for most of their lives. The important thing to remember is that whether or not you masturbate, there is nothing wrong with you.

Are you a pervert if you look at "dirty" magazines, videos, or Web sites?

A magazine or video that shows naked people in a way that is designed to get a person sexually excited is called pornography. Looking at pictures of naked people doesn't make you weird or a pervert. Although it is natural to be curious and interested in the human body, for some people, viewing pornography on a regular basis may have a damaging or negative effect. This is especially true for young people, who are at a stage in life where they are trying to figure out what their roles are when it comes to sex, love, and relationships.

There is much debate over what effect pornography has on a person. Some people who look at pornographic materials can sometimes get hooked. This may cause the person to buy and look at these materials a lot but avoid meeting people and developing relationships.

Many people will deny that pornography has this influence, and understandably so, because this is difficult to prove through scientific research. If you think about it, though, movies, TV, music, Web sites, and books can all have an effect on how we think, how we feel, what we expect from our relationships, and even how we behave. Have you ever seen the movie Rocky or Rocky II? How did you feel at the end of the movie when Rocky achieved what he worked so hard to do? Didn't you feel motivated to conquer the world? Inspired to reach your goals no matter what? Or at least to start working out?

Do you ever listen to songs or watch shows on TV that make you feel or think a certain way? Many times, what a person watches will influence him/her immediately, or influence how he/she sees the world in the future—and not always in a productive or healthy way. For example, pornography may influence males to believe that females want to have sex all the time, be beaten or raped, be very promiscuous (have sex with many different people), and have sex in every way possible. These beliefs may then influence how a male might view females and how he might treat them or expect them to act in the future.

Females who watch pornography may become influenced to think women were put on earth to be sex toys for males (which is not true), that the best sex has to be loud and wild (also not true), or that all women are bisexual, that is, sexually attracted to both males and females (again, not true).

You will also notice I've used the words "may," "might," and "sometimes" a lot. This is because many people are able to look at something pornographic without having too much of a problem at all. It is almost like drinking alcohol. A person who has an occasional drink doesn't usually go on to become an alcoholic. But the person who drinks frequently has a good chance of becoming an alcoholic. The same goes for pornography. If a person comes across something pornographic rarely or occasionally, the chances of the person having a problem are small. But the person who is repeatedly exposed to these types of materials may end up thinking or feeling certain ways that are not realistic or healthy for a relationship.

The bottom line is this: satisfying your curiosity is normal, but beware if you find yourself thinking about or spending many hours per week or day viewing pornography. Most of what you see in pornographic magazines, videos, and Web sites is an act. The images of the actors or models are digitally altered to make them look perfect. Don't confuse this with reality.

Is it normal to have strong urges or desires to have sex?

Yes. Some people have strong urges to have sex. Some people have little or no desire to have sex. Both are normal, and both can change as a person grows older.

Is it normal to have romantic feelings for or "crushes" on adults and teachers?

Yes. Sometimes a young person will develop feelings for an adult. Even though a young person may not really know the adult personally, he or she may fantasize about how the adult may be. Sometimes an adult or teacher may be understanding, nice, or have qualities that you like. It is easy to turn your admiration into attraction. You should realize that the adult has his or her own life and relationships and a personality that may not be what you imagined. You can fantasize, but it's best not to pursue these feelings in reality.

Does intercourse hurt the first time?

Usually not, but it can for some. For a female, her hymen (the thin layer of skin that may cover the vaginal opening) may still be in place. When the erect penis enters into the vagina, it separates the hymen and may cause some pain and even some bleeding. Often, by the time a female has intercourse, her hymen has already been separated through active sports, stretching, or use of tampons, and there isn't any pain or discomfort.

The other cause of pain might be a lack of lubrication. If a female is nervous (the first time or anytime she has sex), then she will probably not produce enough vaginal lubrication. She may not be sexually aroused enough, or she simply doesn't produce lots of lubrication naturally. If there isn't enough lubrication, then intercourse could be painful. It would be important for her to use a personal lubricating liquid, available at drugstores.

Do girls ejaculate?

Not really. A female will produce lubrication or moisture on the inside of her vagina when she is sexually aroused. There might be a little lubrication or a lot. If there is quite a bit of vaginal lubrication, some of the fluid may come out of the vagina, but it is not generally "ejaculated" from the vagina.

Some females, however, do seem to "ejaculate" during their orgasm. There are two small glands called located near the urinary opening. These are called the Skene's glands. In some females, the Skene's glands produce a fluid that will come out or be "ejaculated" during an orgasm.

What is the right age to have intercourse?

Tough question. Your religion and your parents would probably say after marriage, and, of course, that does work very well for some people. But there is no perfect answer or one that will please everyone. There is always going to be a lot of argument over when a person is mature enough to have intercourse.

A person is physically capable of having intercourse at a very young age, as early as nine or ten in some cases, but never is such a preteen ready mentally, emotionally, or financially. Nor is a young person skilled in the knowhow of raising a child effectively or in dealing with any of the other possible results of sex in today's world.

Intercourse is often much more than a physical act. It involves a person's mental and emotional preparedness as well. The act of intercourse can lead to pregnancy and sexually transmitted disease, which can change a person's life forever. Intercourse could also lead to emotional letdowns or even a fixation (which means that all you can think about is that one person or aspect of your life, causing everything else to slip, including family relationships, friendships, school grades, and other development activities).

There's no way of knowing for sure what the "right age" is to have intercourse. If the "after you're married" response doesn't work for you, then a good guide to follow is this: when you are ready to deal with the responsibilities of sex—which include contraception and STD prevention before intercourse takes place, as well as what may happen after sex, such as pregnancy or an STD infection or having your partner dump you or spread rumors about you afterward—then you might be ready for sex. Perhaps the best way to look at this is not to ask what is the right age to engage in intercourse, but when is a person really able to understand and manage everything that goes along with intercourse—physically, psychologically, socially, and emotionally.

When you're ready to deal with the responsibilities of sex, you may be at the right age. Some of the responsibilities of sex include:

- Always using contraception.
- Taking precautions to prevent STDs.
- Being able to communicate openly with your partner before, during, and after sex
- Being able to deal with the possibility of a pregnancy.
- Being able to deal with the possibility of an STD (including AIDS).
- Being able to recover from a heartbreak if you and your partner break up.

This list of sexual responsibilities can be expanded, but if you are not capable of dealing with these basic six, you're probably not at the right age.

Here's an interesting tidbit of information: on a survey I give to my high school students each semester, of the females who have engaged in intercourse, 90 percent say they regret having had sex at an early age and wish they had waited.

Can a girl get pregnant if she has unprotected intercourse during her period, or just after her period?

Yes. A female can get pregnant anytime she has unprotected intercourse. There are certain times during a female's menstrual cycle that she is more likely to become pregnant, but females can and do become pregnant because of unprotected intercourse during a period or just after a period. Contraception should always be used—each and every time!

Can a female get pregnant standing up?

Anytime a female engages in unprotected intercourse, it is possible that she will become pregnant. It doesn't matter when, where, or how—if there is no contraception used, a female can become pregnant. This includes standing up, sitting down, lying down, upside down, in a plane, on a train, in a pool, in the sea, in a tree—are you getting the idea?

Can a female get pregnant the first time she has sex?

Absolutely! A couple must use contraception every time they engage in intercourse—the first time, next time, last time, every time.

Can a female be pregnant and still have her period?

Yes and no. It is possible for a female to release an ovum (egg) just before or during her menstrual period. If she has unprotected vaginal intercourse just before or during her menstrual period, the ovum could become fertilized. So she can be pregnant and still have her menstrual period. A female can also be pregnant and have a small amount of blood/discharge come from her vagina. This isn't her period, but very often the female believes it is. However, usually a female who has her period is not pregnant.

What are the signs of pregnancy?

The first signs of pregnancy are a missed period, frequent urination, nausea, vomiting, and fatigue (feeling tired).

If a female does display these signs, it doesn't necessarily mean she is pregnant. Quite often teenage females will miss a period because of stress, worry, or some type of hormone imbalance and think they're pregnant. Amazingly, right after taking final exams in school or after getting a pregnancy test done, the period returns.

The only sure way a female can know if she is pregnant is by having a pregnancy test done.

Is it harmful to have intercourse during a female's period?

Because of the presence of blood, an HIV-infected female would have an increased chance of infecting her partner during unprotected intercourse. (Other than that, it might just be messy.)

Does a male's penis get larger if he has sex a lot?

No. A male cannot buy anything or do any special exercises to change the size of his penis, either.

What size should a guy's penis be when he's a teenager?

Again, the average adult erect penis is about six and a half inches. This can vary by a few inches more or less. The size of the penis in teen males will be different from guy to guy. What is important to remember is that everyone has growth spurts at different ages. Guys will continue to grow (and so will their penis size) up until about the age of twenty-one.

What can I do to make my penis bigger?

That is like asking how you can make yourself grow to be seven feet tall; if your family genetics don't naturally have a plan for you to grow to be seven feet tall, nothing you do will add that extra height. It is the same with the penis. There are no pills, powders, or potions that a guy can take that will make his penis any different from what his family genetics have determined for him. Even though there are plenty of salespeople out there who want to take your money and who will say and promise that they have a product that will add inches to your penis, this is all just advertising. It's designed to get you to spend your money. Save your money and try to forget about your penis. Nobody really cares about the size of your penis except you.

Is it normal to have two different-size testes?

Yes. Usually one testicle is bigger than the other, and usually one hangs lower than the other in the scrotum.

Is it harmful for a person to swallow semen during oral sex?

Yes and no. If the male has a sexually transmitted infection, the partner can become infected (even if the partner spits it out). If the male does not have any type of STD, the semen is harmless. Using a condom will help prevent most STDs.

Does teenage love have to be "puppy love"?

Puppy love . . . romantic love . . . real love . . . crushes . . . call it whatever you want. If you feel it, then it is real. What a person feels is important, but remember that feelings can change, sometimes very quickly. Sometimes it is best to put feelings up to the "time test" before you act on them. Remember, love does not equal sex, and sex does not equal love.

What is "getting burned"?

"Getting burned" is a slang or street term that usually means a person has become infected with a sexually transmitted disease (STD).

Is too much sex harmful at a young age?

It can be. Teenage females who engage in intercourse at an early age, especially without a condom, have a higher chance of cervical cancer. Both males and females who engage in intercourse frequently increase their chances of STDs and unplanned pregnancy.

If two people are going to engage in intercourse, they should be monogamous (have only one sex partner) and use a reliable form of contraception all the time in order to reduce the risk of unplanned pregnancy and STDs.

What makes the penis hard and erect?

Blood. Basically, blood rushes into the penis while blood flowing away from the penis slows down. When this happens, blood fills the spongy tissue in the penis, and the penis becomes larger and harder. If you can imagine blowing air into a balloon without letting any air escape, the balloon will get larger and harder. With an erection, blood is rushing into the penis to make it larger and harder. There is no bone in the penis.

Why do males have erections when they get up in the morning?

When the male has to go to the bathroom (urinate), his bladder will be full and expand (get bigger). The full bladder will slow blood flow out of the penis and cause blood to stay in the penis. When more blood goes into the penis than comes out, the penis fills and becomes erect. Waking up with an erection is normal.

Is a black man's penis bigger than a white man's?

Sometimes yes, sometimes no. Penis size has nothing to do with the color of your skin. The average size penis is around six and a half inches for black males, white males, and every male of any color. Some black males will have larger penises than some white males, while some white males will have larger penises than black males. Penis size depends on genetics, not skin color.

Is oral sex normal or abnormal?

Normal means that many people do a certain activity. Normal does not mean something is good or right. Abnormal means that only a few people do a certain activity. Abnormal does not mean something is bad or wrong.

Oral intercourse is practiced by many people in the United States, therefore, the answer is that oral intercourse is normal. Although many people engage in and enjoy oral sex, others find it disgusting or wrong. It is up to the couple to decide whether or not they want to engage in a certain type of intercourse.

What counts as having sex?

The three types of intercourse are vaginal (vagina-penis), oral (mouth-genitals) and anal (anus-penis). They are all considered to be sex.

Am I still a virgin if I have oral sex?

"Virginity" is one of those terms that has different meanings to different people. For some, virginity means that a female has not had her hymen separated (which doesn't take into account the fact that the hymen often separates while the female is growing up, nor does it account for a male's virginity!). Another definition describes a virgin as someone who has never engaged in vaginal intercourse (which doesn't take into account those who engage in oral or anal intercourse). Yet another definition is someone who has never engaged in any type of intercourse (vaginal, oral, or anal), but this doesn't account for nonintercourse activities like "outercourse." Or what if a couple begins to engage in intercourse but stops after a few seconds? Does this count? You are free to choose whichever definition makes the most sense to you.

So, yes, if someone engages in oral or anal intercourse, by some interpretations of the term "virginity," they would no longer be virgins. By other interpretations, they would still be considered virgins. Virginity is a term that seems to cause quite a bit of confusion and problems. Choose whichever definition you feel makes the most sense. What is most important is that you know what your beliefs are.

Is oral sex safe?

Neither oral nor anal intercourse will cause a pregnancy, but sexually transmitted germs can be passed from person to person through these types of intercourse. Anytime ANY person engages in ANY type of intercourse, she/he must take precautions to prevent becoming infected with an STD.

Where does the male's penis go during intercourse?

During vaginal intercourse, the male's erect penis goes into the female's vagina. The male will move his penis in and out of the female's vagina, or the female may move herself up and down the male's penis.

How deep is the female's vagina?

On average, the female's vagina is about five-and-a-half inches long. During intercourse, the vagina expands another few inches. The vagina is like a soft, flexible tube. During intercourse, the male and female do not need to worry about a penis that is "too large." The vagina will usually expand to fit most penises. The penis will not fit through the cervix and into the uterus.

Why are teens less respected when they have kids?

There could be many answers to this question, and it would be unfair to say that all teens are less respected when they have kids. However, for the most part, teens who have kids are often looked upon with disappointment because teens are not generally prepared to deal with the responsibilities and challenges of being parents. Our society believes that the teen years should be spent learning, having fun, and preparing for life as an adult—not using that time being a parent. This is probably why people become so disappointed with teens who have kids. It is sadness or anger over the young person's missed or lost opportunity.

Is it possible to be in love with two people at the same time?

There's that word again—love! If we're talking about companionship love or a marriage type of love, then we face a question that has perplexed philosophers for centuries. There is no concrete answer that can be given here.

However, can a person be sexually attracted to or have romantic feelings for two or more people at the same time? Absolutely. Now we really have a problem!

Is intercourse really important?

For continuing the human race, yes. Otherwise, not necessarily. Sex has many purposes, but it is primarily used to make babies or satisfy "biological urges." People also have sex to share romantic feelings or love for one another, or they have sex just for pleasure.

Is sex really important to a relationship?

Two people can share love, intimacy, romance, and pleasure without having sex. If a couple cannot share their love, be intimate, or be romantic without having intercourse, then sex will certainly not improve or sustain that relationship.

Sex never saves a relationship; it often only complicates it. A person should never resort to sex to try and keep a boyfriend or girlfriend, "save" a relationship, or "prove their love."

Most couples in love around the world, married or not, young or old, express their feelings and share intimacy without having sex. Could all these people be onto something?

The flip side to this is that for some people, sex is very important, or not very important at all. If the two people are not sexually compatible (similar or the same), then that could be problem for the relationship. Especially for young people and people who are not married, sex should never be used to "prove love" or to try to save a relationship. A relationship at this stage will usually end in a breakup anyway, with the person who compromised feeling bad and having regret.

Is using a condom "safe sex"?

Technically, using a condom is "safer sex." Condoms are not 100 percent effective against unplanned pregnancy. However, when they are used correctly (see chapter 7), they offer excellent protection against unplanned pregnancy (about 95 to 98 percent effective) and most STDs, including HIV.

Why do parents put down teenagers for having sex when they know, back when they were teens, they did the same thing?

Not all parents put down teens, nor did all parents have sex when they were in their teens. This is a good question, though, because it does happen. Some parents do this because they care about their teens and want to protect them from choices that may put them at risk. Parents may realize how risky their youthful behaviors were, and there wasn't an STD like HIV/AIDS spreading so quickly.

Parents may look back on their experiences and regret some of their actions and want to help you make better decisions than they did—kind of like guardian angels.

Why do females take intercourse more seriously than males?

Not always, but usually a female will engage in intercourse for different reasons than a male might. Stereotypically, a female will engage in intercourse for love, romance, or intimacy, whereas a male might engage in intercourse primarily for pleasure. Of course this is not always true.

For this reason, many times a male will use "romantic" reasoning to convince a female to have sex, and then the female will be disappointed or regretful when she discovers that sex did not provide her with what she was expecting—romance, tenderness, unconditional "true love," or unity with her partner.

Why are there times when a male and female can have unprotected sex and not become pregnant?

This can happen because the female has not ovulated and there is no ovum (egg) to be fertilized by the male's sperm, or sometimes a pregnancy does occur but the female has a miscarriage. Taking a chance that there is no ovum waiting to be fertilized is risky. People who take this needless risk have a very high chance of getting pregnant or infected with an STD. In fact, of every one hundred couples that choose to take this chance repeatedly over a year's time, eighty-five will experience a pregnancy by the end of the year. Contraception should be used every time a couple has sex.

What are blue balls? Does this really happen to guys when they don't have sex?

Ha! This line has been used for years! A guy will sometimes use this line on a female if she doesn't want to have sex with him. While there are times that the male's testes and genital area fill with so much blood and sexual tension that he feels uncomfortable, a girl should in no way feel sorry for him or obligated to administer "sexual healing."

Time or a cold shower can help him get rid of his problem. The old "blue balls" line is just a last-ditch effort to get a female to have sex. If a guy uses this line on you, a nice reply is, "Lucky for you that blue looks good on you," then leave!

Why do people moan and groan during intercourse?

Not all people do, but some people feel the need to moan, groan, grunt, snort, ooh, ahh, and make every other noise during intercourse. There is nothing wrong with this, but some people do it just because they think it's what they're supposed to do.

Other people do this because they feel so good that these sounds naturally come out—kind of like spontaneous cheering at a football game after a touchdown has been scored. Intercourse can be, and often is, very quiet.

Can a couple get pregnant if they are "boning" (rubbing up against each other) and he ejaculates?

In general, the only time a pregnancy can occur is if vaginal intercourse takes place. If the penis does not enter the vagina and release prelubricating fluid or semen, then a pregnancy is unlikely to occur. There may be a very slight chance of pregnancy if semen enters into the vagina through "boning" or "fingering," but there isn't much research to support that this happens. To protect yourself against pregnancy and STDs, a good rule to remember is that you need to be very aware and always prevent another person's prelubricating fluid, semen, vaginal secretions, or blood from entering your body.

Can a couple get an STD if they are "boning"?

For a sexually transmitted infection to take place, someone must already be infected with a sexually transmitted disease. Since boning does not usually involve getting semen, prelubricating fluid, vaginal secretions, or blood into another person's body, many STDs cannot be transmitted by boning. However, there are some STDs that can be transmitted through skin-to-skin contact. These include syphilis, herpes (if the sores are present or are about to appear), genital warts, and crabs. As always, you should assume a partner is infected with an STD and just doesn't know about it. Do what you need to do to protect yourself from infection.

I hear people say things about sex that I now know is not true. In the future, whom should I believe when it comes to sex?

Unfortunately, some adults are more interested in their own values, religious beliefs, agendas (plans to accomplish their personal goals), and power than in providing facts supported by research, equity, people's rights, and the health and lives of others, especially young people. Even some doctors will manipulate facts, spreading inaccurate or twisted information in order to promote their religious beliefs, rather than deliver the facts to young people—and these doctors are very convincing! Beware of where you get your information. Reliable places to get information about sex include the Sexuality Information and Education Council of the United States (SIECUS) (www.siecus.org) and The Alan Guttmacher Institute (www.agi-usa.org). For youth-friendly information, Advocates for Youth (www.advocatesforyouth.org) is a good source, allowing you to ask any question you like, confidentially, and receive a nonjudgmental, accurate response.

If you have more questions about what is normal or about any other sexuality related issue, you can find additional information at Youth Embassy (www.YouthEmbassy.com).

3

Love, Love, Love!

If there is anything that confuses us all, it is love. Since we are talking about sexuality, we will limit our definition of love to one kind of love—romantic love.

Simply put, romantic love is an intense passion toward another person. However, romantic love is far from simple. The intense passion that you feel toward another person may make you feel excited, energized, nervous, depressed, and even obsessed. This has confused each and every one of us. We can feel so many things at one time.

How do you know if you're in love or just infatuated?

The bad news is that it is almost impossible to tell the difference between love and infatuation because they often feel the same. There are a few small differences between the two, but nothing that is easy to see. The good news is that it doesn't really matter which one you're feeling, because both need to be handled the same way. So you will probably save yourself a lot of headaches if you don't try to examine too much whether you are infatuated or in love. Just realize that you have these intense feelings.

Regardless of whether you are in love or infatuated, your feelings are real and special. What is most important is that you manage your feelings and make decisions that will not put you at risk for problems.

Why is love blind?

We say love is blind because it often makes us unable to see things as they really are. This blindness does not go away with age, either. Adults are also victims of this blindness.

I like to think of humans as separated into two parts, the mind and the heart. The mind controls what we think. It is logical and usually makes careful choices and decisions for us. The heart, however, controls what we feel. All our emotions are controlled by the heart. The heart has no need for logic or careful decision making. It just wants to be happy.

The problem here is that the two sometimes don't get along very well. In fact, sometimes they fight against each other or try to control each other.

Love can be very confusing.

Unfortunately, when we are in love or infatuated, we sometimes let our heart make decisions for us instead of our mind. When we let our heart make decisions for us instead of our mind, we usually choose what feels good rather than what is logical and should be done. Later we may look back at our decision and say, "What was I thinking? Couldn't I see what was happening? Was I blind?"

Here are a few examples: Have you ever spent the afternoon with your boyfriend or girlfriend instead of doing your homework or something else that needed to be done? Have you ever stayed up late talking to your boyfriend/girlfriend on the telephone even though you knew you had a difficult exam in the morning? Have you ever become more physically close to your girlfriend/boyfriend than you actually wanted to but felt too much pressure to say no, so you did what she/he wanted instead of what you knew was right for you?

These are a few examples of how we sometimes do what our heart tells us instead of our mind. Usually, when the heart makes the decisions in romantic situations, you can expect that things will probably not turn out the way you wanted them to in the end.

Here is another example of how the mind and the heart do battle in a romantic situation. See if you can tell how each decision is made—with the heart or with the mind?

Felisha and Kevin have been in love (or infatuated) for almost a year. They see each other as much as they can on the weekends and talk on the phone every night. They think about each other all the time, and kissing and holding each other makes them feel warm and sometimes even a bit dizzy.

One Saturday afternoon, while Felisha's parents were away, Kevin came over to be with Felisha and exchange a few loving kisses and caresses, which Felisha didn't seem to mind, either. Like many times in the past, Felisha and Kevin became more and more passionate.

DECISION 1: Kevin's hands began to move over Felisha's breasts and butt. Felisha is a bit uncomfortable but lets Kevin continue.

DECISION 2: Kevin now becomes more excited and begins to unbutton Felisha's pants. Felisha moves Kevin's hand away and thinks that this will let him know not to go any further.

DECISION 3: Moments later, Kevin is trying to lift Felisha's shirt. Once again Felisha slides his hand away. Now Kevin is getting a bit impatient, to say the least, and whispers in Felisha's ear, "What's wrong?" as he continues to kiss her.

Felisha whispers back, "I'm not ready."

Kevin is still impatient and extremely excited and asks, "When will you be ready?"

Felisha is now feeling quite a bit of pressure and is finding it difficult to refuse Kevin's advances. "I don't know, Kevin. I'm just not ready now," she replies.

DECISION 4: Kevin whispers in Felisha's ear, "I love you and would never want to rush you into anything that you weren't ready for. But we've been together for a year and we both know that we will always be together. I want to show you how much I love you."

Felisha loves Kevin and wants to make him happy. She knows that one day they will get married and have a family of their own. But there is something just not right. She is worried and uneasy.

DECISION 5: Felisha whispers back to Kevin, "What if something goes wrong?"

Kevin quickly responds, "Nothing will go wrong. Trust me."

Felisha then softly mumbles, "Okay," and Kevin tells her he loves her again. Felisha and Kevin continue kissing while Kevin begins removing Felisha's clothes.

DECISION 6: Felisha loves Kevin, but she is a bit afraid and definitely unsure. She watches Kevin take off his clothes. Felisha worriedly asks, "But what about a condom?"

"Don't worry about it," Kevin replies.

Minutes later, Kevin and Felisha are finished "making love" and quickly get dressed.

Fear and worry race through Felisha's mind. Will I get pregnant? What will my parents think? What will my friends think? Can I afford a baby? How can I take care of a baby and go to school? Will he marry me? Do I want to marry him? Do I have herpes now? AIDS? Am I infected with anything?

There are any possible number of outcomes to this story. I'll let you fill in the rest.

Before you get too wrapped up in the story, let's see what wins the fight at each decision point—the mind or the heart.

DECISION 1: Kevin begins feeling Felisha's breasts.
The mind says: Stop this here or he may go even further.
The heart says: I love him and this feels good anyway.
WINNER: The heart. She allows him to continue.

DECISION 2: Kevin begins unbuttoning Felisha's pants.
The mind says: I'm not ready to deal with intercourse and its responsibilities.
The heart says: I don't want to lose him.
WINNER: The mind. Felisha pushes Kevin's hand away.

DECISION 3: Kevin tries lifting Felisha's shirt.
The mind says: He doesn't care about what I want. He is just interested in what he wants—I have to tell him that I'm not ready!
The heart says: I don't want to upset him. I don't mind.
WINNER: The mind. Felisha tries to explain that she is not ready.

DECISION 4: Kevin tells Felisha that he loves her and wants to show her his love.
The mind says: What does sex (intercourse) have to do with love? What will my life be like if something happens?
The heart says: I love him so much and I want him to know how much I love him. We're going to get married anyway.
WINNER: The mind. Felisha desperately tries to look for a reason not to have sex.

DECISION 5: Kevin tells Felisha to trust him and that nothing will go wrong.

The mind says: He can't guarantee that nothing will happen. Besides, he isn't ready for what might happen, either.

The heart says: Nothing will happen. This will be a warm, loving experience that we will always remember.

WINNER: The heart. Felisha says okay.

DECISION 6: Kevin and Felisha are about to engage in intercourse without protecting themselves against pregnancy or sexually transmitted infections.

The mind says: You may get pregnant. You may become infected with HIV (the AIDS virus).

The heart says: We've come this far, let him do what he wants. I trust him.

WINNER: The heart. No contraception is used.

As you can see, when the heart makes our decisions for us in romantic situations, it puts us at risk and exposes us to many dangers, some even life threatening.

The fight between the heart and the mind has taken place since the beginning of time. Now it is your turn to choose who will win when these two battle inside of you.

Are love and sex the same thing?

Love is not sex, and sex is not love. Sexual intercourse is a physical act. It is the way humans reproduce. The feelings that may be present when two people engage in intercourse can vary widely. A couple may be in love, or they may just want the physical pleasure that sexual intercourse may bring. Unfortunately, in our society, many people will say that they love another person just so he/she will engage in intercourse.

Love is not a license for sex. Just because people are in love does not mean they should engage in sex. Many times people think that, because they are in love, they should have sex. This is often a big boo-boo. The physical act of intercourse has many responsibilities and risks involved.

Does sex prove your love for someone?

No. A person should never engage in sex to try to prove his/her love. Sex doesn't do many things. Sex does not:

- Prove your love.
- Make you an adult.
- Cure loneliness.
- Make you "cool" or part of the "in" crowd.
- Prove your independence from your parents.
- Make a situation or relationship better. (In fact, it usually complicates it.)

How can I express my love for someone without intercourse?

One of the most popular lines is "If you loved me you would (have sex)." This line almost always works to get a person to engage in intercourse, because it puts pressure on the other person to "prove" his/her love or risk appearing like he/she doesn't really love you. This is an old trick of "either–or," meaning that the person only gives you two options: (1) If you love me then you will do what I want you to do, or (2) If you don't do what I want, then you don't really love me. Doesn't this sound as though the person is being manipulative (being sneaky and trying to trick you into doing what he/she wants)? Actually, there are many other options besides these two. You can certainly love someone and yet not want to have sex or do what he/she wants. In fact, you probably show the person how much you love him/her all the time and don't even realize it. Turn to chapter 10 to check out just a few of the many ways you can show and share your love with someone instead of having sex.

Some people think you need to have sex to express love because of the way we use the term "make love." I put this phrase in quotes throughout the book because there is no such thing as creating love through intercourse. Sex does not make love. If the two people are not already in love before they engage in intercourse, they will not be magically in love after intercourse.

When two people are in love and engage in sex they do not make love. They possibly enhance their love, just as they could through many other activities.

Just a quick note, though: the next time someone says that he/she wants you to prove your love or wants to make love to you, please remember these few things:

- Sex does not make love. Love does not necessarily require sex.
- You should never have to prove your love to someone with sex.
- If the person really loved you, he or she would never pressure or manipulate you into doing anything that you thought was not right.

Am I ready for intercourse?

Most likely you are physically ready for intercourse. But are you ready emotionally and financially?

Intercourse has many responsibilities and risks. You need to ask yourself if you are ready to deal with what could happen. Are you emotionally able to deal with diseases like herpes, chlamydia, AIDS, or any other sexually transmitted infection? Are you financially ready to pay for the costs of tests and treatments if you get a disease? Are you emotionally ready to deal with a pregnancy? Are you financially ready to pay for pregnancy costs and to raise a

Am I ready for intercourse?

If pregnancy occurs:
Can I afford hospital bills?
Can I afford:
  –clothes
  –food
  –medicine
  –home

Can I do what I want while supporting a baby/family?
  –college
  –career
  –entertainment

If infected with an STD:
Am I prepared to deal with
  –cost of treatment
  –having a disease forever
  –possible sterility
  –dying young

Are YOU ready for intercourse?

child? Take a look at the illustration on page 72. If you answer no to any of the questions listed, then you're probably not ready for intercourse. This goes for your partner, as well. Your partner must also be ready, or you might find yourself in a situation that you don't want to be in. If you think your partner will be with you through thick and thin, you might be in for a surprise.

What if my boyfriend/girlfriend and I are in love and we both want to have sex?

There may be a time when you are alone with your girlfriend/boyfriend and you "feel" that the time is right. This is the ideal battleground for your mind and heart.

Your heart pours out feelings of love, passion, and desire—definitely a powerful squad. Your mind sends in logic and education to do combat, which tries to turn the heart's feelings into worry and doubt. The result is a war, which you feel as confusion.

This battle will rage until finally either the heart or the mind is victorious. If you find your heart standing alone and passion leading you down the road to intercourse, then there are a few necessary precautions that you must take—regardless of where your heart is delivering you.

Make absolutely sure you protect yourself from sexually transmitted infections and unwanted pregnancy. Although

When the mind and heart do battle, who will win inside of you?

abstinence (not engaging in intercourse) is the only sure way of protecting yourself, a condom (rubber) will provide excellent protection against both an unwanted pregnancy and most STDs.

If you feel prepared to accept the responsibilities of dealing with what might happen after intercourse, then you must also be willing to accept the responsibilities of dealing with what happens before intercourse. Let me make this simpler:

If you feel uncomfortable using a condom, you will definitely feel uncomfortable with a pregnancy, an STD, or AIDS. To make this simpler still:

If you can't make sure a condom is used before and during intercourse, you can't deal with what might happen after intercourse. You should wait until you are able to behave responsibly, reduce your risks, and better handle these issues around sex.

If you have more questions about love, infatuation, relationships, or any other sexuality related issue, you can find additional information at Youth Embassy (www.YouthEmbassy.com).

4

Healthy and Unhealthy Relationships

A relationship is a connection between two or more people. There are many types of relationships, from friendships to acquaintances (someone you know but don't really consider a friend) to family relationships and romantic relationships. A relationship can be mutually satisfying (where both people feel good about themselves and the other person), or one-sided (where one person gives more of herself/himself than the other). Relationships mix personalities together, which is like mixing food or spices together; sometimes the ingredients blend well and sometimes they don't. The trick is knowing when a relationship is positive and when it is negative.

What is a healthy relationship?

A healthy relationship is one that is mutually satisfying (where both people feel good about themselves and the other person) and that doesn't put the physical, mental, or emotional health of either person at risk.

What are the signs of a healthy relationship?

Some signs of a healthy relationship include:
- You enjoy being with the other person.
- You feel good about yourself when you are with this person.

- You are able to be yourself without feeling as though you have to act like someone else.
- You feel secure and trusting because the person has earned your trust.
- The other person is a positive influence on your life.
- You can continue to grow and reach personal goals.
- The other person respects your personal values and desires.
- The other person respects your wishes to do, or not do, things.
- You feel your relationship needs are being met.
- You are both able to communicate in a way that meets the other's needs.
- You both have similar expectations (same wants) from the relationship.

What is an unhealthy relationship?

An unhealthy relationship is where one or both people involved create physical, mental, or emotional risks or pain by being together.

What are the signs of an "unhealthy" relationship?

Some signs of an unhealthy relationship include:
- You don't enjoy being with the other person.
- You feel inferior, guilty, or worthless when you are with this person.
- You feel as though you have to put on an act to impress this person and keep this person interested in you.
- The other person puts you in situations that create stress or risks in your life.
- Your physical, mental, and emotional health needs are ignored or placed at risk.
- The other person attempts to use guilt or anger to manipulate you into doing things.
- You do not feel as though your relationship needs are being met.
- One or both of you fail to communicate in a way that meets the other's needs.
- You both want different things from the relationship.

How do I improve an unhealthy relationship?

You don't—not alone, anyway. Both people must want to improve the relationship in order for positive changes to occur. If the other person in the relationship isn't willing to meet you halfway, then chances are the relationship will not improve. Even then, improvements in a relationship often depend on a person making certain changes to his/her personality and normal behavior, which is extremely difficult to do.

If both people are interested in improving the relationship, then the first step is to begin finding out what each person wants from the relationship,

→ GO	‹SLOW›	STOP
You Feel:	**You Feel:**	**You Feel:**
Trusting	Guilty	Abused
Respected	Stressed	Controlled
Confident	Worthless	Ashamed
Secure	Manipulated	Threatened
Happy	Dissatisfied	Afraid

You need to be able to read the signs of a
relationship to be safe and happy.

what each person likes about the relationship, and what each person wants to improve in the relationship. You should never be made to feel as though you must sacrifice your integrity or personal values to please another person or prove your commitment to the relationship. If you are being asked to do something that you feel violates or compromises your personal beliefs and values, it is a sign that this may not be the relationship for you.

We love each other but we constantly argue and do mean things to one another. Why is this happening?

We are given the ability to feel love, physical attraction, and other emotions very early in life, but the ability to manage those emotions usually comes much later. So the love may be there, but the relationship skills and compatible personalities might not be there. This happens quite frequently in relationships. You may need to move on to someone who is better at meeting your relationship needs.

The good news is that as most people become older, they learn to manage their feelings better and develop better relationship skills, so relationships tend to go a little more smoothly. Even then, relationships need work. The trick is to gain greater understanding of your emotions and learn to exercise skills that will help you build solid relationships—and to recognize when someone else doesn't possess those skills.

I love my partner, but I want to meet other people. What should I do?

The teen years, at least in the United States, are a special time to learn new things, discover your interests, and meet new people. While commitment in a long-term relationship is important, the teen years are your time in life to meet new people, if that is what you want to do. Enjoy your relationships and meet as many people as you would like; just remember to be honest with everyone, including yourself.

I think this is "the one!" Should I marry her/him?

Love is wonderful, and relationships that involve love can be intoxicating. But again, while you have developed the ability to feel and experience romantic

love, other areas of your personal growth have not fully developed yet. In the years to come, your likes, dislikes, and interests may change, as will your partner's. Although the two of you are completely "in sync" right now, in the future you may want to go in different directions. You may be perfect for one another now, but in other times, as life changes and the two of you change (and you WILL change), you may not be perfect for one another anymore.

Additionally, marriage is a very different relationship than what you are experiencing now. Marriage involves much more than love and enjoying being together—it also involves the ability to exercise healthy relationship skills not only when everything is going well, but especially when things are going badly.

Of course, the question for you is, if he/she IS "the one," then won't he/she still be "the one" five or six years from now? What's the rush to get married? Enjoy your relationship as it is now; time will be your friend in helping you to discover whether it was meant to be.

When should I end a relationship?

You should end or change a relationship if the signs of an unhealthy relationship (listed on page 76) exist. You can change a romantic relationship to a friendship without the romance/intimacy, or the other person can become an acquaintance, or you can cut off all ties and communication with this person.

If my boyfriend/girlfriend cheated on me, should I give him/her a second chance?

Can this person be trusted again? If you don't feel as though this person can be trusted, then you might be better off suffering through a little pain now in a breakup, than a lot of pain later when he/she betrays your trust again.

I know I am in an unhealthy relationship, but I still don't want it to end. Why?

People (of all ages!) tend to cling to things they are used to. Change from what is familiar is often more frightening than staying in an unhealthy relationship. Often people stay in abusive relationships even when they know it is damaging them and creating unhappiness. Many people might stay in unhealthy relationships because they are afraid that no one else will be interested in them or that they will be alone forever. Of course, this is untrue, especially for young people, because there are literally millions of people on this planet to meet and get to know.

Why do healthy relationships end?

Even when relationships are healthy and both people are happy, people change as individuals. Their interests change, goals change, likes and dislikes change. Sometimes these changes cause a person to want things that the relationship simply cannot provide. There isn't anything wrong with either person in that relationship, and there isn't anyone who is at fault—as long as both people are honest about their feelings and with each other.

Another possible reason, especially with young people and young adults, is that some people enjoy romance and the thrill of meeting new people more than they want to have a long-term relationship. This is normal and happens quite frequently. This leads back to an earlier point about knowing what a person wants from a relationship and what her/his expectations for the relationship might be.

How do I know if my boyfriend/girlfriend is honest?

Simple! If people's actions and behaviors match their words, then chances are they are honest. On the other hand, if they lie to other people or don't do what they say they are going to do, then you have good reason not to give them your trust. (A good general rule is that if a person lies to or cheats on someone else, chances are high that he/she will do the same to you when it becomes convenient.)

If you find that your boyfriend/girlfriend makes a lot of excuses for not doing something or not being somewhere, or that he/she always seems to have a story to explain things, again, take this as a sign that the person has some honesty issues.

What is the best way to end a relationship?

There are many ways to end a relationship. It all depends on the individuals involved and what will cause the least amount of emotional pain for the other person. Unfortunately, when some people end a relationship, they think more about what is easiest for them than what's least painful for the other person.

Certainly, the most common way is to ignore the other person, spend less time with him/her, stop taking his/her telephone calls or e-mails, and hope that the person will get the hint and just move on. Unfortunately, this tends to create more stress for the one who wants to break up, and it is emotionally hard on the other person. There are better ways to end a relationship.

Another way is to write a letter. It's not exactly direct, but at least the person knows for sure that you want the relationship to end and what the reasons are.

Yet another way is to be direct. If the relationship didn't last more than a few weeks or months, then some people may choose to use the telephone to break up. If the relationship was very intimate and meaningful, or the other person is likely to be deeply hurt, then a face-to-face is probably the most respectful way to end the relationship. A face-to-face over lunch, in a public area, maybe with friends nearby, might be the best way to let someone know that you want to end the relationship.

Sometimes things can become quite scary! If you feel as though the person might become violent or will not accept an end to the relationship, then this process becomes more difficult. In this case, you want to make sure that two things occur:

• You will be safe at all times while breaking up with this person.
• The person understands that the relationship is over.

In this scenario, using the telephone may be the best way to communicate with the other person and ensure your safety. If the other person will not accept that the relationship is over, then it is usually best to state clearly that it is over and that there is no chance of getting back together. State that you do not want to continue a friendship or communication, and then end the call without allowing the person to draw you into a discussion. This sounds harsh (and it is), but for some people, this might need to happen to get your point across. If all else fails and you find that the person is continuing to try to contact you or is showing up in places where he/she knows you will be, then you may need help. You may need to ask your parent or guardian to step in and contact his/her parents to explain the situation. Hopefully, things will end there and you will not need to involve anyone else like school administrators or the police.

If the person you are breaking up with is less nightmarish, consider his/her feelings when you are communicating with him/her. Talk about the good times and positive aspects of the relationship, but say that you want to focus more attention on other activities like school, hobbies, etc., or that you don't feel your heart is where it should be in the relationship. From there you need to determine whether the two of you can remain friends without causing any lingering emotional pain, or if no communication at all would be best. Many people need "closure" (a clear, definite end) to a relationship in order to lessen the emotional pain and to move on with their social lives and romantic pursuits.

How can I ease the pain of a breakup?

Explore what you are feeling and why you are feeling that way. Life is forever a series of ups and downs—when things are down, you can be sure that your life will pick back up. When things are up, you can be sure that things will slump back down. Remind yourself that you will have other relationships, more happiness, and that in time the pain will fade. Then try to keep yourself busy with friends and family, hobbies, and positive activities that you enjoy.

When is it time to get help?

If your sadness lasts more than two weeks, then it would be a good idea, if you haven't done so already, to share what you are feeling with a trusted adult. Expressing emotions like sadness and anger is a good way of releasing them from your body so they won't cause you such intense pain.

If you feel you are becoming depressed and that talking with a trusted adult isn't providing enough help, then you should ask that adult to arrange a meeting with a trained counselor who can help you clear your feelings.

Should I get back together with my ex?

While some people do, most of the time things rarely change. You may end up having to go through the breakup again, reliving the pain (although there are always exceptions). Your odds of being happy improve if you move on to someone who is a better match for you.

What is an abusive relationship?

Unfortunately, abusive relationships are growing more and more common, especially among young people. Some signs of an abusive relationship include the following:

- Your partner physically abuses you (slaps, hits, kicks, burns, or inflicts any other kind of pain on your body).
- Your partner emotionally abuses you (tells you that you are worthless; tries to make you feel guilty, ashamed, nervous, or afraid; ignores you).
- Your partner socially abuses you (spreads nasty rumors about you or tries to put you down or embarrass you in front of other people).
- Your partner psychologically abuses you (tries to control whom you talk to, whom you spend time with, where you go, what you wear, what you do).
- Your partner sexually abuses you (uses physical force or threats to make you perform any kind of sexual contact or intercourse).
- You feel afraid to say or do certain things around your partner.
- You are worried about what he/she will do to you the next time you are together.
- You feel dependent on him/her to live and survive.
- You make excuses about why this person is the way he/she is.
- You make excuses about why you will not end the relationship.
- You are afraid to break up.

What should I do if I am in an abusive relationship?

Speak to a trusted adult who can help you get out of this relationship. This kind of situation is extremely hard (almost impossible) to get out of on your own. You will need someone else's help to make sure that you stay safe.

If you do not have a trusted adult in your life, contact agencies such as a school counseling office, police department, or health clinic and tell them that you have a domestic violence issue and need help. Trained staff should be able to direct you to community resources that can help. You may also find assistance at Safe Horizon (www.dvsheltertour.org, 1-800-621-4673).

If you have more questions about relationships or any other sexuality related issue, you can find additional information at Youth Embassy (www.YouthEmbassy.com).

5

How to Make Love

If you think you are alone in wondering what happens when two people "make love" or how to engage in sex/intercourse the right way, let me assure you that this question is asked at least once by every person in his/her lifetime. You may be wondering if there are certain moves, positions, techniques, or strategies that you should know in order to be "good" at "making love."

Before we answer these questions, please make sure that you understand what "love" and "making love" mean. If you have not read chapters 3 and 4 about love and relationships yet, you should do so before going on. If you have already read them, then let's get busy.

First of all, intercourse is not an Olympic event. Imagine: She's kissing him passionately, but suddenly, her own drool drips down his lip! She gets a measly 5.5 from the German judges. Or this: It looks like he's on his way to a perfect 10 as he gently caresses her shoulders, but oh no, he miscalculates his position and falls out of bed! Point deductions there, folks!

There will not be a panel of judges in the corner watching for style, technique, and execution. Intercourse is not a competition.

Why do people make so much noise during intercourse?

Believe it or not, the moaning, grunting, screaming, and groaning you see and hear in the movies is not what intercourse is necessarily all about. Intercourse can also be very quiet or silent, and often is. Yelling, screaming, groaning, and moaning do not necessarily improve intercourse, unless that is what the couple wants to do. The sounds you hear on TV and in the movies are the directors' way of making those scenes more interesting, rather than just having silence or playing some kind of music.

Is sex really like it is in the movies?

We live in a media-controlled society (TV, movies, music, Internet, news). The media repeatedly show us sex in ways that are inaccurate, unbelievable, unrealistic, and often harmful to us. Media myths say that in order for the male to be a "stud" he should have a ten-inch monster penis, keep an erection for at

Intercourse is not an Olympic event!

least half an hour, and know where to touch and how to excite his partner. Of course, the male must be aggressive. Media myths say that for the female to excite and stimulate her partner, she should either be aggressive or the exact opposite—passive or dominated. Also, for the female to be a good sex partner, she should know where and how to touch her partner, have big breasts, moan and scream, and, of course, have an orgasm.

Constantly watching these media myths will soon start you thinking that this is how intercourse is supposed to be. This is not good.

Many people have problems with intercourse because of what could be called "performance anxiety." These people believe that if they do not do it "right" (as seen on TV/movies/Internet), it means they are inadequate (terrible lovers) and will be degraded (put down) and embarrassed. To repeat, intercourse is not a performance or an Olympic event. The things that you see on TV and in the movies are faked performances for an audience.

What is the best way to "make love"?

The answer could be a surprise. There is no best way to "make love." At least not the way you are thinking. People are not soda machines. On a soda machine, if you press the soda button, you get soda. The human body does not have buttons you can push to get what you want. There is no orgasm button that you can push on another person and "boom," instant orgasm.

There are no positions or special techniques that you need to know to engage in satisfying or pleasurable intercourse. (There are definitely some responsibilities, though!) It is all a matter of preference. Everyone is stimulated by different things. Caressing the male's penis in a hard or rough manner may stimulate him. However, it may not. It may actually be painful. Perhaps he prefers to be touched softly. Squeezing the female's breast in a hard or rough manner may stimulate her, too. However, it may be painful or uncomfortable. Gentle caresses may be more stimulating.

Each person is different and there is no one position, technique, or place you can touch someone that will definitely be stimulating. In other words, not everyone likes chocolate ice cream. People like different flavors of ice cream. There is no flavor that everyone likes, and there is no one touch that everyone likes. A person needs to find out what his/her partner likes.

Are there different types of intercourse?

The three most common types of intercourse are vaginal intercourse (when the penis is inserted into the vagina), oral intercourse (when the person uses his/her mouth to stimulate another person's genitals), and anal intercourse (when the penis is inserted into another person's anus).

Some of these may sound weird or even disgusting to you. That's okay. Some people enjoy certain types of intercourse while others do not. Some people may enjoy being kissed on the ears or neck while others may not. "Different strokes for different folks," as they say.

How will I know what my partner likes?

The secret is communication. You need to communicate to your partner what you like and dislike. You need to ask what your partner likes or dislikes. I realize that talking may be uncomfortable and nearly impossible, but there are other ways of communicating that don't require talking. What do you think a smile might communicate to your partner? The person may realize that he or she touched you in a way that you liked.

Another way of communicating where and how you want to be touched is by gently taking the person's hand and moving it to the place you want to be touched and showing him/her how you want to be touched. This also works if you are being touched in a place or a way that you don't like. Gently push away your partner's hand or back away from your partner. If your partner still does not get the message, you will probably need to tell your partner to stop or that you don't like what is happening.

You also need to pay attention to the messages your partner is sending you. If your partner says to stop, then stop! Stop means stop.

What do you do when you "make love"?

I will provide you with a framework that may put you at ease. Keep in mind that there are many things two people can do when they "make love." There is no magical position or method for everyone.

Here is a basic framework of what usually happens when a male and female engage in intercourse. (Let's use a married couple wanting to have a baby.)

The couple may begin kissing each other on the lips, face, and neck. As they kiss, they may also caress (feel) each other. The male may caress the female's shoulders, back, arms, chest, breasts, stomach, butt, thighs, or genitals. The female may caress the male's shoulders, back, arms, chest, butt, thighs, or genitals. The couple will then undress. They may either undress each other or undress by themselves, whichever way they prefer. While they undress or after they undress themselves, the couple will continue kissing each other. The male may move his kisses from his partner's lips, face, and neck down to her shoulders and arms. He may also kiss and caress the female's breasts, nipples, stomach, butt, thighs, or genitals. The female may also move her kisses from her partner's lips, face, and neck to his shoulders, chest, stomach, butt, legs, and genitals.

While the couple kiss and caress each other, the male's penis will become hard and erect. If the female is stimulated enough, her vagina will become moist.

Intercourse takes place when the erect penis is inserted into the vagina. The male may continue to slide his erect penis in and out of the female's vagina or the female may slide her vagina back and forth on the male's penis. As the male's penis continues to penetrate into the female's vagina, he will become so stimulated that he will orgasm and ejaculate (release semen from his penis). The female may also feel stimulated during penetration, but may or may not orgasm. The female orgasm may be a quivering of the vagina, anus, or even uterus.

If either or both partners have reached orgasm, the couple may continue kissing, hugging, and caressing each other. This process is usually much slower and more tender than during intercourse.

This is basically what happens when two people "make love." This description was intended to give you a general idea of what takes place. As you might have noticed, I used the word "may" quite frequently throughout this description. The reason is that there are many different things that can happen when two people engage in intercourse.

At this point, a few questions might be running through your head. I will try to answer some of them here.

How much time does it take to have intercourse?

It varies. It can take less than a minute, two minutes, five, ten, fifteen, thirty, or even longer.

What does intercourse feel like?

Again, this varies. Physically, sex can be a pleasurable, wonderful experience. Most times, when two people both want to engage in intercourse and are very aroused by one another, intercourse feels very good.

Sometimes, sex can be uncomfortable or even painful if the female's vagina is not well lubricated and moist. If this happens, the penetration of the penis may be difficult or abrasive (rough rubbing) for both partners. It might be unpleasant when one partner is touching the other in a way that he/she doesn't like.

What is an orgasm?

An orgasm is the release of built-up sexual energy. It is the high-point or peak of sexual excitement. One way to describe it is to compare an orgasm to a bottle rocket—it ignites, rises high into the sky, higher, higher, until finally, it explodes. The explosion would be the bottle rocket's orgasm.

When two people engage in intercourse, feelings of passion may grow stronger and stronger. As these feelings continue, each person may become more and more excited until finally he/she can no longer control this excitement and the body releases all of its built-up sexual energy.

What does an orgasm feel like?

This is a tough one. One way to describe this release of energy is to imagine being tickled. If you have ticklish feet, imagine playing a game where you lie still on the floor and are not allowed to move. Then imagine somebody tickling your feet with a feather. You're not allowed to move your feet or laugh. Take a few seconds to think about how this would feel. Can you imagine all this laughter building up inside of you? When you can't take it anymore and finally move your feet and burst out laughing, this is what an orgasm feels like (except an orgasm is the release of built-up sexual excitement, not laughter excitement).

How do you know when the male orgasms?

Usually, when the male orgasms he also ejaculates. The male may also feel a release of tension from his groin, butt, legs, and back, almost like a chill running up his back.

The male is usually only capable of one orgasm in a short time. It may take a few minutes to a few hours before the male can become excited enough to get another erection and orgasm again. The male's partner can often feel him ejaculate during intercourse.

How do you know when the female orgasms?

For the female, her body becomes tense. The female orgasm occurs when the vulva and even the uterus release their stored sexual tension. The female may feel her vagina, anus, uterus, hips, back, or entire body begin to shake or throb. If you can imagine shivering when you're cold or get a chill, this is similar to what the female may feel through her body (except an orgasm is much more pleasurable and much more intense).

The female is capable of having more than one orgasm in a short time. This is called having a multiple orgasm. The female will feel her vulva and/or body pulsate and then stop, and then feel another wave of orgasm rush through her. This may occur numerous times.

There is no sure way the male can know if the female is having an orgasm or not. Many times the female feels the need to fake an orgasm for her partner's benefit or because she thinks that is what she is supposed to do. There is no way the male can know for sure.

Do females ejaculate?

Generally speaking, no. Most females will produce a little or quite a bit of vaginal lubrication when aroused or sexually excited, but this is not ejaculation.

Some females, however, have "ejaculated" during their orgasm. There are two small glands called the Skene's glands located near the urinary opening. In some females, the Skene's glands will produce a fluid that will come out or be "ejaculated" during an orgasm. It appears that this doesn't happen in most women. This topic is still being studied.

Why do females sometimes fake orgasms?

There could be many reasons for this. Probably the main reason a female may fake an orgasm is because she thinks that a female is supposed to orgasm every time she engages in intercourse and, if she doesn't, then there is something wrong with her or her partner. After all, when you watch sex scenes on TV or in the movies, the female always has what appears to be an orgasm. So rather than have her partner think that there is some kind of a problem with either one of them, she will fake an orgasm and that way there are no questions asked. A female may also fake an orgasm to show that she was very aroused and that her partner was very sexually satisfying.

Most females report they don't always orgasm during intercourse. Females do say that intercourse is still pleasurable even if they do not orgasm.

Is there something wrong with a female if she doesn't orgasm?

No. Many things determine whether or not a female or male orgasms. If the female does not orgasm, it does not make her any less of a female or mean there is something wrong with her or her partner.

How can you make a person orgasm?

You can't—at least not without the other person's help. This is a questionable point, and some people will argue over this, but the only person who can make you feel good or orgasm is you! Read on.

A person can become stimulated from being touched only if that person thinks he/she is being touched in a pleasing way. For example, if your boyfriend/girlfriend were to touch and kiss your lips, you might find it to be very pleasing and exciting. But what if your brother/sister touched you in the same exact way? You probably would not find it very stimulating. What is the difference between the two touches?

The difference between the touches is what you think and feel about your partner and what you think and feel about your sibling. You may be attracted to your partner in a romantic way, therefore his/her touches would feel good. Your sibling is not someone that you are attracted to in a romantic way, therefore his/her touches would not be pleasing.

You think that your partner's touches are exciting, and therefore they are. You do not think that your sibling's touches would be exciting, and therefore they would not be. How a person perceives (sees/thinks about) something is mostly responsible for what a person finds stimulating.

Do all orgasms feel the same?

No. Orgasms can vary from slight feelings of pleasure to an intense and exhausting release of sexual tension. Not all orgasms are the earth-shattering explosions of pleasure portrayed by the media.

What is foreplay?

Foreplay is a general term used to describe sexual stimulation before intercourse. Foreplay can be kissing, hugging, touching, caressing, talking, listening to music, or anything sexually stimulating to the couple. Foreplay usually increases the amount of sexual tension in the couple.

Unfortunately, a common complaint of some sexually active couples is that one person rushes through foreplay and begins intercourse before the other person is ready. Because each person is different, some people become sexually excited quickly, while others take longer.

For this reason, a sexually active person should try to be sensitive to how his or her partner is feeling and continue with foreplay until both people are feeling the same way. Once again, communication is important.

What is outercourse?

"Outercourse" is a term often used to describe when a couple sexually stimulates each other, sometimes to the point of orgasm, without actually engaging in vaginal, oral, or anal intercourse.

Outercourse has many different names like "noninsertive sex," "mutual masturbation," or, as your parents may have called it, "petting" or "getting to first base/second base/third base." ("Going all the way" or a "home run" meant having vaginal intercourse.)

There is debate over what outercourse is, what it includes, and if it is a good idea for young couples. Most people agree that outercourse can include:
- Touching/caressing/stimulating your partner's chest, breasts, butt, legs, genitals, or any other body part.
- Rubbing your bodies against one another (sometimes called "boning").
- Stimulation with all of your clothes on, some of your clothes off, or all of your clothes off.

The advantages include:
+ It can be very pleasurable and sexually fulfilling.
+ There is no chance of pregnancy, unless semen or prelubricating fluid comes in contact with the vaginal opening—then there is a very slight chance.

+ There is very little chance of getting STDs, as long as infected blood, semen, prelubricating fluid, or vaginal secretions do not enter any openings in the body. There is a slight chance of herpes, crabs, or genital warts infections, but this is not a very common way to transmit these infections.
+ A couple can explore each other's bodies, have sexual intimacy, and relieve sexual tension without the risks of intercourse (pregnancy and STDs).
+ It can postpone (put off) intercourse, possibly for years.

Disadvantages include:
− Outercourse can become "out of control" and lead to intercourse.
− A partner may move too quickly, which can lead to touching that one person is not ready for.
− Once started, it may be difficult to stop or cool down if one person changes his/her mind.

Outercourse can be like a campfire in the forest. It can keep you warm and happy as long as you keep it under control. If the flames get too high or too hot, however, you may have a difficult time putting it out before it becomes a disaster.

Are some parts of the body more sensitive than others?

Yes. The largest and most sensitive organ of the body is the skin. The entire outside of the body is loaded with sensitive nerves that can be stimulated. Some of the more sensitive areas of the body include:

Female: Lips, face, breasts, ears, neck, areolae, nipples, shoulders, clitoris, arms/hands, vaginal opening, stomach, anus, back, butt, mons veneris, labia, perineum, inner thighs, feet.

Male: Lips, face, ears, neck, areolae, nipples, shoulders, penis (glans and shaft), chest, testes, arms/hands, stomach, anus, back, butt, thighs, feet.

What each person finds the most stimulating varies from person to person and situation to situation. Touching these different parts of the body does not guarantee that the person will find it stimulating. Remember, the part of the body that usually needs to be stimulated the most isn't between the legs, but rather between the ears!

What pills/vitamins/foods will make a person better sexually?

There aren't any, really. For years, something called aphrodisiacs have been sold. They are said to give people super sexual powers or put people in the mood to have sex, but these claims simply are not true. These are usually just old myths or get-rich-quick scams trying to take people's money.

Oysters, ginseng, Spanish fly, and conch are just a few of the many hundreds of things that are claimed to be aphrodisiacs and that supposedly promise sexual staying power.

Some doctors prescribe drugs that have side effects that affect a person's libido (sex drive) and sensitivity, but these are not sold as aphrodisiacs.

What is Viagra?

Viagra is a drug given to men who are experiencing erection problems. This drug is not given to young males.

What is the best way to make love?

Are you still asking that? There is no one "best" way. There are many books and stories that try to tell people what the best way is, but these are simply untrue. It is up to the couple to decide what is best for them.

If you have more questions about love, infatuation, relationships, or any other sexuality related issue, you can find additional information at Youth Embassy (www.YouthEmbassy.com).

6

How Babies Are Made

The creation of a new person is one of the most beautiful and amazing things that takes place in life. The process from conception to the birth of a child is miraculous, to say the least. It makes building a skyscraper look insignificant in comparison.

A human being is made of billions of cells. Each of us started out as just one single cell. Over a nine-month period, that cell split again and again to make a baby.

In this chapter we will go over how babies are made, from start to finish. It may be a good idea to read the anatomy chapter before you read this so that you know all the parts of the female involved in pregnancy.

How do a female and a male make a baby?

The first thing that happens when a female and male want to have a baby is they engage in unprotected intercourse (no condom or other birth control method). The male moves his erect penis in and out of the female's vagina until he ejaculates (semen comes out of his penis). When the male ejaculates into the female's vagina, between 200 million to 600 million sperm in the semen quickly travel or "swim" through the vagina. (Sperm are the male eggs.)

Where do the sperm go once they are in the female's vagina?

Once the sperm are in the female's vagina, they quickly start their difficult trip through the cervix into the uterus. This is a difficult trip for the sperm

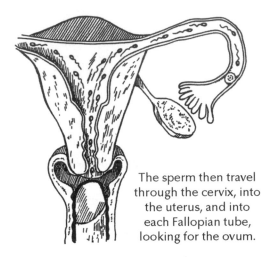

The sperm then travel through the cervix, into the uterus, and into each Fallopian tube, looking for the ovum.

because the environment inside the female tends to destroy sperm. Even by the time the sperm have reached the cervix, many millions of sperm have been destroyed.

The sperm that survive and make it into the uterus travel toward the two Fallopian tubes. Some sperm head into the left Fallopian tube and some go into the right Fallopian tube. Usually only one of the Fallopian tubes will have the female egg (the ovum) traveling through it. The sperm that go into the empty Fallopian tube will soon break apart and be flushed out of the female's body.

The sperm that enter the Fallopian tube with the ovum in it will surround the ovum and try to enter it.

What is conception? Does it mean the same as fertilization?

Fertilization is when a single sperm has just penetrated the ovum. Conception is when a single sperm penetrates the female's ovum, and the two joined cells start to develop (this process takes about twenty-four hours).

As you can see, both terms mean almost the same thing and many people use the terms to describe the same thing.

Remember that the male ejaculates semen that has as many as 600 million sperm in it. By the time the sperm reach the ovum, only about fifty remain. Out of the fifty sperm that surround the egg, only one will be allowed to enter the ovum.

What would happen if two sperm entered the ovum?

That doesn't happen. When the sperm have reached the surface of the ovum, the ovum will start to pull one of the sperm closer and bring it inside. When this happens, a brief electric shock makes the surface of the ovum very hard so that no more sperm can enter. The remaining sperm will soon break apart and be flushed from the female's body.

Just to review, out of 600 million sperm that enter the female's vagina when the male ejaculates, only one will go on to fertilize the ovum, which will then develop into a fetus and then a baby. Imagine—one out of 600 million. Your chances of winning the lottery are about one out of 14 million, which means that you have a better chance at winning the lottery than being born. That's right! Have you heard the saying "You're one in a million"? Actually you're one in 600 million! It would be like going to a Star Search or American Idol audition with 600 million other people and

What is conception?

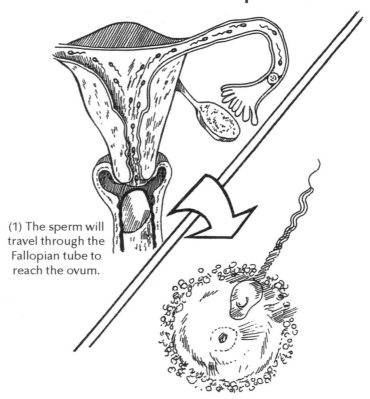

(1) The sperm will travel through the Fallopian tube to reach the ovum.

(2) Conception takes place when a single sperm enters into the ovum.

you were the one selected. You have the genetic information from the one sperm that made it. If any of the other 599,999,999 sperm had made it into your mom's ovum, you might not be here. You are a very special person. Make the most of your life!

(Incidentally, there are about 400 thousand ova that could have matured and been released by the mother. You are a combination of one of 400 thousand ova and one of 600 million sperm. Who said you weren't one heck of a lucky person?)

What is a test-tube baby? IVF or In Vitro Fertilization

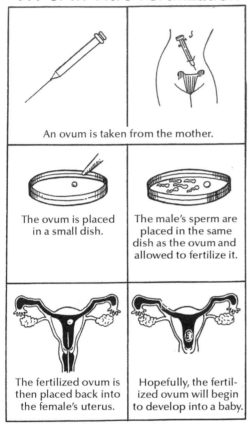

An ovum is taken from the mother.

The ovum is placed in a small dish.

The male's sperm are placed in the same dish as the ovum and allowed to fertilize it.

The fertilized ovum is then placed back into the female's uterus.

Hopefully, the fertilized ovum will begin to develop into a baby.

What is a test-tube baby?

A test-tube baby is made in a laboratory by putting the male's sperm together with the female's ovum in a test tube or small culture dish. This is also known as in vitro fertilization, which means fertilization outside the body. The fertilized ovum is then carefully reinserted, using a medical device, into the female's uterus, where it can grow for nine months.

Couples who are unable to have children by having intercourse can choose from different types of in vitro fertilization. The couple should beware of choosing any doctor or clinic that promises good results. In vitro fertilization is no guarantee that the couple will have a baby. At a cost of $10,000 or more, in vitro fertilization can be very expensive.

The first test-tube baby in history was Louise Brown, born July 25, 1978.

How are twins born?

Twins can develop in two ways. In the first way, after the ovum has been fertilized by the sperm, the ovum may split into two different growing parts. This would cause identical twins to develop. Both brothers or both sisters would look almost exactly alike, and you would have a tough time telling them apart.

The second way that twins can develop is if two ova are released by the mother's ovaries instead of one, and both ova are fertilized by different sperm. For example, if one ovum in the right Fallopian tube is fertilized, and another ovum in the left Fallopian tube is fertilized, this would result in fraternal twins. Fraternal twins—either two brothers, two sisters, or one brother and one sister—would not look alike.

Triplets (three), quadruplets (four), quintuplets (five), and sextuplets (six) can be formed when more than two ova are released by the female and then fertilized by sperm. The record for the most live births is twelve, but only about eight or nine lived. Notice I said "live" births. The problem is, the more fetuses that develop inside the mother's womb (uterus), the more likely it is that one or more of those developing fetuses will not make it to birth. There is also a much greater chance of the mother dying or having a problem giving birth.

How do twins develop?

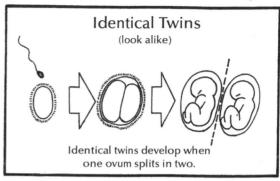

Identical Twins
(look alike)

Identical twins develop when one ovum splits in two.

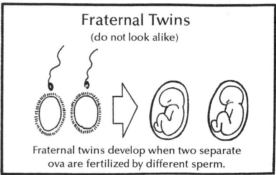

Fraternal Twins
(do not look alike)

Fraternal twins develop when two separate ova are fertilized by different sperm.

Twins seem to run in families. This means that if any of your parents, grandparents, aunts, or uncles has a twin brother or sister, then when the time comes for you to have children, there is a greater chance you will have twins as well.

Today, there are certain types of drugs called "fertility drugs" that females take to help them ovulate (release an ovum from their ovaries). Many times these drugs cause the ovaries to release more than one ovum. When this happens, two or more ova can become fertilized by sperm when a female has intercourse, and twins, triplets, etc. will develop.

What does it mean when a female is pregnant?

When a female becomes pregnant, it means that her ovum has been fertilized by a sperm, and she may have a baby if everything goes well. If the female's ovum becomes fertilized (conception takes place), then she is pregnant.

What happens after conception?

After the sperm has penetrated the ovum, the head of the sperm breaks off and releases the father's genetic information into the ovum. Then this single-celled ovum divides into two cells. Then the two cells divide into four cells. The four cells divide into an eight-cell cluster, then sixteen cells, then thirty-two cells, then sixty-four cells, then one hundred twenty-eight cells, and so on and so on. By the time a baby is born, she/he will be made of billions and billions of cells! And it all started from a single-celled ovum. Amazing, isn't it?

While all the dividing is going on, this cluster of cells is moving through the Fallopian tube toward the womb (uterus). When this cluster of cells, which is now called a blastocyst [blást-oh-sist], finally makes it into the uterus, it will attach itself to the uterine wall, or endometrium. Implantation takes place about ten to twelve days after fertilization. At this point, the blastocyst is starting to receive its oxygen and nourishment from the thick endometrium.

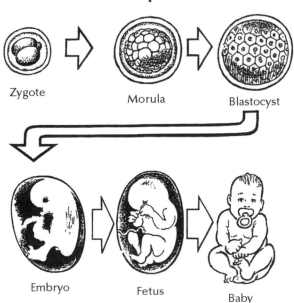

What happens after conception?

Zygote   Morula   Blastocyst

Embryo   Fetus   Baby

After the conception, the fertilized ovum is called the zygote, which develops into the morula, then the blastocyst, then the embryo, fetus, and finally, a baby.

By the fourteenth day after fertilization, the blastocyst is called an embryo [ém-bree-oh], which it will be called up until the end of the eighth week of pregnancy. From the eighth week of pregnancy until birth, the embryo will be called a fetus. Once the fetus is born, it is called a baby. This is a technical and detailed way of identifying different stages of development. Most people just use the term "baby" to describe the developing form inside the female. If you take a look at the list below, you will see the terms used to describe the development of a baby from conception to birth.

ZYGOTE: Fertilization through the first thirty hours.

MORULA: Thirty hours after fertilization to the third or fourth day.

BLASTOCYST: Fourth day after fertilization to the fourteenth day.

EMBRYO: Fourteenth day after fertilization to the eighth week of pregnancy.

FETUS: Eighth week of pregnancy to birth.

BABY: Birth, or the entire development.

How does the "baby" live inside the mother's womb (uterus)?

As the blastocyst implants itself in the wall of the uterus, tiny parts of the blastocyst start to form a soft, cushiony organ called the placenta. Through the placenta, the developing embryo/fetus will get oxygen from the mother's blood as well as nutrients from the mother's food.

Also at this time, a protective bag or sack, called the amniotic sac, starts to form around the fetus. This amniotic sac is made of two thin layers of tissue called the

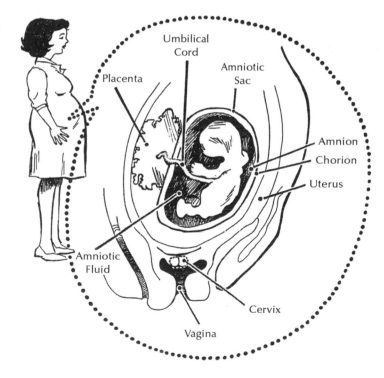

amnion (the inner layer of tissue) and the chorion (the outer layer of tissue). The amniotic sac fills with a warm, thick, fluid called amniotic fluid. The amniotic sac and the amniotic fluid have a few important functions. First, the sac works like a shock absorber that protects the fetus. If mom accidentally bumps into something, the fetus will be protected from getting hurt. The amniotic sac is a lot like a large Ziplock bag filled with honey. If you put an egg into the bag of honey, the egg should be pretty well protected from bumps and bruises. Second, the amniotic fluid keeps the fetus at a nice, warm temperature. Third, because the sac completely surrounds the fetus, it is difficult for germs and bacteria to get close to the fetus.

By the end of the fifth week, a ropelike cord, called the umbilical cord, connects the embryo to the placenta. The umbilical cord has two arteries and a vein inside it that connect the embryo/fetus to the placenta. Through the umbilical cord, the embryo/ fetus will get its nutrients and oxygen from the mother's blood. Also, any waste materials that the embryo/fetus has will pass through the umbilical cord to the mother.

As long as the embryo/fetus is getting enough of the nutrients it needs to develop, and the mother is taking care of herself, the embryo/fetus will start to grow quickly and begin to look like a baby.

When does the baby actually start to look like a baby?

Usually by the eighth week, the embryo starts to take on the shape of a baby, even though it has no chance of surviving on its own at this point.

How does a baby grow?

In the first month, the size of the blastocyst is one millimeter. The heart, brain, digestive system, spinal cord, and nervous system start to develop, and the outline of ears may appear.

During the second month, arm and leg buds develop, the jaw begins to form, and development of the eyes and ears continues. Teeth and facial muscles begin to form. Bones are beginning to develop, and feet can be seen. By the end of the second month, the fetus is about 3 centimeters long (1.2 inches).

Fingernails, toenails, eyelids, and the male or female genitals can be seen in the third month. The major organs are formed, but not completely.

Lips, fingerprints, and hair develop in the fourth month. The fetus begins to swallow small amounts of amniotic fluid (this is known as fetal respiration). The fetus also begins to move. When the mother feels this, it is known as quickening.

By the fifth month, the heartbeat can be heard, and the fetus responds to sound. The fetus may be very active or very still.

By the end of the sixth month, the eyes of the fetus are open. The fetus is about 30 centimeters (12 inches) long and weighs about 1.5 pounds. The fetus has a poor chance of survival if it is born now.

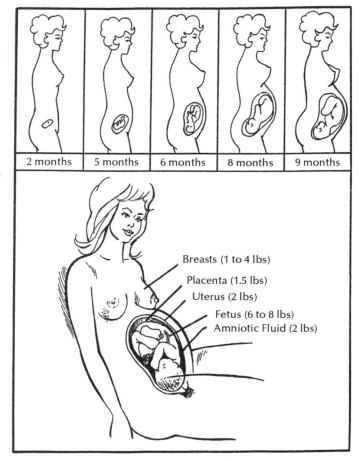

2 months | 5 months | 6 months | 8 months | 9 months

Breasts (1 to 4 lbs)
Placenta (1.5 lbs)
Uterus (2 lbs)
Fetus (6 to 8 lbs)
Amniotic Fluid (2 lbs)

The brain and nervous system are almost completely developed by the seventh month. The fetus has about a 20 percent chance of surviving if it is born now.

In the eighth month, most of the major body systems are developed. The fetus will probably get into a head-down position in the uterus. The fetus has an 85 percent chance of surviving if it is born now.

During the ninth month, the fetus is not as active as it was because there is very little room to move. The eyes are blue. (Other eye colors like brown, hazel, or green will develop after birth when light hits the eyes.)

At the end of the ninth month, the fetus is around 50 centimeters (20 inches) long, and weighs 6 to 7.5 pounds. (Of course, it could weigh a little more or less.)

How long is a female pregnant?

A female is pregnant for about nine months. Sometimes a baby can be born before the nine months is up, but most pregnancies last about nine months.

Quite often you will hear people use the term "trimester" to describe what stage of pregnancy the female or developing fetus is in. A trimester is a three-month time period. Since the female is pregnant for nine months, that is equal to three trimesters. The first trimester is months one, two, and three. The second trimester is months four, five, and six. The third trimester is months seven, eight, and nine.

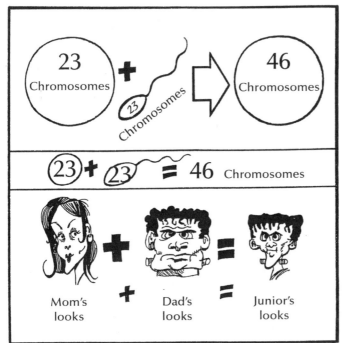

Chromosomes determine what the baby will look like

23 chromosomes from the mother's ovum, plus 23 chromosomes from Dad's sperm, will give the child his/her looks.

What makes a baby a boy or girl?

Chromosomes. Chromosomes are tiny packets of information that determine whether a boy or a girl will be born and what the child will look like. Chromosomes are also called genes.

The mother's ovum has twenty-three chromosomes and the father's sperm has twenty-three chromosomes. When the mother's ovum and father's sperm combine, there are forty-six chromosomes that determine what the baby will look like. Hair color, skin color, height, and everything else that makes a person look the way he/she does are all determined by the parents' chromosomes. Since twenty-three chromosomes come from the father and twenty-three chromosomes come from the mother, the child will usually look similar to mom or dad, or a combination of both.

What determines whether a boy baby or a girl baby is born?

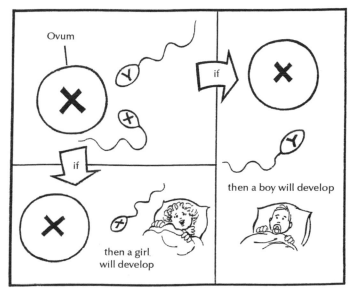

If a Y sperm fertilizes the X ovum, a boy will develop.
If an X sperm fertilizes the X ovum, a girl will develop.

Whether a child will be a boy or girl depends on two chromosomes in particular. One chromosome is the X chromosome and the other is the Y chromosome. The X chromosome causes a girl to develop and the Y chromosome causes a boy to develop. The mother's ovum always has an X chromosome in it. The father's sperm has an X chromosome or a Y chromosome. If a sperm with an X chromosome fertilizes the mother's X chromosome ovum, then a girl will develop. (X + X = girl.) If a sperm with a Y chromosome fertilizes the mother's X chromosome ovum, then a boy will develop. (X + Y = boy.)

So as you can see, the father is responsible for whether the child is a boy or a girl, not the mother, as some people think.

How does the female feel throughout the pregnancy?

This varies from female to female, but let's try to break it down trimester by trimester.

A pregnant female may experience

Morning Sickness

(which can occur at any time of day).

During the first trimester (first, second, and third months of pregnancy), the female may experience "morning sickness," which is nausea (feeling like you're going to throw up) and vomiting (throwing up). The female can experience this any time of day, not just the morning. Not all females will experience this, but most do. Usually within a month or two, morning sickness goes away. Also during the first trimester, the female usually has to go to the bathroom a lot (frequent urination), and her breasts become larger and very tender.

Emotionally, the female may feel very happy and excited that she is going to have a baby. Or, like many teenagers who become pregnant, she may feel sad, depressed, embarrassed, angry, and scared. The female's feelings depend a lot on whether she wanted to have a baby or not and if she feels that she is ready for the responsibilities of being a mother.

During the second trimester (fourth, fifth, and sixth months of pregnancy), the female's body starts to take on a different shape. Her abdomen (the space between the stomach and the genitals) starts to bulge and get bigger as the fetus gets larger. The female's breasts continue to grow, and regular clothes don't fit well anymore. About this time, the female may not be too happy about the way she looks.

Also during the second trimester, the female may experience constipation (she has a hard time going to the bathroom), stretch marks, edema (bloating), and varicose veins (large, painful veins), and her nipples may become larger and darker in color. A fluid called colostrum may start to occasionally come out of the female's nipples. Colostrum is a thin, yellowish fluid that the breasts make before breast milk is produced.

During the fourth month, the female starts to experience quickening, when she feels the fetus moving around inside her uterus. This is usually exciting, and the mother may feel little kicks or hits by the fetus.

During the third and final trimester (seventh, eighth, and ninth months of pregnancy), things are really changing on the female. She has probably gained at least twenty pounds and her abdomen is bulging out. Her back hurts, legs cramp, and she has a difficult time getting comfortable. Many females at this point say they feel like beached whales. The female may become very moody and irritable and cry for no apparent reason. Sleeping becomes difficult, and the female spends a lot of time going to the bathroom.

The female may also begin to feel tired, scared, worried, and depressed (if she is not already). But most females are happy and can't wait for the baby to be born. This is often a very exciting time.

How is a baby born?

Around the ninth month of pregnancy, the female will feel a trickle or a gushing of fluid coming out of her vagina. This means that her "water broke." (Actually, the amniotic sac has burst and amniotic fluid is coming out.) When the "water breaks," it usually means that labor will most likely start within a day. Labor is when the female's uterus starts to squeeze and contract. This is known as a contraction, which helps push the baby out. Labor is when the mother begins to feel discomfort. In fact, labor is downright painful and hard, physical work. Most

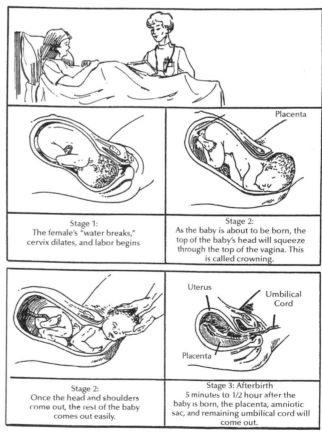

Stage 1:
The female's "water breaks,"
cervix dilates, and labor begins

Placenta

Stage 2:
As the baby is about to be born, the top of the baby's head will squeeze through the top of the vagina. This is called crowning.

Stage 2:
Once the head and shoulders come out, the rest of the baby comes out easily.

Uterus

Umbilical Cord

Placenta

Stage 3: Afterbirth
5 minutes to 1/2 hour after the baby is born, the placenta, amniotic sac, and remaining umbilical cord will come out.

women who have had children will gladly go into great detail to tell what labor pain was like.

While the uterus contracts, the female is also feeling another kind of discomfort. The cervix (the small opening from the uterus to the vagina) starts to spread and widen. This is called dilation. The opening to the cervix is normally as wide as a pencil, but in order for the baby to leave the uterus and go through the vagina to be born, the cervix must spread open ten centimeters (about four inches). Imagine an opening the width of a pencil widening to four inches! Do you think the mother-to-be might be feeling a little pain or discomfort? I think so, too.

Labor can last for many hours. The first time a female is pregnant, labor usually lasts around fourteen hours, but labor can last much longer or not as long. Usually a female's second or third delivery goes much more smoothly and takes far less time.

When the cervix has dilated to ten centimeters, the baby starts its trip out of the uterus, through the cervix, and out the vagina. The first part of the baby that the doctor or midwife hopes to see is the top of the head. When the head starts to squeeze through the opening of the vagina, it is called crowning.

As the mother continues to "push" (she tightens or squeezes her abdominal muscles to help force out the baby), the head will emerge and then the shoulders will follow. Once the shoulders fit through, the rest of the baby tends to slide out a bit more easily.

The doctor or midwife will wipe away any fluid from the baby's face and use a little suction device to suck out amniotic fluid from the baby's nose, mouth, and throat. Once the baby has been born, it will usually take its first breath of air on its own or the doctor or midwife will provide some assistance.

The umbilical cord will be clamped (squeezed shut) and then cut. From there the baby is cleaned up and presented to mom and dad for their first family meeting. As most parents will say, this is an unbelievable rush of excitement like none other in life.

Usually within a half-hour after the birth of the baby, the afterbirth will come out of the vagina. The afterbirth is the placenta and any remains of the amniotic sac and umbilical cord. The afterbirth is then usually thrown away.

The mother's breasts are still producing colostrum (the thin, yellowish, pre-milk fluid) for the baby. After about two days, breast milk will be produced, and the baby will get its nourishment from breastfeeding, or the parents may decide to use a store-bought formula and feed the baby from a bottle.

Can a female have any problems during pregnancy?

Yes. There are a few things that can go wrong during a pregnancy.

Premature babies, or "preemies," are born before the ninth month of pregnancy. Preemies are more likely to have health problems or die because they have not fully developed to the point that they can survive outside of the uterus. This depends a lot on how early the baby is born. If the baby is born during the seventh month of pregnancy, there is only about a 20 percent chance that the baby will live (not good). If the baby is born during the eighth month, there is about an 85 percent chance that the baby will live (very good). Today, hospitals have many different kinds of equipment that help the premature baby survive until it is better developed.

Toxemia is another problem that may arise during pregnancy. Toxemia is when the female suddenly has high blood pressure, severe edema (bloating), and protein in her urine (which is not good). This can cause the mother or fetus to die if it is not controlled. No one is sure what causes toxemia, but if it is treated, it shouldn't cause a serious problem.

Birth defects may cause the fetus to develop abnormally. An example of a birth defect is Down's syndrome. Down's syndrome is a type of mental retardation that is caused by a chromosome disorder. Other birth defects can be caused by infections, drug use, or the age when the female gets pregnant. Some birth defects are simply inherited. To help reduce the risk of some birth defects, folic acid or folacin (which is a B vitamin) is recommended.

Ectopic pregnancy is a pregnancy occurring outside the uterus. When the growing cluster of cells starts to develop in the Fallopian tube instead of the uterus, it puts the mother in great danger. The Fallopian tubes are very thin. If an ectopic pregnancy continues, it will burst the Fallopian tube and the mother may die. Most ectopic pregnancies will not go that far, but some-times the doctor will need to perform surgery to remove the embryo before any damage can be done. The most common cause of ectopic pregnancy is

PID (pelvic inflammatory disease), which causes the Fallopian tube to swell shut so that the fertilized egg cannot pass through.

Miscarriage or stillbirth is when the embryo or fetus dies within the mother's womb (uterus). The mother may see and feel a heavy flow of blood and fluid from her vagina. If this occurs, it is possibly a sign that the female has just had a miscarriage. If a miscarriage occurs in the second or third trimester, the doctor will need to surgically remove the fetus. A female may have a miscarriage for many reasons. Perhaps her diet was poor, or she smoked (anything), or used drugs and alcohol while she was pregnant. Some doctors think that the female will miscarry if the embryo/fetus has a birth defect, but the exact reason is usually never known.

Amniocentesis

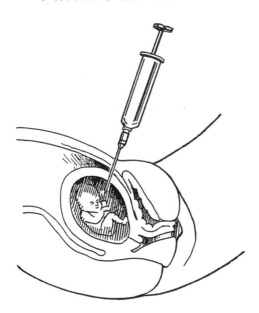

An amniocentesis takes a sample of the amniotic fluid and tests it for birth defects.

Are there any tests to check for birth defects during pregnancy?

Yes. Quite often the pregnant female will have one of three tests done to check the fetus for birth defects.

An amniocentesis is done by inserting a thin needle through the female's abdomen and into the amniotic sac (the sac of skin that surrounds the fetus). Some of the amniotic fluid is sucked out and then tested to see if any birth defects are present. The amniocentesis can tell the parents if the fetus will have Down's syndrome or muscular dystrophy, and even if the fetus is female or male. The amniocentesis cannot be performed until the fourth month of pregnancy.

Chorionic villi sampling, or CVS, can be done as early as the second month of pregnancy. This test uses a thin tube inserted into the female's vagina, through the cervix, and into the uterus. A small sample of the outer layer of the amniotic sac (the chorion) is taken and studied to see if the developing fetus has any birth defects.

An ultrasound can also be done to detect some birth defects, determine if there are twins, and identify the sex of the fetus. The ultrasound uses sound waves to "take a picture" of what the fetus looks like.

It should be noted that there are slight risks involved with these tests, so it is always a good idea to talk with the doctor before these tests are done.

Chorionic Villi Sampling or CVS

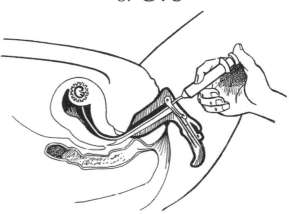

CVS takes a small piece of the chorion (amniotic sac) and tests it for birth defects.

Can any problems occur during childbirth?

A breech birth may occur, which may endanger the lives of both the baby and the mother. A breech birth is when the baby's feet or butt starts to come out first instead of the head. In this case, the doctor or midwife may try to reposition the baby so the head will come out first. If the doctor or midwife cannot reposition the baby, a Cesarean section (surgery) will need to be performed by the doctor.

A prolapsed cord may also endanger the baby's life during birth. A prolapsed cord is when the umbilical cord is wrapped around the baby's neck so that blood flow to the baby through the umbilical cord is cut off. Once again, the doctor or midwife may try to reposition the baby and untangle the umbilical cord, or, if that doesn't work, a Cesarean section will need to be performed by the doctor.

What is a Cesarean section (C-section)?

A Cesarean section, or C-section, operation takes the baby out of the mother through her abdomen. A cut is made across the mother's abdomen with a scalpel (small, sharp knife) and the doctor reaches into the abdomen and removes the baby. Cesareans are done if there is danger to the mother's or baby's health.

Episiotomy

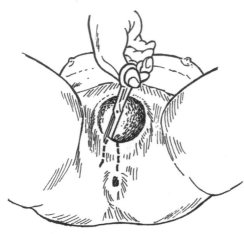

An episiotomy is when the doctor makes a cut from the female's vagina to the perineum if the baby's head and body are too big.

Does the doctor cut the opening to the vagina during birth?

Sometimes the doctor will make a small cut from the opening of the vagina down through the perineum (space between the vagina and the anus). This procedure is called an episiotomy. The doctor may do this to take some of the pressure off the baby's head when it is coming out of the vagina or to prevent tearing of the perineum. Believe it or not, this doesn't usually hurt the mother, and the cut is stitched up after birth.

What should the female do during pregnancy to make sure she has a healthy baby?

Actually, the female needs to start taking care of herself before she becomes pregnant. When the female does become pregnant, how she lives is important to the health of the fetus. How the mother takes care of herself to increase the chances of having a healthy baby is called prenatal care.

When the female becomes pregnant, it is important that she go to the doctor for a checkup and to find out what prenatal care she must follow to have a healthy baby. The kind of doctor she should see is called an ob-gyn [pronounced O-B-G-Y-N], which is short for obstetrician/gynecologist. An obstetrician is a doctor who is specially trained in everything that happens during pregnancy and childbirth. A gynecologist is a doctor who is specially trained to know about the female sexual reproductive organs and hormones and female reproductive health in general. An ob-gyn is trained in both areas of obstetrics and gynecology, so the female gets an all-in-one deal. The ob-gyn will give the female checkups, offer directions for prenatal care, and see that the pregnancy goes along as smoothly as possible.

Here are just a few of the things that the mother-to-be should do to increase her chances of having a healthy baby.

GET REGULAR CHECKUPS AT THE DOCTOR. This will alert the mother-to-be of any problems, give her guidance and direction as far as what she should be doing, and offer support in what she may be feeling.

EAT WELL AND PRACTICE GOOD NUTRITIONAL HABITS. The female will need extra calories from protein foods like meat, chicken, turkey, fish, milk, eggs, cheese, and yogurt, as well as extra calories from carbohydrate foods like vegetables, rice, wheat bread, pasta, oatmeal, potatoes, beans, and fruits. If the female is a vegetarian or has a problem eating a wide variety of foods, it would be a good idea to discuss this with a nutritionist who can develop a healthy eating program for her. The nutritionist will also be able to recommend whether or not a vitamin and mineral supplement should be taken. The female should not just pick up a bottle of vitamins and assume that it is safe for her and the developing fetus. It would be best to talk with the nutritionist or doctor about that.

Sometimes the female may feel that it is okay to eat "anything and everything." Although most doctors recommend that the female gain between twenty to twenty-five pounds by the end of nine months of pregnancy, gaining too much weight (over forty pounds) may not be to the female's or the fetus' advantage—not to mention the difficulty of trying to lose the additional weight after the baby is born.

EXERCISE. Exercise before, during, and after pregnancy is almost always beneficial and usually recommended by the doctor. Most exercises, like walking, stationary bicycling, low-impact aerobics, swimming, and even tennis or jogging, will help the female better prepare for the delivery of the baby. Of course, it is best to use common sense when choosing an exercise activity. Any exercise that may send the pregnant female slamming into trees, walls, or hard surfaces should obviously be avoided. Also, the female needs to remember not to overdo it and exercise with too much intensity for too long. During strenuous exercise, the female's body heats up and she sweats, which is good, but the fetus inside the female has no way of cooling down, which could lead to damage. The pregnant

What should a female do to have a healthy baby?

female should speak with her doctor before engaging in any type of physical exercise and, of course, remember to drink plenty of water when she does exercise.

No smoking anything! Smoking tobacco cigarettes or marijuana (dope, pot, ganja, grass, weed) by the pregnant female or anyone around the female will increase the chances of having a low birth-weight baby (which can lead to the death of the baby), a baby with a lower I.Q. (not as smart as it could have been), a miscarriage, problems during pregnancy and labor, and health problems for the baby after it is born. Cigarettes, cigars, and marijuana contain toxins (poisons). When the pregnant female or someone around her smokes, these poisons go from the mother's lungs into her bloodstream and are then carried to the developing fetus. The mother-to-be must not smoke during her pregnancy and must do her best to avoid situations where people around her may be smoking. Remember, the fetus cannot protect itself—only mom and dad can protect it.

NO DRUGS. This includes drinking any type of alcohol, like beer, wine, wine coolers, or hard liquor. All illegal street drugs (like cocaine, heroin, ecstasy, and LSD, just to name a few), as well as legal prescription drugs and pills you might find in a drugstore, can cause miscarriage, premature birth, low birth weight, deformities (abnormally shaped body parts), and problems after birth.

Is it okay to have intercourse when the female is pregnant?

Most of the time the answer is yes. The couple can continue to engage in intercourse with no problems at all up until the eighth or ninth month of pregnancy. The only difference is that the couple may need to be a bit more creative. No, the penis will not damage the developing fetus. (Remember, the penis enters the vagina, and the fetus develops in the uterus. These are two different places.) Some couples may also engage in oral intercourse during pregnancy with no problems.

The only time the couple should not engage in intercourse during pregnancy is when the female has a history of miscarriage. As always, the couple should discuss this with the doctor.

How does a female know if she is pregnant?

A female will know if she is pregnant by getting a pregnancy test. Until she gets a pregnancy test, she will not know for sure. The signs of pregnancy include a missed period, frequent urination (the need to pee a lot), nausea (feeling sick to your stomach), vomiting (throwing up), and fatigue (feeling tired).

Even if the female has all these signs, it does not mean she is definitely pregnant. Quite often diet, stress, worry, and changes in hormone levels will bring about these signs as well. Many times a female who has engaged in intercourse will have one or more of these signs and think she's pregnant. It may turn out that she is not pregnant—just worried or under a lot of stress.

Sometimes a female who has engaged in unprotected intercourse may not have any of the five signs, except for a missed period, and actually be pregnant. The only way to know for sure if a female is pregnant is to have a pregnancy test done.

How can you get a pregnancy test done?

A pregnancy test can be done at a doctor's office, health clinic, or by purchasing a home pregnancy kit at a drugstore or supermarket. The most accurate way is to go to a doctor or health clinic and have the test done there.

If the female thinks she might be pregnant, she can go to a doctor or health clinic and have the test done quickly and accurately without anyone else knowing or finding out. The female will simply go into the office, and the doctor/nurse will ask her to urinate in a little cup. From there, the urine will be tested to see if it has a chemical in it called HCG. HCG stands for human chorionic gonadotropin. If the female is pregnant, the placenta will produce this HCG, which will show up in her urine. If HCG is in the urine, the doctor will say that the female's pregnancy test is positive: she is pregnant. If the doctor comes back and says that the test is negative, it means she is not pregnant.

The cost of having a pregnancy test done varies. It can range from free to $15 or more, depending on where the test is done and in what part of the country the person lives. The best thing to do is call your local health department and ask around. Other organizations, like Planned Parenthood can provide pregnancy tests or information on where to get one done. Anyone, regardless of age, can get a pregnancy test done.

Are the home pregnancy kits accurate?

Yes. The home pregnancy kits are usually very reliable, although they are sometimes difficult to interpret (understand the results). The nice thing about home pregnancy kits is that the female can do the test in the privacy of her own home without having to wait at a clinic or schedule an appointment at a doctor's office. The downside is that if the test shows up positive (the female is pregnant), then another test will need to be done at the doctor's office anyway, just to be sure. The cost of most home pregnancy tests is from $10 to $15. Anyone can buy a home pregnancy test.

Home pregnancy tests work in a similar way to the pregnancy test given at clinics and doctors' offices. The directions should be read and followed closely to make sure that the results are as accurate as possible. Most tests have the female urinate in a tiny cup and then mix a couple of drops of the urine with the chemicals in the pregnancy kit. The results are usually ready in five to ten minutes.

Can a female get her period even though she is pregnant?

It is possible to have a fertilized egg in a Fallopian tube while the female is shedding her uterine lining during the first month, but a reddish or mucous discharge (fluid) may come out of the vagina during pregnancy, and this is not her period. In some women a discharge can appear during pregnancy, but once again, this is not a period.

If a female has had a positive pregnancy test (meaning she is pregnant), and then there is a flow of blood or an unusually heavy discharge coming from the vagina in the weeks following, then the female should see her doctor or midwife immediately. She may be having a miscarriage.

Are there any warning signs that something may be wrong with the pregnancy?

There are a few signs that may signal a problem. They include:
- Heavy vaginal discharge or any vaginal bleeding.
- Swollen face or fingers.
- Bad headaches all the time.
- Blurred vision.
- Abdominal pain and chills or fever.
- Painful urination.

What is a midwife?

A nurse-midwife is specially trained in helping females through pregnancy and childbirth. Midwives are experienced in delivering babies and will usually stay with the pregnant female during her entire labor, unless there is a life-threatening situation or a Cesarean section is needed. For normal births, the midwife is there to comfort, guide, and assist the female through the experience. Many people choose to have their babies delivered by midwives.

Does the female really get food cravings during her pregnancy?

Most females will experience a strong desire to have certain kinds of foods during pregnancy. It does not necessarily have to be weird food combinations like pickles and ice cream, although it can be, but just a strong urge to have a certain kind of normal food.

Quite often the female will also have a strong dislike for a food that she normally enjoys. Sometimes just the thought of a certain food may make the female sick to her stomach.

Some doctors think that food cravings are the way the body lets the female know what nutrients she needs.

Will the father feel any sickness during the female's pregnancy?

Some men feel what their wives are going through during the first trimester. This is called couvade syndrome. The husband may feel nauseated and experience vomiting, bloating, and even some food cravings. No one knows why this happens.

What are natural childbirth and Lamaze classes all about?

Natural childbirth and the Lamaze methods are alike in that they try to reduce stress and pain during childbirth. Lamaze classes are offered so that the parents-to-be can prepare for childbirth by learning ways of relaxing through special breathing techniques, physical exercises, and focusing.

If you watch a lot of TV, you have probably seen shows where a couple sits on the floor in a room with other pregnant couples and breathes in funny ways. That is a natural childbirth class, also called a Lamaze class.

Couvade Syndrome

Couvade syndrome is when the male feels the same things as the pregnant female.

What's wrong with him?

Natural childbirth usually means that when the female is about to have the baby, she won't use any drugs to lessen the pain. That is the reason the couple goes to natural childbirth or Lamaze classes; the female learns how to breathe and focus her attention to handle the pain.

Even though natural childbirth is intended to be a birth without the use of painkillers, as long as the female goes to the classes and practices her breathing techniques, even if she does get pain-killing drugs at the time of birth, some people still consider it natural childbirth. A common painkiller used today is called an epidural. The epidural injection is placed in the mother's back and keeps her from experiencing any pain below her abdomen.

Natural Childbirth or Lamaze Classes
help the mother prepare for childbirth.

If the mother does have painkillers given to her during labor, there is no shame in it, nor does it mean that she is a wimp or sissy. Labor pain varies from female to female, and if you can try to imagine blowing an orange out your nose, you might be able to understand what every mom must go through during a vaginal childbirth. Go find Mom and give her a big kiss!

If you have more questions about how babies are made, pregnancy, prenatal care, birth, or any other sexuality related issue, you can find additional information at Youth Embassy (www.YouthEmbassy.com).

7

Contraception (Birth Control)

Here you are! It's good that you have taken the first step in being responsible and are finding out how to protect yourself and your partner from some of the consequences of sex. Before we find out some of the best ways to protect against unwanted pregnancy and STDs, I should probably tell you a little about what will happen in your life. Put your fingertips on the page so I can feel your cosmic energy. Are your fingers on the page? Ah, yes, I can see it now.

The Facts of Life

FACT 1: You will sometimes meet people you should not trust.

You will meet people with good looks, warm smiles, and charming personalities. But the fact is, many people simply don't care about pregnancy or STDs, maybe even the person who you feel is that special someone.

This does not mean all people will try to take advantage of you, but you should realize that some people will say and do anything to get what they want. Sometimes it is difficult to know who is being honest with you and who is just feeding you lines. Regardless, you always need to look out for your own protection and not depend on anyone to do it for you when it comes to intercourse, your body, and your life.

FACT 2: There will be times when you become confused and unsure of what to do. Everyone has experienced difficult situations and needed to make tough decisions (especially regarding sex); you will be no different. One way to get through these rough times is to follow a three-step plan:

1. Prepare yourself. Get all the facts (which you are doing by reading this book) and develop a plan for when you are faced with a tough situation. (In other words, know what you are getting into and what you want to do before anything happens.)

2. Take control. Once you're in a confusing situation, take control of yourself and follow your game plan.

3. Protect yourself. Remember, there will be times when you will be on your own and nobody will be there to stick up for you and what you want. You need to stand up for yourself and make sure your partner doesn't endanger your health or your future. Make sure you clearly communicate your feelings and what you want.

FACT 3: You may feel pressure to have sex just to make your boyfriend/girlfriend happy. Sometimes we feel the need to be loved and accepted by another person, so we think we should do whatever he/she likes to make him/her happy.

If you feel this way, reread facts 1 and 2 and remind yourself that if the other person really cared about you, he/she would not want to make you feel uncomfortable or push you into doing anything you didn't want to do.

Almost every person who has made the mistake of having sex with someone for this reason has looked back at the decision and regretted it. This would be a good opportunity to learn from another person's mistakes and not engage in intercourse just to "keep" your partner or make him/her happy.

Wait! Do I see more? Is someone calling you Mommy or Daddy? Are you very pale and covered with open sores from an STD? It's very fuzzy and unclear. I guess your decisions will determine what happens.

What is contraception (birth control)?

Contraception (birth control) is a way of preventing unwanted pregnancy and, in some cases, sexually transmitted diseases (STDs). Some contraceptives are excellent at preventing unwanted pregnancy and STDs, while others are excellent at preventing unwanted pregnancy, but not STDs. Some are not very good at preventing either.

Many contraceptives, when used correctly each and every time a couple engages in intercourse, will provide good protection against unwanted pregnancy and most STDs. The amount of protection varies from contraceptive to contraceptive. Although only one form of contraception provides 100 percent protection—abstinence—there are many others that provide excellent protection, even though they are not perfect.

Most contraceptives are inexpensive and available to young people, and many are quick and easy to use with a little practice.

Why don't some people like using contraception?

Some people make excuses for not using contraceptives. Some of the more common excuses are:
- It spoils the romance and spontaneity of the moment.
- It lessens the sensitivity, feeling, and enjoyment.
- It costs too much.
- It means you don't trust your partner.
- It's not natural.
- It's embarrassing.

Some people give many other reasons for not wanting to use contraception, but they are all just excuses to cover up the real reasons. Here are a few of the real reasons why some people don't want to use contraception.

THE PERSON DOES NOT KNOW THE RISKS INVOLVED IN UNPROTECTED INTERCOURSE. Many people are not as educated as you are becoming about the risks involved in unprotected intercourse. Some people still don't know that unprotected intercourse can lead to pregnancy and sexually transmitted diseases. People will make excuses for not wanting to use contraception because they don't believe in the possible dangers involved. If you come across a person like this, educate him or her, and, of course, protect yourself.

THE PERSON DOES NOT CARE ABOUT THE RISKS INVOLVED IN UNPROTECTED INTERCOURSE. Believe it or not, some people could care less if their partner became pregnant or infected with an STD, even one that could lead to AIDS. This is sad, but true. These people will use every excuse in the book not to use contraception. Be prepared and protect yourself!

THE PERSON BELIEVES THAT UNPLANNED PREGNANCY AND STD INFECTION ONLY HAPPEN TO OTHER PEOPLE. If you know someone like this, or you believe this yourself, it's time to wake up and smell the coffee. Even though each person is unique, each person has something in common with everyone else—a human body that can get sick.

Anyone who participates in unprotected intercourse is asking for an unplanned pregnancy or STD. Certainly you may beat the odds for a while, but not every time. An unplanned pregnancy or STD will change your world forever.

Regardless of where a person is from, on this planet, no one is immune to unplanned pregnancy and STDs. Protect yourself.

THE PERSON DOES NOT KNOW HOW TO USE CONTRACEPTION. Once again, many people have not received the type of information that you will read about contraception. Nobody likes to admit they don't know something, especially when it comes to intercourse. So rather than show off their ignorance, they will make up excuses to avoid using contraception. If you are going to engage in intercourse, be sure you know how to use at least one form of contraception. If you think your partner might not know how to use a form of contraception, be prepared to use your own. Protect yourself!

THE PERSON IS NOT CONFIDENT USING A CONTRACEPTIVE AND FEELS EMBARRASSED. The best solution for this problem is practice. The more times a person does something, the better at it he/she becomes—more confident and comfortable. The more confident and comfortable a person is doing something, the more likely he/she is to make it a positive habit.

Remember the first time you tried tying your shoe? You were probably all thumbs, and it took you awhile to get it right. After ten or twenty tries, tying your shoes became a bit easier. Soon you could tie your shoes with your eyes closed and without even thinking about what you were doing.

Whichever form of contraception you choose, sit at home, by yourself, and practice using it over and over and over again until you can do it quickly and with your eyes closed. Practice, be confident, and protect yourself.

If you ever hear someone give you an excuse for not using contraception, remember some of the real reasons why he/she may not want to use contraception, and be ready to protect yourself.

Who is responsible for contraception—the male or female?

Both. Since a pregnancy or an STD will affect both the male and the female, both are equally responsible for protection against unwanted pregnancy and STDs.

However, who is the person who becomes pregnant for nine months? Ladies, this is not a sexist remark, but since it is you who might become pregnant and must deal with the situation immediately, you need to protect yourself at all costs. Do not count on your partner to be responsible, regardless of how you feel for him romantically.

Guys, you are not off the hook. Even though the female becomes pregnant, you are still responsible for the care of a child, which lasts many years—much longer than the sex did. You will be legally required to pay eighteen years of child support, and the responsibility of caring for a child will dramatically change your plans for your education, career, financial situation, and family life. Protect yourself.

Why should I use contraception?

Can you imagine what would happen to a police officer who didn't wear a bullet-proof vest in a shoot-out? How about a race car driver who did not wear a seat belt and helmet during a high-speed race? Think about what would happen if a professional football player didn't use a helmet and shoulder pads during a bone-crushing game. As you might imagine, these people would be taking a risk by going into a situation without protection. Contraception is the protection that is needed to engage in intercourse. Just like playing in the Super Bowl without wearing a helmet and the proper protective equipment would be foolish and dangerous, so would having sex without using contraception.

Even though there are no contraceptives that offer 100 percent protection (except for abstinence), using contraception during intercourse will provide you with excellent, good, or at least much better protection against unplanned pregnancy and STDs than not using anything at all. Why should you use contraception?

- Contraception helps prevent unplanned pregnancy.
- Using condoms correctly every time you engage in intercourse will help protect against most STDs, including HIV/AIDS.
- Contraception offers "peace of mind," helping you and your partner to relax and enjoy the experience without having to worry.
- Using contraception shows your partner that you care enough about his/her health and future to prevent an unplanned pregnancy or STD.
- By using contraception you show that you know what the possible consequences of intercourse are, what contraception is, and how to use an excellent form of contraception.
- Using contraception shows that you are mature enough to realize contraception is needed and that you are responsible enough to protect yourself and your partner's health and future.

This list can go on and on, but you should get the idea by now. You don't jump out of a plane without a parachute, and you don't have sex without contraception.

Are contraceptives easy to use?

Yes. With a little practice, most contraceptives are easy to use and can be applied in only a few seconds.

What are the most effective forms of contraception?

At the end of this chapter is a list of the contraceptives available in the United States. Other contraceptives used or tested in Europe are not included in the chart.

Abstinence

Abstinence means not engaging in intercourse. This is the only method that offers 100 percent protection against unwanted pregnancy and STDs. Abstinence is a good idea since STDs are quickly spreading, and unplanned pregnancy, especially among teens, is still far too common.

How well does it prevent unplanned pregnancy?

Abstinence is 100 percent effective all the time.

How well does it protect against STDs?

Offers 100 percent protection all the time.

How do I use it?

The decision to abstain sometimes takes great discipline and an ability to resist pressure, especially during the teen years when hormones, feelings, and peer pressure are at an all-time high.

The following points may help you remain logical and stick to your decision to abstain. A pregnancy would jeopardize:
- The fun you could have during the rest of your teen years.
- Your plans to get your high school diploma.
- Your plans to get a college degree or career training.
- Your career and the money you could earn over a lifetime.
- Your freedom to do what you want.
- Your reputation.
- Your relationship with your parents or friends.

A sexually transmitted disease could:
- Be painful.
- Cause you to feel sick.
- Cause you to be sterile (no children when you want them).
- Require lifelong treatment.
- Cut your chances of having a healthy baby later in life.
- Shorten your life.

Remember, you can engage in intercourse later in life, when you and your spouse/partner are better prepared. You can be affectionate and loving in ways other than sex. And by abstaining from sexual intercourse, you will be doing what YOU want to do, not what someone else wants you to do.

How does it work?

By not engaging in intercourse, there is no chance for the male sperm to fertilize the female ovum and cause pregnancy. Also, there is no contact with body fluids that may have sexually transmitted germs.

What are its side effects?

None.

Where can I get it?

It's within your willpower.

How much does it cost?

It's free.

What are its disadvantages?

You may feel pressure from your friends or partner, or you may feel that everybody else is doing it (which is far from the truth) and that you're missing out on something. Also, some people may decide to be abstinent but end up having sex anyway, often without any contraception.

What are its advantages?

You protect your health and future, and you don't need to worry about what may happen or what people might think.

Do I need parental consent?

Are you kidding?

Any recommendations?

For ways to say no to sex, read the chapters about STDs and How to Say No to Sex.

Birth Control Pills (BC-Pills)

Birth control pills (BC-pills) are one of the most popular contraceptives used today. BC-pills are also one of the most effective nonsurgical methods of preventing pregnancy available.

How well does it prevent unplanned pregnancy?

BC-pills are highly effective at preventing unplanned pregnancy (more than 99 percent effective).

How well does it protect against STDs?

BC-pills do not offer any protection against STDs. Therefore, you should also use another method of contraception that protects against STDs, like a condom.

How do I use it?

BC-pills come in a one-month supply of twenty-one or twenty-eight tiny pills, individually wrapped in little packets. BC-pills are reliable and easy to use. The most difficult part is remembering to take one pill each day.

The female must remember to take one pill each day so that the amount of hormone stays at a level that prevents ovulation. If the female forgets to take her pill one day, she should take two pills the next day. If the female forgets to take her pill two days in a row, then she should take two pills as soon as she remembers, and then two pills again the next day. The female should then continue to take one pill a day. Because missing two days in a row may lower the level of hormone in the female's system, she should use another form of contraception for the rest of her cycle.

If the female forgets to take the pill three days in a row or forgets to take the pill three or more times during her cycle, she should use another form of contraception to prevent pregnancy for the rest of her cycle and closely follow the instructions that came with the pills.

The female can start using a new supply of BC-pills at the beginning of her next period. BC-pills should not be shared with anyone.

Important note: The female must use BC-pills every day for one month before she can rely on them to prevent pregnancy. During this month, she should use another form of contraception to prevent pregnancy.

BC-pills should not be used just on the days the female is going to have sex! BC-pills need to be taken every day, even if the female is not going to engage in intercourse.

How does it work?

BC-pills are made of hormones or hormone-like chemicals called estrogen and/or progestin (like the female hormone progesterone). These hormones are found in the female's body and prevent the ovaries from ovulating. If there is no ovulation (release of an ovum), then no egg can be fertilized by the male sperm. If the ovum can't be fertilized, the female cannot become pregnant.

What are its side effects?

Some are good, some are not so good. Females who use BC-pills may experience one, a few, or none of the following:
- Nausea.
- Breast tenderness.
- Edema (bloating).
- Rash.
- Weight gain or weight loss.
- Spotting (slight vaginal bleeding during the month).
- Headaches.

Other side effects have been studied since the pill was introduced in 1960, but these side effects are very rare or not proven to be linked with BC-pills.

Many users of BC-pills don't experience any side effects. If the female does experience side effects, especially spotting and headaches, she should go back to her doctor or clinic. Most times, a simple change in the dose (strength) of the pills will relieve the side effects. Also, taking the BC-pill at the same time each day can help diminish side effects.

BC-pills have good side effects as well. BC-pills may benefit the female by reducing her risk of:

- Ovarian cancer.
- Endometrial cancer.
- Ovarian cysts.
- Benign breast tumors (noncancerous lumps).
- PID (pelvic inflammatory disease).

BC-pills also benefit females by keeping the menstrual cycle more regular (the female will have her period each month at about the same time) and reducing cramping and the amount of menstrual flow.

When you talk to the doctor or nurse about BC-pills, ask about the possible side effects and what you should do if you experience any of them.

Where can I get them?

You can get BC-pills at just about any health clinic or doctor's office. If you go to a doctor's office, the doctor will probably give you a prescription you can pick up at the drugstore.

There are also clinics where young people can access different types of contraception. One nationwide organization is Planned Parenthood (1-800-230-7526). You can call this toll-free number to find out if there is a Planned Parenthood near you.

Sometimes health teachers or counselors can give you information on health clinics in your area. You can ask parents, aunts, uncles, or school officials (if you have a good relationship with them) if there are any health clinics in the area where you can get information.

You should not get BC-pills from any place other than a doctor's office, clinic, or drugstore (with a prescription).

How much does it cost?

The price can range from free to $5 or $30 per month, not including the price of a doctor's visit and checkup. Usually health clinics will give you the first month or two of BC-pills for free. Public health clinics often have the best prices, while doctors' offices and Planned Parenthood tend to be more expensive.

What are the disadvantages?

– Must remember to take one pill per day.
– Possible side effects.
– Must go to a doctor or clinic to get a prescription.
– Does not protect against STDs.

What are the advantages?

+ Highly effective at preventing unwanted pregnancy.
+ Easy to use.
+ Can be inexpensive.
+ May offer health benefits.

Do I need parental consent?

This varies from state to state, but in most states parental consent is not necessary.

Any recommendations?

Have a qualified health practitioner/doctor/nurse explain all the possible effects the BC-pill may have and how to use the pill correctly.

Buy a one- or two-month supply of BC-pills in advance so you never run the risk of missing a day taking the pill.

Keep your BC-pills in a place that will help remind you to take one each day. A popular place is an underwear drawer.

A condom should also be used to protect against STDs, unless you and your partner have been tested for STDs and are in a monogamous relationship.

Females who smoke, especially women over age thirty-five, should not use birth control pills. Better still, they should quit smoking! Then they can use birth control pills.

Ortho Evra, or "The Patch"

Ortho Evra (The Patch) is like birth control pills, except the female doesn't swallow any pills. Instead, she places the thin, 1 $^3/_4$-inch by 1 $^3/_4$-inch patch on her stomach, upper arm, back, chest, or butt. The Ortho Evra patch releases hormones into the body through the skin, and, as with birth control pills, ovulation (the release of the egg/ovum) is prevented.

How well does it prevent unplanned pregnancy?

The Ortho Evra patch is highly effective at preventing unplanned pregnancy—more than 99 percent.

How well does it protect against STDs?

Ortho Evra does not provide any protection against STDs.

How do I use it?

The Ortho Evra patch is worn for one week at a time and is replaced on the same day of the week with a new patch for three weeks in a row. The fourth week is "patch free." The female can wear the Ortho Evra patch on one of these areas: her stomach, upper arm, back, chest, or butt. The patch stays attached to the skin even while she is bathing, swimming, exercising, or sweating.

How does it work?

The Ortho Evra patch releases hormones through the skin and into the body to prevent the ovaries from ovulating (releasing an ovum/egg). If the female does not release an egg, then a pregnancy cannot take place.

What are the side effects?

The side effects are similar to those of birth control pills:
- Nausea.
- Breast tenderness.
- Edema (bloating).
- Rash.
- Weight gain or weight loss.
- Spotting (slight vaginal bleeding during the month).
- Headaches.

There may be good side effects as well. The benefits of the patch are still under research, and may be similar to birth control pills. The Ortho Evra patch may benefit the female by reducing her risk of:
- Ovarian cancer.
- Endometrial cancer.
- Ovarian cysts.
- Benign breast tumors (noncancerous lumps).
- PID (pelvic inflammatory disease).

These benefits still need to be confirmed through further research by the manufacturer.

Where can I get it?

Clinics and doctors' offices.

How much does it cost?

The price can range from free to $30 per month, not including the price of a doctor's visit and checkup. Usually health clinics have the best prices, while doctors' offices tend to be more expensive.

What are its disadvantages?

– Must remember to change the patch each week.
– Possible side effects.
– Must go to a doctor or clinic to get it.
– Does not protect against STDs.

What are its advantages?

+Highly effective at preventing unwanted pregnancy.
+Easy to use.
+Can be inexpensive.
+May offer health benefits.
+Does not need daily attention (just weekly).
+Offers the same benefits as birth control pills, but you don't have to swallow a pill or get an injection (shot).

Do I need parental consent?

This varies from state to state, but in most states parental consent is not necessary.

Any recommendations?

Have a qualified health practitioner/doctor/nurse explain all the possible effects the Ortho Evra patch may have and how to use the patch correctly.

Buy a one- or two-month supply of patches in advance so you don't run the risk of missing a week.

Keep your patches in a place that will help remind you to change them each week.

Another form of birth control (abstinence or condoms, for example) should be used for the first week that a female uses the Ortho Evra patch. After that first week, the female can rely on the patch alone to prevent unplanned pregnancies (but not STDs).

A condom should be used to protect against STDs, unless you and your partner have been tested for STDs and are in a monogamous relationship.

As with birth control pills, females who smoke, especially women over age thirty-five, should not use Ortho Evra. Better still, they should quit smoking; then they can use the Ortho Evra patch.

NuvaRing

NuvaRing is a soft, flexible plastic ring that is about two inches wide. It is placed inside the vagina where it releases hormones (like birth control pills) that prevent ovulation. Only one NuvaRing is needed each month to provide excellent protection against unplanned pregnancy.

How well does it prevent unplanned pregnancy?

NuvaRing is highly effective at preventing unplanned pregnancy—between 98 and 99 percent.

How well does it protect against STDs?

NuvaRing does not provide any protection against STDs.

How do I use it?

The female squeezes the flexible ring and places it into her vagina. The NuvaRing does not need to be fit into any special place in the vagina, so it is easy to use. The ring stays in the vagina for three weeks and is removed at the beginning of the fourth week. Pregnancy prevention is provided for the entire month (four weeks). The female can remove the NuvaRing for as long as three hours during intercourse, if she wants, and then must place it back into the vagina. The female inserts a new NuvaRing each month.

How does it work?

The NuvaRing releases hormones into the body to prevent the ovaries from ovulating (releasing an ovum/egg). If the female does not release an egg, then a pregnancy cannot take place.

What are the side effects?

The side effects are similar to those of birth control pills:
- Nausea.
- Breast tenderness.
- Edema (bloating).
- Rash.
- Weight gain or weight loss.
- Spotting (slight vaginal bleeding during the month).
- Headaches.

There may be good side effects as well. The benefits of the NuvaRing should be similar to those of birth control pills. The NuvaRing may benefit the female by reducing her risk of:
- Ovarian cancer.
- Endometrial cancer.
- Ovarian cysts.
- Benign breast tumors (noncancerous lumps).
- PID (pelvic inflammatory disease).

These benefits still need to be confirmed through further research by the manufacturer.

Where can I get it?

Clinics and doctors' offices.

How much does it cost?

The price can range from free to $30 per month, not including the price of a doctor's visit and checkup. Usually health clinics have the best prices, while doctors' offices tend to be more expensive.

What are its disadvantages?

– Must remember to put in a new NuvaRing each month.
– Possible side effects.
– Must go to a doctor or clinic to get it.
– Does not protect against STDs.
– The female may feel uncomfortable inserting something into her vagina.

What are its advantages?

+Highly effective at preventing unwanted pregnancy.
+Easy to use.
+Can be inexpensive.
+May offer health benefits.
+Does not need daily attention (just monthly).
+Offers the same benefits as birth control pills, but you don't have to swallow a pill or get an injection (shot).

Do I need parental consent?

This varies from state to state, but in most states parental consent is not necessary.

Any recommendations?

Have a qualified health practitioner/doctor/nurse explain all the possible effects the NuvaRing might have and how to use it correctly.

Buy a one- or two-month supply of NuvaRings in advance so you don't run the risk of missing a month.

Keep your NuvaRings in a place that will help remind you to change it each month.

Another form of birth control (abstinence or condoms, for example) should be used for the first week that a female uses the NuvaRing. After that first week, the female can rely on the NuvaRing alone to prevent unplanned pregnancies (but not STDs).

A condom should be used to protect against STDs, unless you and your partner have been tested for STDs and are in a monogamous relationship.

As with birth control pills, females who smoke, especially women over age thirty-five, should not use the NuvaRing. Better still, they should quit smoking; then they can use the NuvaRing.

IUD (Intrauterine Device)

An IUD (intrauterine device) is a small, plastic object that looks like the letter T with a string on the bottom of it. It is inserted into the female's uterus by a doctor to prevent pregnancy. Depending on the type of IUD, it can stay in the uterus for one, five, or ten years, or until the female wants it removed.

How well does it prevent unplanned pregnancy?

The IUD is 99 percent effective at preventing unplanned pregnancy.

How well does it protect against STDs?

The IUD does not provide any protection against STDs.

How do I use it?

The female must go to a doctor or trained healthcare professional and have the IUD inserted into her uterus. This process may cause some discomfort but not pain. If the female wants, she can be given a medication to help her relax.

A thin tube with the IUD inside it will be inserted through the female's cervix and into her uterus. When the IUD is positioned at the top of the uterus, the doctor will slide the tube out of the uterus and cervix, leaving the actual IUD in the uterus with the thin string coming through the cervix.

The doctor will show the female how to check for this string to make sure that the IUD stays in place in the uterus. Although it is rare that an IUD slips out of place, it can happen. If this does happen, the female should go back to the doctor to have it checked out and possibly have the IUD reinserted.

Once the IUD is inserted, the female can engage in intercourse with good protection against an unwanted pregnancy.

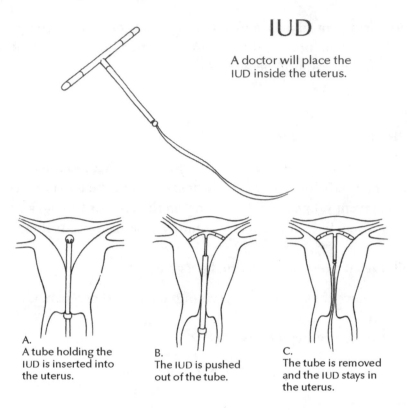

IUD

A doctor will place the
IUD inside the uterus.

A.
A tube holding the
IUD is inserted into
the uterus.

B.
The IUD is pushed
out of the tube.

C.
The tube is removed
and the IUD stays in
the uterus.

How does it work?

The IUD prevents pregnancy by blocking sperm from reaching the female's ovum and preventing a fertilized egg from attaching itself to the uterine wall (endometrium) if an ovum does become fertilized.

What are its side effects?

Here are a few of the things that could happen:
- Tearing of the uterus (which may happen while the doctor is inserting the IUD).
- Heavier and longer menstrual periods (depending on the type of IUD).
- Spotting between periods (menstrual bleeding during the month).
- Increased chance of PID (pelvic inflammatory disease).
- Abdominal cramping (although some IUDs come with a hormone that may reduce menstrual cramps).

Where can I get it?

You can get an IUD at a doctor's office or health clinic.

How much does it cost?

The price for the insertion/removal of an IUD varies from doctor to doctor and clinic to clinic. You can expect to see prices from $175 to $400. This does not include the price of the doctor's visit or checkup. The price could be less if you can show you don't make much money and if the clinic uses what is called a "sliding scale."

What are its disadvantages?

- Side effects mentioned above.
- Does not protect against STDs.
- Requires insertion by a doctor or health professional.
- Needs to be checked to be sure it is still in place.
- Initial cost may be high.

What are its advantages?

+ Highly effective at preventing unplanned pregnancy.
+ Once inserted, the female does not need to worry about pills, patches, rings, or inserting anything before intercourse.
+ Easily removable by a doctor.

Do I need parental consent?

This varies from state to state, but in most states parental consent is not necessary. IUDs are usually only provided to teens who have babies or to adult women.

Any recommendations?

Use a condom to protect against STDs unless you and your partner have been tested for STDs and are monogamous.

Have the doctor explain the possible side effects, how to check if the IUD is still in place, and what to do if there are problems.

Diaphragm

The diaphragm is a round, soft rubber dome that the female inserts into her vagina before she engages in intercourse. The diaphragm must be used with a spermicidal gel and kept in the vagina for at least six hours after sex.

The diaphragm can be used over and over again, usually up to a year, if it is taken care of properly.

How well does it prevent unplanned pregnancy?

The diaphragm is a good contraceptive that works effectively when used correctly. It is not nearly as effective as the surgical methods (explained later), BC-pills, patches, vaginal rings, the IUD, or even condoms, but it is a reliable way to prevent unplanned pregnancy—80 to 94 percent effective.

How well does it protect against STDs?

The diaphragm may protect against a few STDs, but HIV (the AIDS virus) is not one of them. The diaphragm is not considered very good protection against STDs.

How do I use it?

The diaphragm can be inserted into the vagina just before intercourse takes place or up to two hours before the female has sex. Before the diaphragm can be inserted, however, it must be lubricated with a spermicidal gel. The female will squeeze some gel into the dome-shaped diaphragm and spread the spermicide over the entire diaphragm, including the inside, outside, and rim.

When the diaphragm is lubricated with the spermicide, the female will use her fingers and thumb to squeeze the rim of the diaphragm, making it narrow. The female will insert the diaphragm into her vagina and gently push it downward and as far back into the vagina as possible. Once the diaphragm is fully inserted, the female must make sure it is completely covering her cervix.

When the female is sure her diaphragm is fitted properly, she can engage in intercourse. After intercourse, she must not remove the diaphragm for at least six hours. If the couple wants to have sex again within six hours, the female must reapply (add) more spermicidal gel to her diaphragm. To do this without removing the diaphragm, she must use a plastic applicator to apply the spermicide around the diaphragm.

After at least six hours have passed since the couple had sex, the female can use her fingers to remove the diaphragm, wash the diaphragm with cool water, and place it back into its holder until she wants to engage in intercourse again.

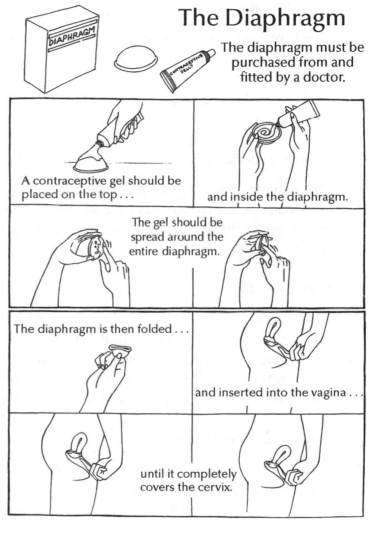

The Diaphragm

The diaphragm must be purchased from and fitted by a doctor.

A contraceptive gel should be placed on the top . . .

and inside the diaphragm.

The gel should be spread around the entire diaphragm.

The diaphragm is then folded . . .

and inserted into the vagina . . .

until it completely covers the cervix.

The female can use the diaphragm many times, but she should go back to her doctor/clinic to get another diaphragm or be refitted if a puncture develops in the diaphragm or if she loses or gains fifteen or more pounds.

How does it work?

The diaphragm covers the cervix so that sperm cannot get into the uterus. If the sperm cannot get into the uterus, the ovum cannot be fertilized and there will not be a pregnancy.

Because the diaphragm may not always cover the cervix perfectly, a spermicide is used for added protection.

What are its side effects?

There are no common side effects associated with using the diaphragm. On rare occasions the female may have an allergic reaction to the spermicide or the rubber of the diaphragm, or she may develop a vaginal or bladder infection if the diaphragm is not cleaned properly.

Where can I get it?

You can get a diaphragm from a doctor or health clinic. There are different size diaphragms, so the doctor/healthcare professional will find out which diaphragm is the best fit for you. He/She will show you on a diagram how to use it, then have you practice inserting it correctly into the vagina. The doctor will also show you how to clean the diaphragm.

How much does it cost?

Prices vary, but expect somewhere in the range of $15 to $50. A spermicide gel must also be used with the diaphragm. A tube of spermicide costs $8 to $15 at the drugstore. The couple must buy more spermicidal gel when it runs out.

What are its disadvantages?

- Requires a visit to a doctor or health professional.
- Takes practice to use correctly.
- May slip out of place during intercourse.
- The female may feel strange inserting something into her vagina.
- After the female engages in intercourse, she must reapply spermicide if she wants to engage in intercourse again.

What are its advantages?

+Good form of contraception.
+Offers some protection against STDs, pelvic inflammatory disease, and cervical cancer.
+Harmful side effects are unlikely.

Do I need parental consent?

No.

Any recommendations?

Use a diaphragm along with a condom to improve effectiveness against unplanned pregnancy and STDs.

Practice using the diaphragm until you feel comfortable wearing it. Plan ahead and carry the diaphragm in a purse or knapsack, even if there is only a slight chance that you may have sex.

Make sure to stock up on spermicidal gel.

Depo-Provera (DMPA), or "The Shot"

Depo-Provera is an injection (shot) of hormone that prevents ovulation for three months.

How well does it prevent unplanned pregnancy?

Depo-Provera is an excellent method of contraception, more than 99 percent effective.

How well does it protect against STDs?

Depo-Provera does not provide any protection against STDs.

How do I use it?

Once the female receives the shot of Depo-Provera, she does not need to do much except protect herself from STDs when she engages in intercourse (and, of course, remember to get another shot in three months).

How does it work?

The female will receive an injection of Depo-Provera from the doctor. It will prevent ovulation for three months. DMPA is totally reversible.

What are its side effects?

Possible side effects may include:
* Spotting (irregular menstrual bleeding).
* Lighter or heavier menstrual periods.
* Amenorrhea (no menstrual periods).

Where can I get it?

A female can get a Depo-Provera injection at a doctor's office or health clinic.

How much does it cost?

Depo-Provera may cost $35 or more for each shot every three months. There will also be an office visit charge, which can range from free to over $100 per visit.

What are its disadvantages?

– Initial cost may be high.
– Possible side effects.
– The female must go to a doctor or clinic for the injection.
– Doesn't protect against STDs.
– May cause amenorrhea (missed menstrual periods).

What are its advantages?

+ Highly effective at preventing unplanned pregnancy.
+ Easy to use.
+ Lasts three months.
+ May cause amenorrhea (missed menstrual periods).

Do I need parental consent?

This varies from state to state, but in most states parental consent is not necessary.

Any recommendations?

Use along with a condom to protect against STDs.

Lunelle

Lunelle is another type of injection (shot) of hormone that prevents ovulation for one month.

How well does it prevent unplanned pregnancy?

Lunelle is an excellent form of contraception, more than 99 percent effective.

How well does it protect against STDs?

Lunelle does not protect against any STDs.

How do I use it?

Once the female receives the shot of Lunelle, she does not need to do much except protect herself from STDs when she engages in intercourse (and, of course, remember to get another shot in a month).

How does it work?

The female will receive an injection of Lunelle from the doctor/nurse, and it will prevent ovulation for one month. Lunelle is totally reversible.

What are its side effects?

Some possible side effects include:
- Spotting (droplets of blood in the middle of the month).
- Weight gain or weight loss.
- Breast tenderness.
- Nausea (feeling sick to your stomach).

Where can I get it?

A female can get a Lunelle injection at a doctor's office or health clinic.

How much does it cost?

The cost of Lunelle varies from $30 and up for each shot every month. There will also be an office visit charge, which can range from free to over $100 per visit. Some clinics offer sliding scales, which means that if you are a student without a job, you might pay less.

What are its disadvantages?

- Possible side effects.
- The female must go to a doctor or clinic for the monthly injection.
- Doesn't protect against STDs.

What are its advantages?

+ Highly effective at preventing unplanned pregnancy.
+ Easy to use.
+ Lasts an entire month.
+ May include some protection against PID (pelvic inflammatory disease), certain types of cancers, and some of the problems of premenstrual syndrome.

Do I need parental consent?

This varies from state to state, but in most states parental consent is not necessary.

Any recommendations?

Use along with a condom to protect against STDs.

Cervical Cap

The cervical cap is small, thimble-shaped, and made of soft, pliable latex (or rubber) or of harder plastic. The cervical cap works like a suction cup that the female inserts into her vagina and snugly fits over her cervix. It is a smaller version of the diaphragm.

How well does it prevent unplanned pregnancy?

The cervical cap is a good method for preventing unplanned pregnancy, although it's not one of the best methods. It is up to 91 percent effective when used correctly.

How well does it protect against STDs?

Not well at all. If a spermicide is used with the cervical cap, the spermicide may offer some protection against STDs.

How do I use it?

The cervical cap must be inserted into the vagina and placed over the cervix at least thirty minutes before intercourse. The cervical cap should be left in the vagina for at least eight hours after intercourse but can be left in for up to two days.

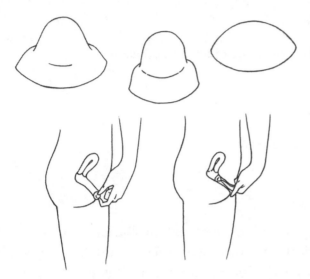

The Cervical Cap

The cervical cap is purchased at a doctor's office or clinic.

The female will insert the cap into her vagina and, with a small amount of suction, apply it over the cervix.

The female should follow the directions of her doctor closely.

How does it work?

The cervical cap is known as a mechanical barrier, which blocks sperm from getting through the cervix and into the uterus. The cervical cap uses suction on the cervix to stay in place. If sperm cannot get into the uterus, the female ovum cannot be fertilized and pregnancy will not occur.

What are its side effects?

There may be cervical irritation and slight discomfort. A cervical cap that is properly fitted will reduce the chances of this happening. There are no proven side effects associated with the cervical cap.

Where can I get it?

A doctor's office or clinic.

How much does it cost?

The cost varies, but the average price of a cervical cap is about $50. This does not include the cost of an office visit and checkup, which can range anywhere from free to over $100.

What are its disadvantages?

- Doesn't protect against STDs.
- Can be dislodged from the cervix during intercourse.
- Requires a visit to a doctor or clinic.
- Takes practice to use correctly.

- The female may feel weird or uncomfortable inserting something into her vagina.
- The female must get a checkup every three months.

What are its advantages?

+ Can be used many times.
+ Can be used without a spermicide. (With the use of a spermicide, the cervical cap becomes more effective at preventing unplanned pregnancy.)

Do I need parental consent?

No.

Any recommendations?

Use with a condom and spermicide in addition to help protect against STDs, unless you and your partner have been tested for STDs and both of you are monogamous.

Today Sponge

The contraceptive Today Sponge is a soft, disposable, polyurethane foam disc that contains the spermicide nonoxynol-9. After it is moistened with water and inserted into the vagina, the Today Sponge immediately becomes effective in providing protection against pregnancy for the next twenty-four hours. There is no need to add spermicidal cream or jelly, even with repeated acts of intercourse.

The Today Sponge is easier to use than the diaphragm or cervical cap and is thrown away after it is used.

How well does it prevent unplanned pregnancy?

The Today Sponge, when used correctly, works fairly well (85 to 90 percent effective) at preventing unplanned pregnancy. This is not the best method for people who do not want to become pregnant, especially teens.

How well does it protect against STDs?

The Today Sponge does not provide any protection against STDs.

How do I use it?

First, the sponge is moistened with a little bit of tap water. Then it is squeezed a few times to get the excess water out, which will cause it to become a bit foamy. This activates the spermicide in the sponge.

The sponge should be folded, with the string facing down, and inserted into the vagina. The sponge should be placed as far back into the vagina as it will go, completely covering the cervix. The female can engage in intercourse many times without having to reapply a spermicide.

In order for the Today Sponge to be effective, the female must leave the sponge in her vagina for at least six hours after she has had intercourse. To remove the sponge, the female simply pulls on the string loop attached to the sponge, and the sponge will slide out.

How does it work?

The Today Sponge prevents pregnancy by blocking the cervix so sperm cannot enter the uterus to fertilize the ovum. The sponge also contains a spermicide that helps to destroy sperm.

What are its side effects?

The most common side effect is a mild irritation of the vagina or penis because of the spermicide, but this seems to occur in only 5 percent of the people who use the sponge.

The only other known possible side effect is TSS (Toxic Shock Syndrome), which is caused by a bacteria. This is extremely rare.

Where can I get it?

It can be ordered online at any number of Web sites that offer contraceptives (for example, www.birthcontrol.com). Soon it will be found in just about every drugstore, in the condom section.

How much does it cost?

The price may vary, but you should expect to pay about $3 or more per sponge.

What are its disadvantages?

- Must be inserted correctly.
- Does not protect against STDs.

What are its advantages?

+ Offers fair protection against unplanned pregnancy.
+ Easy to use.
+ Fairly inexpensive.
+ Can be ordered online or bought at a drugstore.

Do I need parental consent?

No.

Any recommendations?

Be sure to read the instructions on the package, and use the sponge with a condom to protect against STDs.

Condom

The condom is a sheath (covering) that fits snugly over the penis during intercourse. When used correctly, the condom provides excellent protection against unplanned pregnancy and most STDs, including HIV. For this reason, condoms are becoming more and more popular. Condoms are often the preferred choice of contraception for young people because they work well and are easy to buy, easy to carry around, and easy to use.

How well does it prevent unplanned pregnancy?

The condom is an excellent contraceptive for preventing unplanned pregnancy. When used correctly, it is 95 percent effective or more.

How well does it protect against STDs?

Other than abstinence, the condom is the best contraceptive to use to protect against most STDs, including HIV (the AIDS virus).

How do I use it correctly?

With a little practice, anyone can use a condom correctly and quickly.

The first thing to remember is to put on a condom when the penis is erect (hard) but before any intercourse takes place. This means that if a male and a female are going to engage in vaginal intercourse, the male (or female) should put the condom on his penis after it becomes erect but before his penis enters her vagina.

Sometimes a couple will make the mistake of having the male penis enter the female vagina a few times, then put on a condom before he ejaculates. Don't do it! Sometimes, long before the male actually ejaculates, he will release prelubricating fluid from his penis. Neither the male nor the female will feel this prelubricating fluid come out of the penis, but this fluid may have sperm in it. Sperm may be deposited into the vagina and can go on to fertilize the ovum. Females can, and do, become pregnant this way. Therefore, put on a condom before the penis enters the vagina.

For a condom to provide protection against unplanned pregnancy and most STDs, you should become an E.X.P.P.E.R.T. at using condoms. Here are the steps for becoming a condom E.X.P.P.E.R.T.:

ERECTION: When the penis becomes erect (hard), the condom should be put on.

EXPIRATION DATE: Before using any condom, check the box or condom package for the expiration date. If the condom is old, there is a greater chance that it will break. Do not use any condoms that have expired.

PILLOW OF AIR: Use your thumb and forefinger and gently squeeze the center of the condom package, feeling for a pillow of air. If there is a pillow of air, the condom package does not have a hole in it and has not been worn down by heat or pressure. If there is no pillow of air, do not use the condom. Throw it away and use a different one.

PINCH THE TIP OF THE CONDOM: Pinch the tip of the condom as you place it over the end of the penis. Uncircumcised males should pull back on the foreskin first.

EASE THE CONDOM ALL THE WAY DOWN TO THE BASE OF THE PENIS: While you continue pinching the end of the condom, ease the rest of the condom all the way down to the base (bottom) of the penis to the pubic hair. Try to squeeze out any air that may be in the condom. This will increase sensitivity and help prevent the condom from breaking. Now the couple can engage in intercourse.

REMOVE THE CONDOM AND THE PENIS FROM THE VAGINA AT THE SAME TIME: Once the male has ejaculated, the male or female should hold the condom at the base of the penis, and remove the condom and the penis at the same time. This will help prevent the condom from slipping off and staying inside the female, or semen from coming out of the condom and entering the female's body.

THROW AWAY THE CONDOM: Once the condom has been removed, throw it away. It is also a good idea to wash your genitals with soap and water (or at least water) to protect against germs that may be lingering on your skin.

Many people mess up on the R step, the removal of the condom and the penis from the vagina at the same time. Sometimes the male may want to leave his penis inside his partner after he ejaculates, but after the male ejaculates, his penis quickly becomes flaccid (soft). If the male pulls out when his penis is flaccid, the condom may slip off. If this happens, the semen inside the condom will spill into his partner, defeating the purpose of the condom. Sperm will be on their way to the uterus, and an STD infection is possible.

Also, it may be a little embarrassing if the male pulls his penis out and the condom is gone. If this does happen, the female will need to feel inside her vagina for the condom and pull it out. This is a real mood spoiler!

How to Use a Condom Like an E.X.P.P.E.R.T.

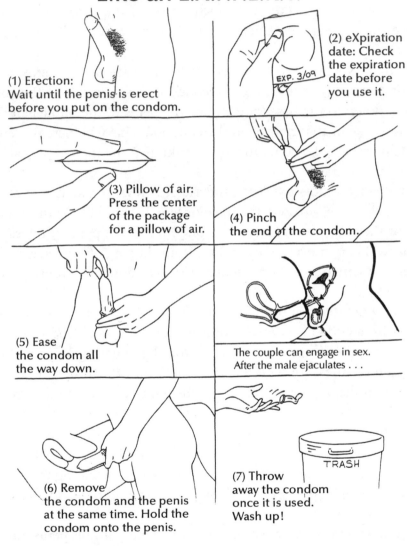

(1) Erection: Wait until the penis is erect before you put on the condom.

(2) eXpiration date: Check the expiration date before you use it.

EXP. 3/09

(3) Pillow of air: Press the center of the package for a pillow of air.

(4) Pinch the end of the condom.

(5) Ease the condom all the way down.

The couple can engage in sex. After the male ejaculates . . .

(6) Remove the condom and the penis at the same time. Hold the condom onto the penis.

TRASH

(7) Throw away the condom once it is used. Wash up!

How does it work?

The condom helps prevent pregnancy by keeping the male's sperm (and pre-lubricating fluid) from entering the vagina.

When the male ejaculates, his semen will stay in the pinched (receptacle) end of the condom. This keeps sperm from entering the female's vagina. If there are no sperm to travel into the uterus and Fallopian tubes, the ovum cannot be fertilized.

Latex and polyurethane condoms (but not lambskin) protect against most STDs by not allowing any body fluids, which may contain bacteria or viruses, into the body. A condom prevents the male's semen and prelubricating fluid from entering another person's body. A condom also prevents the other person's fluids (blood, vaginal lubrication) from entering the male's body. When a condom is used correctly, both people are well protected against most STDs.

What are its side effects?

Some people have reported an allergic reaction to the latex of the condom or to the spermicide that lubricates some condoms. These may cause an irritation of the penis or vagina, but this isn't too common.

Where can I get it?

You can get condoms at drugstores, health clinics, and sometimes even vending machines. Anyone can get condoms. Try not to be shy or embarrassed about buying condoms, especially you ladies. Almost half of all condoms sold are purchased by females! Condoms are sold to males and females, young and old. There are no laws prohibiting you from buying condoms, and usually the experience of buying condoms is disaster free.

How much does it cost?

Anywhere from free to $2 each. At health clinics, condoms are usually provided for free. At drugstores, condoms can be sold in a box of three, six, twelve, or twenty-four. The price can vary from brand to brand, store to store, and according to different features the condom may have.

What are its disadvantages?

- Could break (although this doesn't happen very often if the condom is used correctly).
- Easily damaged by heat, age, Vaseline, baby oil, or any other type of oil.
- Must be used every time a couple engages in intercourse.
- The couple must have a condom with them to engage in intercourse.
- Takes a few moments to put it on.

What are its advantages?

+ Works well to prevent unplanned pregnancy.
+ Works well at protecting against most STDs.
+ Easy to get.
+ Inexpensive.
+ Easy to carry.
+ May help to keep the male from ejaculating too quickly.
+ Lubricated condoms may help make intercourse more comfortable if the female does not have a lot of vaginal lubrication.
+ Helps the couple feel safe from unplanned pregnancy and most STDs.

Do I need parental consent?

No.

Any recommendations?

Before ever engaging in intercourse, practice saying the steps of being an E.X.P.P.E.R.T. and practice using a condom in the dark and in a hurry.

Latex condoms coated with spermicide are best. Do not use any oil-based lubricants (Vaseline, mineral oil, suntan oil, hand or face creams) on a condom. Do not leave condoms in a warm place.

Buying condoms isn't this hard or embarrassing.

Condom Facts

CONDOM SIZE: If you were to take a condom and fit it over your fist, you could pull it all the way down to your elbow. In the store you might see large or extra large condoms, but for the most part, this is just a marketing/sales technique to encourage males with that monster-size ego to buy that kind of condom. Large condoms generally sell to the male's ego size, not his penis size. You do not need to worry about condom size. One size fits all.

LUBRICATED OR NONLUBRICATED: Lubricated condoms have a water-based lubricant (slippery gel) that makes penetration of the male's penis into his partner easier. Some couples don't like the way these condoms feel. If the female produces enough vaginal lubrication, there shouldn't be any problems, and nonlubricated condoms can be used.

RIBBED CONDOMS—FOR HER PLEASURE: Not really. This is more of a marketing/sales technique than anything else. Once again, the male may want to please his partner as much as possible, or the female may want to enjoy the experience as much as possible. They think that buying these condoms, which have thin little grooves along the sides, will help bring the female to orgasm. This is not the case. Most females cannot tell the difference between a ribbed condom or a regular one. But if it is ribbed condoms you want, there is no harm done. Go ahead and use them.

SPERMICIDES: A spermicide is a chemical that helps destroy sperm. Most lubricants on condoms today also contain spermicides to add further protection against unplanned pregnancy.

Nonoxynol-9 is a common spermicide found on condoms. It has recently been shown to help reduce the chances of pregnancy but not of STDs, including HIV.

EXPIRATION DATE: The expiration date will let you know if the condom is still safe to use. If today's date is past the expiration date on the condom package, do not use it. Throw it away. You may lose a dollar, but you save yourself from a possible unplanned pregnancy or STD.

STORAGE: Do not keep condoms in a car or other hot place or in your wallet for extended periods of time. Do keep condoms in a cool, dry place.

Always keep a good supply of condoms so you will never run out when you need one. Once you get down to your last three condoms, that is the perfect time to get more.

RESERVOIR TIP OR REGULAR TIP: Some condoms come with a reservoir tip (a little added space at the tip of the condom) to hold the semen when the male ejaculates. If the condom does not have a reservoir tip, pinching the tip of the condom (as it is put on the penis) will create a bit of a reservoir tip.

MULTICOLORED CONDOMS: Once again, just a little added incentive to encourage a person to buy or use a condom. As long as the condoms are latex and made by a well-known company, they should work just as well.

DIFFERENT FLAVOR/DESIGN CONDOMS: Some people may use a flavored condom if they are going to engage in oral intercourse. Be sure that a condom has been tested to be used for intercourse and is not just a novelty toy or fun item. It should say on the package if the condom is a novelty item or not. If the condom is a novelty item, do not use it.

LUBRICANTS: Do not use oil-based personal lubricants on condoms. Lubricants made with oil weaken the latex in a condom and cause it to break. Never use petroleum jelly, baby oil, vegetable oil, butter, hand and facial creams, or massage oils with a condom.

If a couple wants to use a lubricant, it should be a water-based lubricant. You can purchase water-based personal lubricants at the drugstore. The most popular is called K-Y Lubricating Jelly.

USE LATEX CONDOMS: Latex condoms prevent unplanned pregnancy and most STDs, including HIV. Lambskin condoms are porous (have microscopic holes), allowing many STDs, including HIV and hepatitis B, to pass through them, so don't use them. Throw away any condom after it is used.

NEW PLASTIC CONDOMS: Polyurethane (plastic) condoms are now available. These new condoms have several advantages:
- They can be used by people who are allergic to latex.
- They are possibly stronger than latex condoms.
- They may provide greater sensitivity than latex condoms.
- They can be used with any type of personal lubricant.
- They don't break down as easily if left in the heat.

Although all the test results are not in yet, the new polyurethane condoms look like they may become very popular. The price is a bit higher than for latex condoms, but you may enjoy some of the advantages.

TO INCREASE/DECREASE SENSITIVITY: Many people don't know that using condoms can actually increase sensitivity (the amount of feeling against the penis or vagina) during intercourse.

If the male wants to have more sensitivity during intercourse, he (or his partner) should put a small amount of water-based personal lubricant (like K-Y Jelly or Astroglide) on the glans penis (the head of the penis) just before putting the condom on. This will increase the amount of sensitivity dramatically. Putting additional lubrication on the shaft of the penis before the condom is put on may cause the condom to slide off during intercourse—so you will not want to do that!

Once the condom is put on, pinch the receptacle end of the condom, making sure to squeeze all the air out. This will also increase sensitivity, and it will help keep the condom from breaking.

By following these tips, some males say using a condom feels better than not using a condom. (Plus it offers great protection against unplanned pregnancy and most STDs.)

For females, using a lubricated condom or adding lubrication to the outside of the condom will help reduce any friction or discomfort if there is not enough natural vaginal lubrication.

Many males experience premature ejaculation. This is when the male gets so aroused or excited, he ejaculates before intercourse takes place or just a few seconds after intercourse has begun. In this case, the male may be better off with less sensitivity and could use a nonlubricated latex condom. This will decrease the amount of sensitivity the male feels and will often delay his orgasm and ejaculation.

A NOTE TO THE GENTLEMEN: There are a number of advantages to using a condom like a pro. First, you appear confident and sure of yourself. Second, you impress your partner by showing that you are responsible and you care about your partner's protection (as well as your own). Third, you help your partner relax by not having to worry about pregnancy or STDs.

As you can see, there are advantages to using a condom like a pro besides protecting yourself from unplanned pregnancy and STDs. Practice using a condom until you feel comfortable using it under any condition.

A note to the ladies: Whether or not your partner wants to use a condom will help you identify how emotionally mature and responsible he is. Unfortunately, many males do not use condoms because they don't know how or do not feel comfortable using them. But you must protect yourself even if the male does not want to. For this reason, it is important that you be able to use a condom like a pro. If you are going to engage in intercourse, make sure you have condoms with you. If the male seems to be having a problem using the condom, be prepared to put it on for him and to remove the condom and penis from your vagina after he ejaculates. The best way to be prepared is to practice putting a condom on something that resembles the shape of a penis.

Be a condom pro, even if the male isn't. If he says condoms lessen his enjoyment, ask him if he thinks not having sex would lessen his enjoyment even more.

Female Condom

The female condom is designed for the female vagina instead of the male penis. The male condom covers the outside of the penis, whereas the female condom covers the inside of the vagina. The female condom is a hollow tube with one closed end that is placed into the vagina.

How well does it prevent unplanned pregnancy?

The female condom is an excellent method of prevention against unplanned pregnancy, up to 95 percent effective.

How well does it protect against STDs?

The female condom, like its brother, the male condom, offers excellent protection against most STDs.

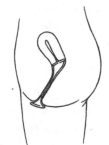

The Female Condom

The female condom can be purchased at the drugstore. The directions inside the box should be followed closely.

The female condom is a thin, strong, polyurethane tube that is placed inside the vagina before intercourse begins.

How do I use it?

The female condom is a hollow, polyurethane (thin, soft, strong) tube, about seven inches long, with a flexible ring at each end. One end of the tube is open and the other end is closed. The closed end of the female condom is inserted into the vagina and placed at the cervix like a diaphragm. The open end of the female condom remains outside the vagina. The walls of the condom protect the inside of the vagina. The female condom can be inserted well before intercourse, but must definitely be put in before there is any genital contact.

During intercourse, the male's penis will enter the female condom. The male can ejaculate into the female condom, and the semen will stay inside the condom and not spill into the vagina.

After intercourse, the female can remove the condom and throw it away just like the male condom. If the couple engages in intercourse again, a new female condom should be used.

How does it work?

The female condom prevents unplanned pregnancy by keeping the male's sperm from entering the vagina.

The female condom protects against most STDs by keeping body fluids (like blood, prelubricating fluid, semen, and vaginal secretions), which can be infected with bacteria or viruses, from entering the other person's body.

What are its side effects?

The only known possible side effects are irritation of the vagina or penis from an allergic reaction to the lubricant or the polyurethane.

Where can I get it?

The female condom is available in health clinics and drugstores.

How much does it cost?

At health clinics, the female condom may be distributed for free or at a reduced price. At drugstores, the female condom will probably cost between $2 and $3.

What are its disadvantages?

- More expensive than the male condom.
- May look frightening to some females.
- The female may feel weird or uncomfortable inserting something into her vagina.
- Can only be used once and then must be thrown away.

What are its advantages?

+ Easy to get.
+ Stronger than the male condom.
+ Protects against unplanned pregnancy.
+ Protects against most STDs.
+ Can be inserted well before intercourse begins.

+Allows the female to protect herself without depending on her partner.

+Good for partners who may have erection problems from time to time.

Do I need parental consent?

No.

Any recommendations?

Practice using the female condom before you actually engage in intercourse.

Use a water-based lubricant. If you are sexually active, keep a good supply of female condoms so you don't run out. Do not use with a male condom.

Spermicide

Spermicide is a chemical inserted into the vagina to help destroy sperm entering it. Spermicides vary in form and effectiveness, when they should be used, and how they should be used. Some spermicides come as foam, jelly, cream, tablets, suppositories, or thin squares of paper called vaginal contraceptive film.

Even the best spermicides are only fair at preventing unplanned pregnancy and protecting against some STDs.

How well does it prevent unplanned pregnancy?

Each form of spermicide has a different level of effectiveness at preventing unplanned pregnancy. Foams and suppositories tend to be the best spermicides, but even if they are used correctly, they still tend to be only fair at preventing unplanned pregnancy.

How well does it protect against STDs?

Spermicide may provide some protection against gonorrhea, PID (pelvic inflammatory disease), and some vaginal infections, but it is not considered to be highly effective protection against STDs.

How do I use it?

Each spermicide is used differently. Some spermicides need to be applied fifteen minutes before intercourse to be effective, whereas other spermicides are effective immediately after insertion. Due to the number of different types of spermicide available, the user should carefully read the instructions on the package.

Spermicide is only effective for a certain period of time, so the couple must engage in intercourse within a certain time period after the spermicide is applied in the vagina. Each time the couple wants to engage in intercourse, the female must apply more spermicide.

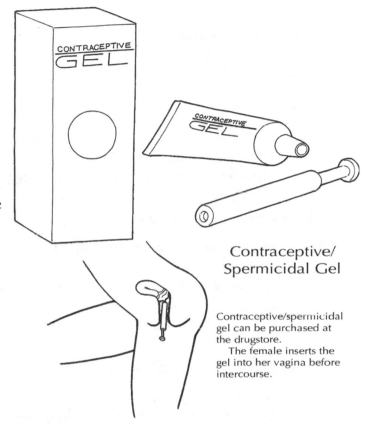

Contraceptive/ Spermicidal Gel

Contraceptive/spermicidal gel can be purchased at the drugstore.

The female inserts the gel into her vagina before intercourse.

How does it work?

Spermicide contains chemicals that destroy sperm. It may also block the sperm from entering the cervix. In this way, spermicide may prevent unplanned pregnancy.

What are its side effects?

About one in twenty people (5 percent) who use spermicide may feel a burning or irritation of the vagina or penis, but sometimes changing the type of spermicide relieves the problem. Otherwise, there are no known side effects.

Where can I get it?

Health clinics and drugstores.

How much does it cost?

The price of spermicide can vary from product to product. Health clinics may provide spermicide for free or at a low price. Drugstore prices may range from $5 to $15 for different types of spermicide.

What are its disadvantages?

- Only provides fair prevention against unplanned pregnancy.
- Can be messy.
- The female may feel weird or uncomfortable inserting something into her vagina.
- Not very effective against STDs.

What are its advantages?

+ Easy to get.
+ Provides additional protection when used with another contraceptive.
+ May offer some protection against STDs.

Do I need parental consent?

No.

Any recommendations?

Use with another form of contraception and read the instructions in the package very carefully.

Tubal Ligation (Tubes Tied)

When a female has her "tubes tied," it means that she has had a surgical operation known as a tubal ligation. Tubal ligation is also known as sterilization, because it permanently prevents the female from becoming pregnant by cutting, tying, or burning the Fallopian tubes closed with a laser.

How well does it prevent unplanned pregnancy?

Next to abstinence, both tubal ligation and male vasectomy (see page 173) are the most effective methods of preventing pregnancy.

How well does it protect against STDs?

Although tubal ligation is excellent at preventing unplanned pregnancy, it offers no protection against STDs.

How do I use it?

Under anesthesia, the female will have a small incision (cut) about one inch long made in her belly button. A tube-like instrument with lights and a viewer, called a laparoscope, is inserted through the belly button incision and moved toward the Fallopian tubes. The Fallopian tubes will then be cut and burned so ova can no longer pass through.

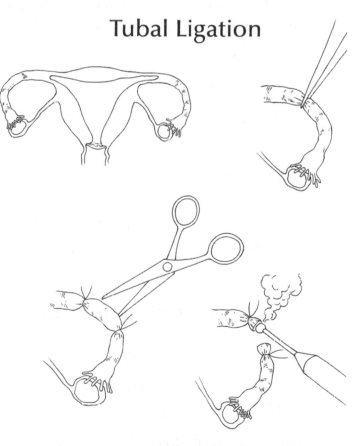

Tubal Ligation

The Fallopian tube is tied, cut, or burned closed so the ovum cannot travel through it.

How does it work?

A tubal ligation blocks the Fallopian tubes so that an ovum cannot be fertilized by a male sperm.

What are its side effects?

None, other than soreness around the incision and possible infection or bleeding after surgery.

Where can I get it?

A tubal ligation can be performed by a doctor at a hospital or health clinic. This method is available only to women who have decided they do not want any additional children. It is not provided to teens in most cases.

How much does it cost?

The price, of course, will vary from doctor to doctor; prices are $600 to over $1,000.

What are its disadvantages?

- May not be reversible.
- Does not protect against STDs.
- High initial cost.

What are its advantages?

+ Highly effective for preventing unplanned pregnancy.

Do I need parental consent?

Yes. This procedure is not generally recommended or made available to young people.

Any recommendations?

A condom should also be used to prevent STDs.

Vasectomy

A vasectomy is the male version of the female tubal ligation. A vasectomy is a quick and simple surgical procedure that cuts and burns (with a laser) the male's vas deferens so sperm cannot pass through.

A vasectomy is also a form of sterilization because it is permanent, although there is a good chance the vasectomy can be reversed.

How well does it prevent unplanned pregnancy?

A vasectomy is almost perfect at preventing unplanned pregnancy. Only abstinence works better.

How well does it protect against STDs?

Although a vasectomy is almost perfect at preventing pregnancy, it offers no protection against STDs.

How do I use it?

The male will have a local anesthetic (painkiller) used for this fifteen- to twenty-minute procedure. A small incision (cut) is made in the scrotum, and the vas deferens is cut, tied, or burned shut so sperm cannot reach the urethra.

The male can go home immediately after the procedure and return to strenuous activities in a few days.

The male will still have some sperm left in his

Vasectomy

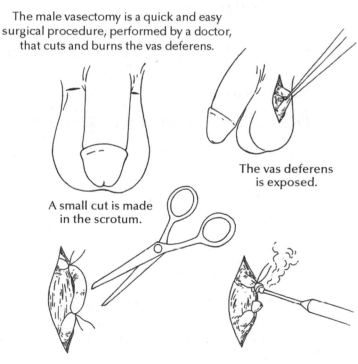

The male vasectomy is a quick and easy surgical procedure, performed by a doctor, that cuts and burns the vas deferens.

A small cut is made in the scrotum.

The vas deferens is exposed.

The vas deferens is then tied and cut.

The vas deferens may then also be burned closed.

semen for about twelve ejaculations (or six to eight weeks), so he must use another form of contraception until there are no longer any sperm in his semen.

How does it work?

Cutting the vas deferens keeps sperm from traveling from the epididymis to the outside of the body. If sperm cannot leave the male's body, the female's ovum cannot be fertilized and pregnancy will not occur. The male can still ejaculate semen, but the semen has no sperm in it.

What are its side effects?

The male may be a little sore around the incision for about ten days after the surgery, but otherwise there are no side effects.

Where can I get it?

A doctor can perform the procedure at a hospital or clinic. This method is not intended for or made available to young men.

How much does it cost?

Prices can range anywhere from $250 to $900.

What are its disadvantages?

- May not be reversible.
- Does not protect against STDs.
- High initial cost.

What are its advantages?

+Highly effective at preventing unplanned pregnancy.

Do I need parental consent?

Yes. This procedure is not recommended or made available to young people.

Any recommendations?

A condom must still be used to protect against STDs.

Emergency Contraception, or "The Morning-After Pill"

Emergency contraception will prevent a pregnancy if a condom breaks or any type of unprotected intercourse takes place. If either of these situations occur, the woman or couple can go to a health clinic or doctor's office and receive emergency contraception (the morning-after pill).

How well does it prevent unplanned pregnancy?

Very well if taken within seventy-two hours (about three days) after intercourse. It works best the day after intercourse, however.

How well does it protect against STDs?

Emergency contraception does not provide any protection against STDs.

How do I use it?

If the female believes there is a possibility she may become pregnant, she can visit a health clinic, doctor, or Planned Parenthood within three days from when the intercourse took place. The female will be given two pills to swallow and two more to take about twelve hours later.

How does it work?

The morning-after pill is a high dose of hormones that may keep the ovum from becoming fertilized by the sperm, or it may make the lining of the uterus unable to support a fertilized egg.

What are its side effects?

Mostly nausea and vomiting. The doctor will provide information about any other side effects.

Where can I get it?

A doctor's office, health clinic, and some Planned Parenthood offices. A toll-free number for locations around the country is 1-888-NOT-2-LATE or 1-800-584-9911. On the Web, visit ec.princeton.edu.

How much does it cost?

About $10 to $20, depending on where you go. This does not include the charge for the doctor/clinic visit. As with many clinics, the charge may be less for people who cannot afford it.

What are its disadvantages?

- Side effects.
- Must be used as soon as possible after unprotected intercourse (within seventy-two hours, or three days, after intercourse).

What are its advantages?

+ Very effective at preventing an unplanned pregnancy.
+ Available in case of an emergency.

Do I need parental consent?

No.

Any recommendations?

Know the location of the nearest clinic that offers emergency contraception so you can get there quickly and not spend time searching for a location while you are worried. The Emergency Contraception hotline (1-888-NOT-2-LATE or 1-800-584-9911) is available for additional information and locations near you. This is a free phone call.

Repeated use (abuse) is not recommended. Ask the doctor about side effects.

Do Not Use the Following Methods!

Pull-Out Method

The pull-out method is not a reliable method of contraception. If you are concerned about pregnancy or STDs, do not use this method. The pull-out method is when a male and female engage in intercourse without any contraception, and the male pulls his penis out of the vagina before he ejaculates. He thinks if he doesn't ejaculate in the female's vagina, sperm will not pass through the cervix and into the uterus, and the female will not get pregnant. This thinking has major problems.

If the male and female engage in intercourse, the male will discharge a prelubricating fluid from his penis. This prelubricating fluid may contain sperm that can cause the female to become pregnant. The male does not feel this prelubricating fluid coming out of his penis. Also, this method relies on the male's ability to know when he is about to ejaculate semen and then "pull out" before it happens. This can be a problem for some males, especially those who have been drinking alcohol or using drugs or who just don't have that kind of control. So the female has to rely entirely on the male to protect her sexual health and future, which isn't responsible or smart.

On top of all this, the pull-out method does not protect against STDs.

Recommendations? Don't ever use the pull-out method—unless you can afford to become pregnant, you have both been tested for STDs, and you are both monogamous!

Rhythm Methods

People who use the rhythm methods try to find out which days during the female's menstrual cycle are "safe" for intercourse. During the "unsafe" days, when the female is likely to be ovulating (releasing an ovum), the couple must abstain (not have intercourse). On the "safe" days, when there isn't an ovum present or being released, the couple believes they can engage in unprotected intercourse. The three most popular rhythm methods are:

- Calendar method: Uses calculations based on the number of days in the female's usual menstrual cycle.
- Temperature method: This involves taking the female's basal temperature each day to identify when it is "safe" to have intercourse.
- Ovulation method: This method looks at the female's vaginal discharge of cervical mucus to see when it is "safe" to have intercourse.

Although a few studies claim that using the rhythm methods correctly are somewhat effective at preventing unplanned pregnancy, the overwhelming majority of statistics show the rhythm methods to be very risky. In addition, the rhythm methods do not provide any protection against STDs.

Recommendations? Do not use any rhythm method by itself. Use rhythm with a reliable source of contraception. Only couples who want to risk having a child should use this method.

Douching

Douching after intercourse is another method that doesn't work to prevent unplanned pregnancy. A douche is a plastic bottle of fluid that the female squirts into her vagina for hygienic purposes (which also is not very effective). Some females believe that if they douche immediately after sex, they will wash all of the semen/sperm out of the vagina, and therefore pregnancy will not occur.

This doesn't work. When the male ejaculates into the vagina, some sperm enter the cervix almost immediately. Once sperm enter the cervix, no douching or washing will flush them out. The sperm are on their way to the uterus and Fallopian tubes, where a pregnancy can occur. Douching also does not provide reliable protection against STDs.

Recommendations: use a different, reliable method of contraception.

If you have more questions about birth control, sexually transmitted diseases, or any other sexuality related issue, you can find additional information at Youth Embassy (www.YouthEmbassy.com).

Guide to Contraceptives (Birth Control)

TYPE	EFFECTIVE?	STDS?	COST	GET IT FROM	MORE INFO
Abstinence	The best	Yes	$0	—	Page 129
Morning-after pill	Excellent	No	$10*	Clinic/Doctor	Page 175
Depo-Provera	Excellent	No	$35*	Clinic/Doctor	Page 147
Lunelle	Excellent	No	$30*	Clinic/Doctor	Page 149
Birth control pills	Excellent	No	$0–$30*	Clinic/Doctor	Page 131
NuvaRing	Excellent	No	$0–$30*	Clinic/Doctor	Page 138
Ortho Evra	Excellent	No	$0–$30*	Clinic/Doctor	Page 135
Condom	Very good	Yes++	$0–$2	Drugstore/Clinic	Page 155
Female condom	Very good	Yes++	$2–$3	Drugstore/Clinic	Page 165
Diaphragm	Good	No**	$15–$50*	Clinic/Doctor	Page 144
Spermicide	Fair	No**	$5–$15	Drugstore	Page 168
Cervical cap	Fair	No	$50*	Clinic/Doctor	Page 151
Today Sponge	Fair	No	$3	Internet/Drugstore	Page 153

NOT RECOMMENDED FOR YOUNG PEOPLE

Vasectomy	Excellent	No	$250–$900*	Clinic/Doctor	Page 173
Tubal ligation	Excellent	No	$600–$1000*	Clinic/Doctor	Page 171
IUD	Excellent	No	$175–$400*	Clinic/Doctor	Page 141
Pull-out ‡	Poor	No	$0	—	Page 177
Rhythm methods ‡	Poor	No	$0	—	Page 177
Douching ‡	Poor	No	$2	Drugstore	Page 178

++	Protects against most STDs, including HIV, but not all.
*	The price doesn't include the cost of the doctor/clinic visit, which could be anywhere from $10 to over $100. Also, some clinics have a "sliding scale," which means that people who do not make a lot of money (such as teens) will pay less, or very little.
**	Only protects against a few STDs.
‡	Very risky method!

8

Sexually Transmitted Diseases and HIV/AIDS

Can you imagine having small, bubbly blisters that are itchy and painful around your vagina or penis? How about a thick, white, cheesy discharge/fluid coming out of your vagina? Or how about a large, soft, pus-filled crater on the tip or shaft of your penis? Would you prefer a small organism that silently destroys your insides, causing you to become sterile (unable to have children), blind, paralyzed, insane, or even dead? Sounds like fun, doesn't it? Actually, this happens to millions of people each year who engage in unprotected intercourse. This is real! Regardless of who you are, the color of your skin, and whether you are rich or poor, young or old, weak or strong, smart or not—if you engage in unprotected vaginal, oral, or anal intercourse, you are at risk of becoming infected with a sexually transmitted germ and developing a serious disease.

Intercourse is a lot like rolling dice. With each roll of the dice, you take your chances on what number comes up. Each time you engage in unprotected intercourse, you take your chances on what might happen.

With all the wonderful feelings intercourse may bring, the germs that can be passed from one person to another during unprotected intercourse can also cause a variety of sores, blisters, discharges, or physical changes that are embarrassing, painful, and even life threatening.

Let's not forget that the male and female also risk becoming responsible for a child if pregnancy occurs, but this chapter will focus on germs like bacteria, viruses, and fungi that can be spread from person to person during intercourse. These types of germs are called sexually transmitted diseases or STDs for short. STIs (sexually transmitted infections) is another term used to describe germs that can be passed from one person to another through sex. Either abbreviation is acceptable. STD also used to be called venereal disease (VD), but that name was phased out quite a few years ago. If you ever see or hear the terms STD, STI, or VD, just remember that they all mean the same thing—germs that can be spread from person to person during intercourse.

How are STDs spread?

STDs are mostly spread through certain body fluids such as blood, semen, vaginal fluid, and prelubricating fluid. When two people have sexual contact (vaginal intercourse, oral intercourse, anal intercourse), and sometimes just close skin-on-skin contact, these fluids can enter the body through microtears in the skin of the vagina, penis, anus, or mouth. The tears are so small that they cannot be felt or seen.

How many STDs are there?

Believe it or not, over twenty different sexually transmitted germs and other physical conditions can be passed on from one person to the next through unprotected intercourse. A few of the more common STDs and their treatments are listed on page 186–188.

Can you develop an immunity to STDs?

The sad thing about STDs is that your body doesn't build up an immunity to them. This means that you can catch them again and again, and even more than one at the same time.

It doesn't stop there. Some STDs, as you can see from the chart, have no cure; once you get them, they are yours for life. (Doesn't this sound like something you would hear about in a horror movie?) The fact is that STDs are very real and change the lives of millions of people each year. Are you next?

What do people with STDs look like?

You should have it clear in your head: people who have STDs look 100 percent normal, and there is no way of knowing who is infected or not. Quite often infected people do not even know that they are infected. A person can look normal, feel normal, and have no signs or symptoms, and then infect other people without even knowing it. Of course, there are also those people who know they are infected but lie about it and infect other people. (Yes, there are some very sick people out there!)

How do STDs spread so quickly?

STDs spread quickly throughout a society. Let's say that Monique had unprotected intercourse with just one guy named Chad. Can Monique become infected with an STD? Let's see.

Chad had intercourse with two other females before Monique. Their names were Aisha and Louise. Aisha had intercourse with three other guys after Chad. Their names were Jimmy, Sean, and Tom. Louise had intercourse

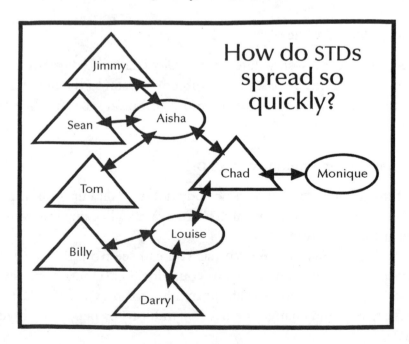

with two other guys before Chad. Their names were Billy and Darryl. Now this can go on forever, but let's stop here. Much of the spread depends on when who had intercourse with whom first, but let's assume that Darryl was infected with herpes and infected Louise. Louise then had intercourse with Billy and then Chad. Could Billy and Chad also be infected with herpes now? You bet. Now Chad has intercourse with Aisha. Could she be infected? Yes. Aisha then had intercourse with Jimmy, Sean, and Tom. Could they be infected now, as well? Yes. The million dollar question is, can Monique be infected with herpes? Yes, yes, yes. This is a simple model, but hopefully it gives you an idea of how STDs are spread.

The more people that you engage in intercourse with, the greater your chances of becoming infected with an STD.

Is it dangerous to have sex with a prostitute?

A prostitute (also known as a hooker, whore, ho, working girl, lady of the evening, or escort) is a person who has sex for some type of payment, usually money, often to satisfy his or her drug addiction. Prostitution has been around for centuries, along with the debate about whether prostitution should be legalized.

One thing is for sure, however; because prostitutes engage in intercourse with so many different people, it is very likely they have one or more sexually transmitted diseases. Even if a prostitute says she/he uses a condom all the time, some STDs, like herpes and genital warts, can be caught even if a condom is used.

Going back to what was mentioned earlier, the more people you have sex with, the greater the chance of catching an STD. Many prostitutes have sex with as many as six or seven different people per day—figure out how many different people that comes out to per year. And this is not to overlook the fact that many prostitutes use IV drugs. Their habit puts them at an extremely high risk of becoming infected with HIV and hepatitis. As you can see, sex with a prostitute, regardless of how she/he looks, is a very risky behavior. Seeing as most prostitutes are infected with an STD at one time or another, and the risk of HIV/AIDS still continues to grow, do you think sex with a prostitute is worth the risk?

When should I go to a medical clinic or doctor?

If you engage in intercourse and later notice any of these signs, you should visit a doctor or clinic immediately:
- Discharge from the penis or vagina.
- Itching around the genital area.
- Burning urination.
- Skin changes around the genital area (bumps, blisters, rash).

These signs may disappear on their own, but the germs will continue to live inside your body and will not go away without treatment.

How can you avoid getting STDs?

Easy. The number one way not to get STDs is abstinence (not engaging in any type of intercourse). But if you do engage in intercourse, here are a few ways to help prevent STDs, even though they're not 100 percent effective.

CONDOMS. Use a condom! Even though it is not 100 percent effective against genital herpes, genital warts, syphilis, or pubic lice, condoms provide you with some protection against these infections and excellent protection against all the other STDs. You must use the condom correctly, however, and the condom must be latex or polyurethane. (Please turn to the contraception chapter to find out how to use a condom correctly.)

MONOGAMY. This is a big word that usually means being in a romantic or sexual relationship with just one person and having sex only with that person. Being promiscuous (which is another big word that means engaging in intercourse with many different people) puts a person at a much higher risk for becoming infected with a sexually transmitted germ. The more people you engage in intercourse with, the higher the chances are that you will get an STD.

ASSUME YOUR PARTNER HAS AN INFECTION. Remember, there is no way of knowing if a person is infected with an STD or not. He or she can look as sweet and innocent as an angel but still be infected. Always assume the person is infected and protect yourself. Using condoms and washing or showering after intercourse may be helpful.

TAKE YOUR PARTNER TO BE TESTED. I know, you're sitting there saying, "Yeah, right." What you may find over the next few years, as the spread of

Having sex is like
rolling dice;
anything can happen!

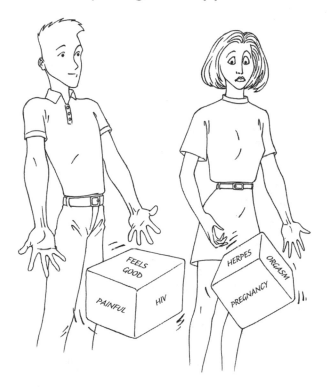

STDs like HIV/AIDS gets worse, more and more people will be strolling down to the local clinic or doctor. I'm just letting you know of ways to prevent getting STDs. You make your own decision.

If I have sex with someone who is infected with an STD, does that mean I will definitely get it?

No. You could get lucky, but your odds are not good. Why take the chance? Remember, some STDs can be spread through skin-on-skin contact, but most enter the body through infected blood, semen, vaginal fluid, or prelubricating fluid. You could be fortunate enough not to come in contact with these germs or have any of these fluids get into your body. Why risk it, though?

Sexually Transmitted Disease Guide

DISEASE	HOW DO I KNOW IF I HAVE IT?	WHAT WILL HAPPEN IF I DON'T SEE A DOCTOR?
AIDS	4–6 weeks after infection there may be flulike symptoms (fever, tired, swollen glands), but then no symptoms usually occur until AIDS develops.	Death (almost always).
Chlamydia	MALE: Painful urination and watery discharge (fluid) from the penis. Sometimes there are no symptoms. FEMALE: Sometimes itching, burning, or discharge (fluid) from the vagina. Usually there are no symptoms.	Possible sterility (no children). Possible sterility (no children).
Genital herpes	Painful, bubbly blisters on the genitals. Often there are no signs or symptoms.	Blisters may disappear and come back again. Possible damage to developing fetus (brain damage or "still birth").
Genital warts	Small cauliflower-like bumps on the genitals.	May spread or lead to cervical cancer in females.
Gonorrhea	MALE: Usually no symptoms, but may have a burning discharge (fluid) from the penis. FEMALE: Usually no symptoms. Possibly a discharge (fluid) from the vagina.	Sterility (no children). Sterility (no children).

DISEASE	HOW DO I KNOW IF I HAVE IT?	WHAT WILL HAPPEN IF I DON'T SEE A DOCTOR?
Hepatitis B	Yellowing of the skin and eyes, fever, nausea. Usually there are no symptoms.	May not cause any harm, but may cause liver damage or possibly death.
Non-gonococcal urethritis	MALE: Thin, clear, watery, or milky discharge from the penis. FEMALE: Burning urination.	Sterility (no children) or possibly arthritis. Sterility (no children) or possibly arthritis.
Pubic lice* (crabs)	Severe itching and possibly tiny blood spots on underwear.	Severe itching will continue.
Syphilis	FIRST STAGE: Chancre (a painless sore that will go away). SECOND STAGE: Rash will develop on palms of hands and body. THIRD STAGE: Insanity, paralysis, death.	Death.
Vaginitis* (also referred to as yeast infection or *Candida albicans*)	MALE: Possibly no symptoms, or red and tender skin on the penis. FEMALE: Pain, irritation, redness, itching, odor, different types of discharge from the vagina (thin and foamy; thick, white, and cheesy; or greenish in color). Common in females.	Symptoms will continue. Symptoms will continue.

*These conditions are not always transmitted sexually. Vaginitis may occur when the female is taking certain antibiotic drugs. Pubic lice may be spread through contact with infected pubic hair, infected towels, or infected bedding.

STD Cures and Treatment Guide

DISEASE	IS IT CURABLE?	HOW IS IT TREATED?
AIDS	No	Healthy lifestyle, antiviral drugs, or anti-infectant drugs to help prevent infections.
Chlamydia	Yes	Antibiotics such as tetracycline.
Genital herpes	No	Acyclovir will help heal the blisters.
Genital warts	No	Liquid nitrogen, laser surgery, or podophyllin liquid will all help remove the warts, but the warts may grow back.
Gonorrhea	Yes	Antibiotics such as penicillin G, or ceftriaxone and doxycycline.
Hepatitis B	No	There are no treatments. A drug called Hepatitis B vaccine will prevent a person from getting Hepatitis B.
Non-gonococcal urethritis	Yes	Antibiotics.
Pubic lice (crabs)	Yes	Kwell or malathion (sold at drugstores).
Syphilis	Yes	Antibiotics such as penicillin. (If you are allergic to penicillin, other antibiotics can be used.)
Vaginitis	Yes	Flagyl or Monistat.

What is the most common STD?

The most common STD is a bacteria called chlamydia. Often a person becomes infected with chlamydia and doesn't even know it until he/she is tested. This is a problem, because if the chlamydia is not treated, it can lead to infertility (inability to have children) in both males and females.

Can I get tested for STDs without my parents knowing?

Almost always, yes. This is a bit touchy in some states, though. Also, for some treatments of STDs, you may need your parents' permission. You might want to call around to different clinics in your area and ask about their policies.

If I am infected with an STD, when can I infect other people?

Immediately. Because the exact time is not known for sure, it is assumed that as soon as you become infected, you can infect others as well. Unfortunately, you may not know if you are infected and you may spread the disease without knowing it.

Where can I call to get more information about STDs?

Try the National STD and AIDS Hotline (1-800-227-8922). Someone at this number will be able to give you general information as well as the names of support groups and people who can help you in your area.

HIV/AIDS

Unless you've been living in a cave and haven't watched TV, read newspapers, or gone to school, you have most likely heard about HIV/AIDS. Are you a little confused about what HIV/AIDS is and how it works? Most people, both young and old, are unsure of what HIV/AIDS is and what it does to the body. There are so many stories people hear about HIV/AIDS that it is sometimes difficult to get accurate information about this disease. Let's see if we can make this as clear and as accurate as possible.

What does AIDS stand for?

AIDS is short for Acquired Immune Deficiency Syndrome. Now, if you're like most people, you just read that and have no clue what it means. So, let's break it down and figure out what this is all about.

    ACQUIRED: This means a person develops a condition over time.

    IMMUNE: In this case, immune refers to our body's defense system, which protects us from germs and disease and keeps us from getting sick. This system is called our immune system.

    DEFICIENCY: Means weak. (When you combine "immune" and "deficiency," it means that your body's immune system is weak.)

SYNDROME: For our purposes, syndrome means a physical condition. (Actually, syndrome refers to a group of characteristics that the condition displays.)

When all the words are back together again, you should be able to put the meaning of the term together also. Acquired Immune Deficiency Syndrome—a condition that develops over time because of a weak immune system.

What is AIDS?

AIDS is a term used to describe when a person's immune system is so weak that it cannot protect the body from germs. Without a strong immune system to fight germs, the person can get sick very easily and even die.

Only a trained professional like a doctor can determine if a person has AIDS. When a person has AIDS, he/she often becomes very sick with rare diseases such as:

- *Pneumocystis carinii* (a type of pneumonia).
- Tuberculosis (usually a lung infection).
- Kaposi's sarcoma (a type of skin cancer).
- Meningitis (a brain infection).
- Cervical cancer.

Where did AIDS come from?

No one knows for sure where this disease originated. Many scientists believe the virus developed over many years in monkeys. There may have been some sort of crossover into humans. From there the disease spread, but this is just a theory.

Although the first cases of the rare diseases *Pneumocystis carinii* and Kaposi's sarcoma were found in a few men in 1979, we didn't start calling this condition "AIDS" until 1982.

How many people have died of AIDS?

This is a trick question. The literal answer is none. Nobody has really died of AIDS. People with AIDS die of rare diseases like *Pneumocystis carinii*, tuberculosis, Kaposi's sarcoma, meningitis, or cervical cancer, not of HIV/AIDS itself.

Remember, HIV/AIDS is a condition where the body's immune system is so weak that it cannot protect itself from harmful diseases. When you hear on the news that someone died of AIDS, what this really means is that the person died of something like Kaposi's sarcoma because he/she had AIDS.

When a person has HIV/AIDS, the immune system can no longer protect the body from disease. This allows diseases to enter the body and grow until they eventually kill the person.

In the United States, nearly one million people have been infected with the virus that causes HIV/AIDS, and nearly half of them have died from AIDS-related illnesses. In some countries in Africa and Asia, the number of people infected with HIV and dying from AIDS-related illnesses is much higher, reaching into the tens of millions.

What is the immune system and how does it work?

The immune system is our body's defense system against germs like bacteria, fungi, protozoans, and nasty little viruses. Whenever a germ enters our body, the immune system surrounds it and destroys it before it has a chance to grow and spread. If our immune system does not destroy the germ, the germ will spread until it kills us. So it is very important that we have strong immune systems to protect us.

When a germ enters the body, it usually finds its way into the bloodstream. In the bloodstream there are little cells that act like soldiers making sure no enemies are around. These little soldiers are called white blood cells, or more specifically, T-lymphocytes (T-cells for short). These T-cells protect us from disease by attacking germs that find their way into the body. Normally, T-cells will surround the germ and try to destroy it before the germ can spread and multiply. While the T-cells are busy attacking the germ, the body will also produce antibodies. Antibodies act like enemy uniforms or flags that surround the germs, making it easier for the T-cells to find those germs and destroy them. When the T-cells see an antibody uniform/flag, they know that an enemy germ is inside it, so they attack and destroy it. Eventually the enemy germs are killed off and the person doesn't get sick or begins to feel better. This happens every single day inside your body without you even knowing it.

What causes a person to develop AIDS?

The majority of scientists believe the virus that causes AIDS is called HIV.

HIV stands for human immunodeficiency virus. Once again, you read that and perhaps didn't understand it too well. To put it simply, human immunodeficiency virus means this virus weakens the body's immune system. The virus begins to destroy the person's immune system until the body cannot protect itself from disease. When the immune system is so weak that it cannot protect the body, we say the person has HIV/AIDS.

How does HIV destroy the immune system?

HIV destroys the T-cells. Without T-cells there is no immune system to protect the body. Then germs get in, spread, and the person can die.

HIV will enter the body, and the T-cells will attack it. Antibodies are produced to identify the HIV so the T-cells can attack it more easily. But this HIV is very tricky. Instead of the T-cells attacking and destroying HIV, the HIV manages to get inside the T-cells and multiply! Soon, HIV has reproduced itself so many times in a T-cell that the T-cell explodes and releases all the newly produced HIV into the body, where it will try to find more T-cells and repeat the process. As more T-cells are destroyed, the immune system becomes weaker. A person has AIDS when his or her T-cells are down to only about 200 per cubic millimeter of blood. (In a healthy human there are between 1,000 and 2,000 T-cells per cubic millimeter of blood.) Once there

HIV kills T-cells

Then germs can spread through the body.

are only about 200 or so T-cells left, the immune system is so weak that the body can no longer defend itself from disease, and the person can become sick very easily and die.

If you're still a little confused about how HIV destroys the immune system, read the story "AIDS in the Castle of Bodi." See if you can match the characters in the story to the AIDS terms we've gone over.

AIDS in the Castle of Bodi

Once upon a time there lived a noble and very wealthy king named Liferous.

King Liferous lived in the beautiful Castle of Bodi, which his parents had built for him before he was born. The Castle of Bodi was truly magnificent. From the high points of the castle one could see for miles into the kingdom. In the summer the castle was cooled by soft afternoon rains, and in the fall the sweet smells from the surrounding fruit orchards filled the air.

Yes, King Liferous of Bodi was a happy man. But King Liferous did have his problems from time to time. For throughout the land lived small, wandering nomads who were fierce warriors. These warriors searched the land for castles to destroy and take over as their own. The three deadliest warriors were the red-and-purple-spotted Cancerites, the coughing Pneumatics, and the swollen-brained Meningites.

For years the Cancerites, Pneumatics, and Meningites tried to enter the Castle of Bodi and kill King Liferous, but each time they tried, they were defeated by the king's guards, the Tea-Sells.

A thousand Tea-Sells patrolled the castle and protected the king. From the time they were born, the Tea-Sells were raised to recognize the enemy nomads and destroy them. The king and his castle were safe as long as the Tea-Sells were there.

One day, after the Cancerites, Pneumatics, and Meningites took a particularly brutal beating from the Tea-Sells, the leaders of these nomads decided to meet and develop a plan that would once and for all kill King Liferous and get them the Castle of Bodi.

"If we could just defeat those Tea-Sells, we could easily destroy King Liferous and take over his castle," said the leader of the Meningites.

"But the Tea-Sells are too smart, too well-trained, and too many!" replied the Pneumatic leader.

"What we need is a way to destroy those Tea-Sells so that we can reach the king," said the leader of the Cancerites.

The three leaders pondered how the Tea-Sells might be reduced in number so they could kill the king.

Suddenly, the leader of the Cancerites remembered hearing of a young and handsome nomad named

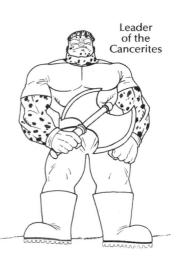

Leader of the Cancerites

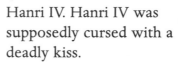

Hanri IV. Hanri IV was supposedly cursed with a deadly kiss.

Leader of the Meningites

"If we could find this Hanri IV," said the leader of the Cancerites, "we just might be able to get him into the Castle of Bodi to kill the Tea-Sells with his kiss."

Well, no sooner than it was said, the three nomadic leaders began to search high and low throughout the land looking for Hanri IV. The three looked for days and weeks, but Hanri IV could not be found. "Is Hanri IV just a myth?" they wondered.

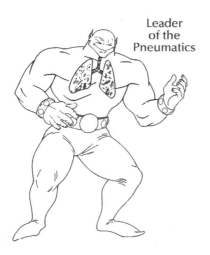

Leader of the Pneumatics

Just when the three nomadic leaders were about to give up, there, in a broken down, crumbling castle tower, sat the most elegant and handsome man the nomads had ever seen. His hair was long, ebony black, and flowed down to his shoulders. His emerald-green eyes sparkled, casting a spell over whomever gazed upon them. His lips were hypnotizing and, ultimately, deadly. Full, ruby red lips that seemed to call out to be kissed.

The three nomads, stunned by the young man's features, asked if he was indeed the Hanri

IV they had heard about. With a smooth, easing curve of his lips, he smiled and then bellowed, "I am Hanri IV. Why do you search for me?"

The three nomads explained their plot to overcome the Castle of Bodi and make it their own, and how Hanri IV could help. The plan was to have Hanri IV enter the castle and, with his exquisite looks and charm, get as many of the Tea-Sells to kiss him as he could. Once the majority of the Tea-Sells were dead and out of the way, the Cancerites, Pneumatics, or Meningites would easily overcome the Castle of Bodi and kill King Liferous. In return for Hanri IV's help, he would be allowed to live in the Castle of Bodi for as long as he liked.

Tea-Sell

The Charming but Deadly Hanri IV

Hanri IV was very tired of living in the shambles of the castle he was in, so he decided to help.

One dark night, as the Cancerites, Pneumatics, and Meningites hid and waited patiently, Hanri IV approached the entrance to the Castle of Bodi and knocked on the huge oak doors. One of the guard Tea-Sells asked in a threatening voice, "Who stands before this door?"

Hanri IV answered, "My name is Hanri IV and I have traveled from a land very far away. I am hungry and tired and am in need of your generosity. May I please come in?"

The Tea-Sell guard answered abruptly, "Be gone! You cannot enter!"

Hanri IV replied, "I can go no further. I will gladly give you anything you please for just one night's stay"

The Tea-Sell guard thrust open the huge oak door in anger and was about to behead the nomad, but just as she was about to strike, she glanced into the eyes of Hanri IV and was spellbound. Her anger quickly turned to desire. He was the most beautiful creature she had ever seen. Her glossy eyes peered helplessly into his, and she was suddenly overwhelmed by his presence. The Tea-Sell guard quickly took Hanri IV into the Castle of Bodi and comforted him. She provided him with food and drink and warm clothing.

Hanri IV told the guard that he was grateful for her kindness and put his arms around the strong Tea-Sell's shoulders for what appeared to be a loving hug. As the guard felt his arms around her, she gazed into his mesmerizing eyes—a fatal mistake. His lips pressed against hers, and, after a moment of warm, passionate bliss, she dropped dead to the floor like a sack of cement.

Hanri IV began to move through the large castle quickly and quietly. Each time a Tea-Sell approached him, he seemed to know just what to say to charm and captivate her until the kiss of death took its toll. One by one, the protectors of the castle were destroyed. Soon, only two hundred Tea-Sells remained to protect King Liferous and the Castle of Bodi.

Realizing what was happening, the Cancerites, Meningites, and Pneumatics quickly assembled outside the walls of the castle. Each nomadic group of warriors knew that its time had finally come; there were not enough guards to protect King Liferous. The first to reach and destroy the king would rule the castle.

Like bloodthirsty hounds the warriors ravaged their way through the Castle of Bodi, destroying whatever came across their paths. Finally the leader of the Cancerites found what he had been looking for. For so many years the Cancerites had dreamed of such a moment. King Liferous knew he was defeated. As the leader of the Cancerites smiled and looked upon the king one last time, he raised his arm and struck the king a final blow. King Liferous was dead, and the Castle of Bodi now belonged to the Cancerites.

At this point you may be wondering "What in the world does this story have to do with HIV or AIDS?" I hope you're not saying that, but if you are, try changing a few of the characters in the story to terms we have gone over concerning AIDS.

Instead of:	**Use:**
King Liferous	Life (a human life)
Castle of Bodi	Body (a human body)
Tea-Sells	T-cells
Hanri IV	HIV
Cancerites	Cancer (Kaposi's sarcoma)
Meningites	Meningitis (brain infection)
Pneumatics	Pneumonia (*Pneumocystis carinii*)

AIDS in real life works a lot like it does in the story. Enemy germs try to attack the body and destroy life all the time, but the T-cells protect us by defeating those enemy germs. Then a virus comes along (HIV) that destroys our T-cells until there are only a few left. Our body and our life can no longer be protected, and the enemy germs come in and easily defeat us.

How do you catch AIDS?

You don't catch AIDS, remember? You can develop AIDS. AIDS is the condition the body is in when it has a weak immune system. You can't catch AIDS from someone—but you can catch HIV, the virus that may lead to AIDS.

How can I become infected with HIV?

You can become infected with HIV only by getting someone else's HIV-infected body fluids into your body. The body fluids that can have enough HIV in them to infect you are blood, semen, prelubricating fluid (the fluid that comes out of the penis before ejaculation), vaginal secretions, and breast milk.

Other fluids from the body like saliva and tears do not have enough HIV in them to infect someone. Even if you were to have deep, wet ("French" or "tongue") kisses with your boyfriend/girlfriend who was infected with HIV, there would not be enough HIV in the saliva to infect you. (If there was a little bit of blood mixed with the saliva, it would be possible to transmit HIV, but to date there are no known infections from wet kissing.) If you really don't want to take any chances, save your wet kisses for someone who has tested negative on an HIV test.

For HIV to enter into your body, infected fluids must enter a cut, tear, or other opening in your body where there is broken skin. These are the ways that HIV is transmitted (caught) and these are the fluids:

Ways	Fluids
Vaginal intercourse (penis entering the vagina)	Blood, semen, prelubricating fluid, vaginal secretions
Oral intercourse (using the mouth to stimulate the genitals)	Blood, semen, prelubricating fluid, vaginal secretions
Anal intercourse (penis entering the anus)	Blood, semen, prelubricating fluid
Drug use (sharing IV drug needles)	Blood
Blood transfusion (receiving blood)	Blood
Breastfeeding	Breast milk
Mother to unborn child	Blood
Ear/body piercing (if infected piercing tools are reused)	Blood
Tattooing (if infected tattooing needles are reused)	Blood

There have also been some medical accidents where nurses or doctors have accidentally stuck themselves with used needles or sharp objects that had HIV-infected blood on them.

Unprotected intercourse (of any kind) and sharing IV (in the vein) drug needles are the two most common ways of becoming infected with HIV.

Unprotected intercourse is responsible for 70 percent of all HIV infections in the United States. Sharing infected IV drug needles is responsible for 25 percent of all HIV infections in the United States.

During intercourse, there may be microscopic tears on the penis (around the opening of the penis) or in and around the vagina. The person can't see or feel these microscopic tears. If infected blood, semen, prelubricating fluid, or vaginal secretions come in contact with those openings in the skin, HIV may enter the body, and the person can become infected.

People who engage in anal intercourse are especially at risk because the layer of skin around the anus and colon is very delicate and thin, so it tears easily. Anal intercourse is likely to cause tears in the skin as well as bleeding. If either partner is infected, there is a good chance that the other person can become infected.

If you do engage in vaginal, oral, or anal intercourse, a condom will provide excellent protection against HIV infection when it is used correctly. Although a condom is not 100 percent effective in preventing HIV (it may break or the person may not use it correctly), it is the best way to prevent getting HIV other than abstinence. (Abstinence is not having any kind of sexual intercourse at all.)

Sharing infected IV drug needles also puts a person at risk of becoming infected with HIV. The IV stands for "intravenous," which means "in the vein." People who use drugs such as heroin, cocaine, or steroids, for example, will fill up a needle (also called a syringe) with the drug and then stick it into a vein in the arm or another body part. Now, what is in your veins? Yes, blood. If an HIV infected person sticks the needle into his/her vein, what will be on the tip and inside the needle? Yes, blood. Infected blood! If he/she passes the needle to someone else to use, and if that person sticks the needle into his or her own vein, then guess what happens? The infected blood in the needle is now in that person's body, and he/she is now infected with HIV.

If you are an IV drug user and you don't use anyone else's needles, you don't need to worry about becoming infected with HIV. You just need to be worried about all the other negative effects of using drugs! If you share needles with other people, thoroughly rinse the inside and outside of the needle with a bleach and water mixture. This will remove any infected blood and destroy the HIV.

The good news is this: If you do not engage in any of these risky behaviors, you do not need to worry about becoming infected with HIV. This is important enough to say again:

If you do not engage in intercourse, use other people's used drug needles, or receive blood transfusions, do not worry about becoming infected with HIV!

What are the most risky and least risky behaviors for HIV infections?

BEHAVIOR	VERY RISKY	SOME RISK	NO RISK
Abstinence (from sex and drugs)			X
IV drug use	X		
Anal intercourse	X		
Oral intercourse	X		
Vaginal intercourse	X		
Mother to unborn child	X		
Tattooing		X	
Ear/body piercing		X	
Wet kissing (open mouth)		X	
Social kissing (dry)			X
Blood transfusion (receiving)		X	
Donating blood			X
Shaking hands			X
Hugging			X
Toilet seats			X
Swimming pools			X
Sneezes/coughs			X
Sharing the same glass			X

How is HIV not spread?

HIV is not spread by casual contact. You can live with, work with, go to school with, and show affection for (hug and kiss) people who are infected with HIV, or who even have AIDS, without becoming infected yourself. In fact, you probably come in contact with people who are infected with HIV each and every day without even realizing it.

HIV does not spread through the air. It is not like the common cold or flu. It spreads only by getting someone's infected body fluid into your system.

HIV is not transmitted by:

- Eating with the same forks, knives, spoons, napkins.
- Using the same exercise equipment.
- Going to the same school.
- Mosquitoes.

Who can become infected with HIV?

Anyone who engages in any risky behavior, like unprotected intercourse or sharing infected IV drug needles, can become infected—and yes, that includes YOU!

It isn't who you are, but what you do that puts you at risk of becoming infected. Whether you are white, black, Hispanic, Asian, Indian, rich, poor, heterosexual (attracted to the opposite sex), homosexual (attracted to the same sex), bisexual (attracted to both sexes), smart, not-so-smart, beautiful, not-so-beautiful—if you engage in risky behaviors like unprotected inter-course or sharing infected IV drug needles, you are at risk of becoming infected with HIV.

How do people know when they have AIDS?

Once again, only a trained medical professional like a doctor can determine when a person has AIDS, but when a person has the following three symptoms, he/she is said to have AIDS:

- 200 or fewer T-cells (on average, a normal, healthy person has between 1,000 and 2,000 T-cells) per cubic millimeter of blood.
- HIV-positive (the person has HIV in his/her body).
- One or more diseases like Kaposi's sarcoma, meningitis, *Pneumocystis carinii,* tuberculosis, or cervical cancer are present.

When a person has all three of these symptoms, he/she is said to have AIDS.

What does a person with HIV look like?

He/She looks normal. There is no way you can
tell if someone is infected with HIV by looking
at him/her. The person looks fine, feels fine,
and may not even know that he/she is infected.
If you are going to have intercourse with someone, use a condom—even if that person looks
sweet and innocent. Assume the person is
infected and doesn't know it.

Anyone can become
infected with HIV!

Can you get HIV/AIDS from someone who doesn't have it?

No. A person who is not infected with HIV cannot infect other people. However, the problem
is that most people who are infected with HIV don't even know it.

    The only way you can know for sure if a person is infected or not is if
the person tests negative on an HIV test, assuming the person has not tested
during the "window period."

What is the "window period?"

It is possible for a person to be infected with HIV but still test negative for
HIV. When a person becomes infected, it takes about six weeks before the
HIV will show up on a test, and it can take as long as six months. This is
called the "window period." The danger is that an HIV-positive person can
take an HIV test, have it turn out negative (no HIV was detected), and then go
on to infect other people, thinking that he/she is not infected with HIV.

What tests are done to check for HIV?

The two tests most often used to check for HIV in the body are the ELISA
and the Western Blot. Both of these tests are called antibody tests because
they check the blood for a buildup of antibodies that are produced when
HIV is present. When HIV enters the body, antibodies will be produced
within just a few hours. However, it usually takes between six weeks to six

months for enough of the antibodies to show up in the ELISA or Western Blot tests. (Sometimes enough antibodies will appear after two weeks, but this is rare.)

The first test that is usually performed is the ELISA. If the ELISA comes back positive (which means there are antibodies in the blood), then a Western Blot test will be done just to be sure that the ELISA was correct.

How much do HIV tests cost?

The costs for the antibody tests (ELISA and Western Blot) can range anywhere from free to around $40 or more, depending on where you have the test done. Public health clinics will probably have the cheapest prices, while private doctors will be more expensive.

Can I get an HIV test without anyone finding out?

Yes. There are two ways the tests can be given. One is confidential and the other is anonymous. You want anonymous testing if you do not want anyone to know who you are.

When you arrive at the clinic for anonymous testing, the counselor will probably ask you a few general questions, like what area you live in, and a few personal questions, like how many people you have had sexual contact with. You will not be asked your name, nor will they find out who you are from the information that you give them. When the test is done, the nurse will put a bar code on your blood sample and give you a matching bar code to keep. (Bar codes are the box of black lines on items you purchase that the cashier runs across a scanner.) This works nicely because when you come back for your results, you show the counselor your bar code and she/he will match it up to the bar code on your results. She/He still does not know your name.

One big problem, however, is that anonymous testing is becoming harder and harder to find. You may have to really hunt around for a place that offers anonymous testing.

Once the results are given to you, the counselor will probably want to talk with you. If you test positive, she/he will discuss setting up a Western

Blot test just to be sure the ELISA test was correct. If the Western Blot results come back positive, she/he will discuss with you different types of treatments and what you can do from there.

If your results come back negative, the counselor will briefly go over ways of preventing HIV infection and give you some informational pamphlets to take with you.

Confidential testing works a bit differently. First of all, your name will be asked, and a form of identification, like a driver's license, will be needed so the staff can see that you are who you say you are. Second, if your test comes back positive, your name goes on record and it is sent to the CDC (Centers for Disease Control). Also, if you are using medical insurance to cover the cost of the test, your name will be sent to the insurance company. This is not usually good news to the insurance company. In fact, your insurance company may drastically increase your rates, or it may try to find a way to drop you altogether.

The bottom line is, if you would rather not have people know your identity, try to find a clinic that offers anonymous testing.

How long do I have to wait for the results of my HIV test?

This depends on the clinic/doctor. Some places offer same- or next-day results; at others you can expect to wait up to a week for your results. There are now rapid tests that can tell you your results in only a few minutes, but it might be hard to find a clinic that offers these.

Can I call on the phone and get my HIV test results?

No. You must go in person to get your HIV results from the clinic. The results will not be given to you over the phone.

How would I know if I became infected with HIV?

You wouldn't know unless you went for an HIV test. In fact, many people don't realize they are infected with HIV until they develop AIDS and go to the doctor to find out what is wrong with them. By then, the situation has become much more difficult to manage.

The only signs or symptoms that might appear would show up about four to six weeks after you were first infected. You would probably feel like you had the flu, but that would go away, and you would probably never suspect that you had been infected with HIV. After that, you would look and feel absolutely normal. Once you developed AIDS, your T-cell count would drop to 200 or less and the lymph glands in your neck and underarms would get swollen. You would experience fever, night sweats, fatigue, nausea (feeling like you want to throw up), diarrhea, skin rashes, tiredness, and weight loss. During this time other diseases could enter your body and start to spread, like *Pneumocystis carinii*, Kaposi's sarcoma, meningitis, tuberculosis, and cervical cancer.

How long does it take to develop AIDS once I have been infected with HIV?

This varies from person to person. Half the people who become HIV-positive will develop AIDS eight to eleven years after they become infected. The other half will develop AIDS sooner than eight years or else after eleven years. Some will develop AIDS just a few months after they become infected. However, there are people who have been infected with HIV for sixteen years or more and still have not developed AIDS.

Why do some people with HIV develop AIDS after just a few months and others not for years?

This depends largely on the type (or strain) of HIV a person is infected with, how well a person takes care of his/her health, and whether or not the person is able to get and use the best medications available.

Once a person develops AIDS, how long does he or she have to live?

This also varies, but usually the person will die between one and two years after AIDS has developed. Generally, one of the "opportunistic" diseases like *Pneumocystis carinii*, Kaposi's sarcoma, meningitis, tuberculosis, or cervical cancer kills the person.

Is there a cure or treatment for HIV or AIDS?

There is no cure for HIV or AIDS. That's why it's best not to get it in the first place. There are medications today that help to keep the HIV from spreading and weakening the immune system. Because of this, many people who have become infected with HIV are living longer than they would have if these medications were not available. Unfortunately, it seems as though these medications lose some of their strength and effectiveness as the years go by, and people go on to develop AIDS. Also, these medications are very expensive and not available to those who cannot afford them. An additional problem is that these medications are very harsh on the body and can cause many nasty side effects. If you would like to know more about treatments, you can call AIDS Info (1-800-448-0440). This is a free and confidential call.

After a person is infected with HIV, when can he/she infect others?

Immediately. Even though no one knows for sure the exact time a person becomes infectious, it is assumed that once a person has been infected with HIV, he or she is immediately able to infect others.

Will I definitely get infected if I have unprotected intercourse with someone who is infected?

No. There is a chance that you won't become infected, but why take a chance?

Should I get tested for HIV?

Yes! If you have ever engaged in unprotected vaginal, oral, or anal intercourse without a condom, or if you have ever used an intravenous drug, then you should take an HIV test.

Should I stay away from people with AIDS?

Absolutely not! People with AIDS are human beings just like you, and they need love, attention, and care, just like every other human being. Let your knowledge about AIDS guide you in treating people with AIDS as you would anyone else. Unfortunately, sometimes people who do not know about AIDS become frightened and will neglect, avoid, or mistreat people with AIDS (or who are HIV-positive). Don't let ignorance cause you to stop treating people with HIV/AIDS as human beings. People who are infected with HIV or who have AIDS especially need your kindness and understanding.

Where can I get more information about AIDS and HIV?

Call the National HIV, AIDS, and Sexually Transmitted Disease Hotline (1-800-342-AIDS). This is a free call available twenty-four hours a day, every day, to answer any questions you have about AIDS.

If you have more questions about sexually transmitted diseases or any other sexuality related issue, you can find additional information at Youth Embassy (www.YouthEmbassy.com).

9

Abortion

As you probably know, abortion is a hot issue, and everyone seems to have a point of view and a convincing argument to go along with it. Should abortion be legal? Should it not be allowed under any circumstances? Should it be allowed only in certain cases? Is abortion safe? What would happen if abortion was not legal? There are many things to consider in this issue. Where do you stand?

What is an abortion?

An abortion is the termination of a pregnancy. An abortion can be performed through either a surgical procedure or the use of certain types of medication.

Are abortions legal?

Abortions are legal in the United States due to a landmark Supreme Court decision in 1973 called *Roe v. Wade*. The outcome of this case gave pregnant females the right to a legal termination of their pregnancies.

Are abortions safe?

An abortion performed by a qualified doctor early in pregnancy is safe. In fact, a legal abortion performed by a qualified doctor is safer than a full-term pregnancy and childbirth. An illegal abortion performed by a person who is not a qualified doctor is very dangerous.

Where can a female go to have an abortion?

Depending on where you live, finding a place where abortions are performed by a qualified physician may sometimes be difficult. Not every place that says it offers abortions is qualified to do so or actually performs abortions at all.

Probably the best place to start is your local Planned Parenthood center. Not all Planned Parenthood centers perform abortions, but they do offer counseling, support, and information on qualified abortion clinics in your area.

If the female does not want to have an abortion, Planned Parenthood also provides support and prenatal counseling. By calling 1-800-230-7526, a person can ask for the local Planned Parenthood chapter. Another toll-free number is the National Abortion Federation at 1-800-772-9100.

How is an abortion performed?

There are a variety of abortion methods. The most widely used method is called a vacuum aspiration. During this procedure, the female will lie down on the doctor's table as though she were going to have a pelvic exam or Pap smear done. The doctor will insert a thin tube into the vagina and through the cervix. Once the thin tube is inside the uterus, the doctor will use a little bit of suction to remove the contents of the uterus, almost like a gentle vacuum. The actual procedure usually takes about five to fifteen minutes, and the female will rest for at least an hour before she is able to go home. The female can expect to be at the clinic anywhere from two to six hours from start to finish. Vacuum aspirations are usually done between the eighth and twelfth week of pregnancy.

Another type of procedure that may be used is called a dilatation and evacuation (D&E). A D&E will usually be performed if the female doesn't find out she is pregnant until her twelfth week of pregnancy. A D&E is usually performed between the twelfth and twenty-fourth week of pregnancy. A D&E will open (dilate) the cervix and use suction to extract the contents of the uterus. Because the pregnancy is at a later stage, a curette (a small, sharp instrument) will be used to gently scrape the walls of the uterus to make sure the uterus is completely empty.

Isn't there a pill you can take?

Yes. A medicinal abortion usually uses a pill called mifepristone (formerly called RU 486). Sometimes another pill, methotrexate, is used instead of mifepristone. Either medication may be used to end a pregnancy.

A doctor will counsel the female and then perform a pelvic examination. If the woman wants a medicinal abortion, she will then be given either mifepristone or methotrexate. A few days after taking the mifepristone or methotrexate, the woman takes another medication called misoprostol to complete the abortion. Several days later, the woman returns to the doctor's office or clinic for a checkup to make sure the abortion is complete. This type of abortion can be performed forty-nine to sixty-three days (roughly seven to nine weeks) after the female's last period.

Can a female do an abortion herself?

No. Unfortunately, some pregnant females don't have safe abortion methods available to them, and they will try to perform an abortion on themselves. This is extremely dangerous. The female who tries to perform an abortion on herself may make herself sterile (unable to ever have children) or even die in the process. Just like any other surgical procedure, an abortion should only be performed by a qualified doctor.

Does drinking vinegar cause an abortion?

No, vinegar does not cause an abortion. There are many myths floating around that say if a female does this or drinks that, it will cause an abortion. Again, a female who is considering an abortion should contact Planned Parenthood (1-800-230-7526) or the National Abortion Federation (1-800-772-9100) to work through the decision-making process. If the female then decides to have an abortion, these organizations will help locate a doctor who is able to perform an abortion safely.

Can the female have children later in life if she has an abortion?

Yes. Legal abortions do not cause any fertility problems later in life. The female is able to have children the way she normally would at a later time.

Do abortions cause breast cancer?

No, abortions do not cause breast cancer.

Is it right to have an abortion?

This certainly depends on whom you ask. In case you don't already know this, there is a lot of argument in the United States over whether or not abortions should be allowed. Here are the two major groups arguing whether abortions should be performed:

PRO-LIFE. People who have the pro-life point of view believe that a human life begins once conception has taken place. Therefore, the pro-life group believes the mother has no right to have an abortion or "kill the human life" developing inside of her. People who are pro-life believe that regardless of how or why the female became pregnant, she has no right to terminate a pregnancy or "life": she should give birth and raise the child or put the child into the adoption system.

PRO-CHOICE. People who have the pro-choice point of view believe the female should have the legal right, or choice, to decide to have an abortion if she wishes. The pro-choice position allows for various beliefs regarding when life begins and how it is defined. People who are pro-choice believe that females should have safe, legal abortion methods available to them.

In America, you are free to think what you like. Just remember, if someone has a different point of view, it doesn't make him/her a bad person, just someone with different thoughts and feelings from yours. You can still love or be best friends with someone who has a different point of view, and there is never any reason for hostility or violence.

Should I have an abortion?

Here are questions you will want to ask yourself:
- Am I ready (financially, emotionally, mentally) to raise a person from birth to adulthood?
- What kind of support would I get from the baby's father?
- How would I feel if I placed the child for adoption?
- Is an abortion right for me?
- How will I feel if I have an abortion?

Does this sound like a tough decision to make? It is! You may want to seek help from a nonbiased, nonjudgmental adult. The problem, however, is finding such an adult who is able to help you figure out what you want and what is best for you, rather than impose his/her beliefs or wants on you. Again, Planned Parenthood (1-800-230-7526) or the National Abortion Federation (1-800-772-9100) have professional counselors who can understand your situation, explain all your options, and help you work through your decision without pushing you one way or the other.

Beware: There are some places that call themselves "Crisis Pregnancy Centers" or other such sounding names that attempt to get pregnant females to come to their offices so they can scare them, harass them, and get them to make the decisions that they want pregnant females to make. These places seem to be popping up more and more, so beware. By contacting Planned Parenthood or the National Abortion Federation, you will be able speak and sit down with someone who is fair and who will help you with whatever YOU decide, including birth, adoption, or abortion.

Why would a female want an abortion?

There are many reasons why a female may consider abortion.
- She may not feel emotionally ready to be a parent.
- She may not have the emotional or financial support to raise a child.
- She may feel that she cannot provide the kind of life she would want for her child.
- She may not have the skills or resources needed to provide a safe and healthy environment for her child.
- She may have educational or career goals that she does not want to postpone.
- Her partner might not want to have a child or might not have the skills or resources to be a good father.
- She may not have the emotional resources to complete a pregnancy and give birth.
- She is the victim of rape or incest.

These are just a few of the reasons for an abortion. There are nearly one million legal abortions performed each year in the United States. Each of these females must face this very difficult decision, hopefully with the help of someone who is understanding and supportive.

Would my parents need to know?

Some states now have laws that say a parent must give permission for a female under age eighteen to have an abortion. Contact Planned Parenthood (1-800-230-7526) or the National Abortion Federation (1-800-772-9100) to find out what your state laws are.

What other options are there besides abortion?

Fortunately for females who become pregnant, another choice is adoption. Adoption services will present the baby to a couple or family who may be better prepared to raise a child to adulthood. To find out more about the possibility of adoption, call the National Adoption Information Clearinghouse (1-888-251-0075).

If you have more questions about abortion, adoption, or any other sexuality related issue, you can find additional information at Youth Embassy (www.YouthEmbassy.com).

10

How to Say No to Sex

You are a special person with your own thoughts, feelings, and beliefs. Throughout your life you will be challenged to defend what you think, feel, and believe. Sometimes this battle will be easy, but most of the time the pressure to conform, be like "everyone else," or do what someone else wants you to do is difficult to overcome.

As more and more pressure is put on you to forget about what you think, feel, or believe, you will be tempted to take the easy way out and give up on your beliefs to make another person "happy" or just to stop her/him from pressuring you.

We have all been pressured into doing something we didn't really want to do. Almost always, we felt embarrassed, ashamed, and angry at ourselves because of it. The trick to becoming successful in life is to learn from our mistakes and, most important, to learn from other people's mistakes.

If you can learn from another person's mistakes, you will be able to avoid a lot of headaches in your own life. Unfortunately, millions of young people each year learn the hard way about teenage pregnancy and STDs (like HIV/AIDS) because they refuse to learn from other people's mistakes. Here is a popular Basso saying that might help: "An intelligent person learns from his or her mistakes. A wise person learns from the mistakes of others." Which will you be?

Contrary to popular belief, not all teens are having sex. In fact, in surveys I give my fifteen- and sixteen-year-old students who live under some of the harshest conditions in America, only about 35 percent of the females have had sex, which means that 65 percent have not. Interestingly, of the 35 percent who had sex, 90 percent said they regretted it and wish they had waited.

Now, before you think my young ladies are lying, you should know that the surveys are anonymous (no names) and are completed in a way that no one can see what the next person is writing. Each year, just about the same results show up.

The guys are different. About 60 percent of my fifteen- and sixteen-year-old males report that they have had sex (40 percent have not). These percentages are pretty close to results from similar surveys given around the nation. Not everyone is having sex!

More important than what other people do is what you are going to do. Do you want to avoid an unplanned pregnancy? Do you want to avoid becoming infected with an STD (including HIV/AIDS)? Would you rather postpone intercourse until you're older? If you answered yes to these questions, you and millions of other teens just like you should take pride in who you are and learn how to defend and protect your thoughts, feelings, and beliefs. You can do it! You will be happy you did.

So how can I get out of having sex if I don't want to have sex?

Before you get into a high-pressure situation, you should do the following:

PLAN AHEAD. Know where you are going and what you will be doing before you go out.

LOOK FOR SIGNS OF A POSSIBLE PROBLEM. There are a few things that can lead to a problem situation. Beer, wine coolers, alcohol, marijuana, or other drugs being bought or used may lead to trouble.

AVOID "HOT SPOTS," places where there are no people around (such as a house where no adult is home or empty parks/beaches at night).

KNOW HOW TO COMMUNICATE YOUR FEELINGS. Practice assertive communication and body language, using "put off" words and moves (actions that get you out of the situation). Each of these communication skills should be practiced until you know them like your ABCs. Go somewhere by yourself and practice verbal messages and "put off" lines until there are at least two or three that you say very well. You will probably feel stupid standing in a room talking to yourself, but after memorizing and saying each line ten or twenty times, it gets easier to do. You may think, "I don't need to do this" or "When the time comes, I'll be ready." This would be a big mistake. When you're in a high-pressure situation, your mind tends to freeze up and you don't usually think very clearly. Let's not forget you're in the middle of a heart-and-mind battleground.

Once you get good at repeating what you really want to say, try it in front of a mirror. Then make it more difficult by adding body language. Make believe you are your favorite actor/actress acting in a big movie.

Here are descriptions and a few tips for each communication skill you should practice.

Verbal messages are any spoken words that say what you feel or think. Repeat verbal messages if necessary. After giving a verbal message, you could ask, "Do you hear me?" or "Do you understand me?" You do not have to explain why you do not want to have sex. "No" is good enough.

More important, when you say no verbally you must also say no with your body. Body language is what your body says through facial expressions, hand gestures, how close you sit/stand next to someone, or any body movement or stance. Gestures and expressions are forms of body language. Your body language should match your verbal message.

"Put off" moves are any words or actions that interrupt what the other person is saying and doing. These moves give you a chance to get out of the situation, giving you time to think, leave, or calm down. Examples of "put off" moves are:

- "Not now. Let's go somewhere."
- "I have to go."
- "Not tonight. I feel like I'm going to be sick."
- "I have to call home."
- "I have to go to the bathroom."

If you want to be successful in doing what you believe is best for you, practice your communication skills. It's like having a big test at school; study until you know the material backward and forward. You will still feel emotional pressure, but if you know your lines, this will help ease some of the pressure on you to have sex.

How can I let my partner know how I feel about sex?

Make your feelings known early in the relationship. An important factor in most successful relationships is the ability to communicate. Verbally let your boyfriend/girlfriend know where you stand.

Equally important is not to send the wrong body messages. If your mouth is saying one thing and your body is saying another, your partner may become confused. Body language is any nonverbal message a person sends with his/her facial expressions, gestures, body posture, body movements, body closeness, touches, and clothes, to name just a few.

When body language and verbal language are different, people can get the wrong idea or message. Here are some examples of confusing messages. See if you can understand what the person wants or is trying to communicate.

Verbal Message	+ Body Language	= Message
"Don't touch me there."	Continue kissing	He/She isn't serious.
"Stop!"	Smile	He/She is just playing.
"Stop trying to take my clothes off."	Continue kissing and stay seated.	He/She is playing hard to get.
"I don't want to have sex."	Stay seated and continue to kiss and caress.	He/she must be teasing me.

If you want to be clearly understood, your body language must agree with your verbal language. Notice how these next messages are much clearer and easier to understand.

Verbal Message	+ Body Language	= Message
"Don't touch me there."	Push his/her hand away	I don't feel comfortable being touched there.
"Stop!"	Serious or angry look on your face.	I don't want you to do that.
"Stop trying to take my clothes off."	Stop kissing and back away.	I don't want this to go any further.
"I don't want to have sex."	Back away, get up, and walk away.	Stop ignoring what I feel, or I won't be here for you to ignore.

Probably the best time to verbally tell your boyfriend or girlfriend how you feel is when you are by yourselves but in a public place, like in study hall, walking home, at a restaurant, or at a movie. Let your boyfriend/girlfriend know how much you enjoy being with him/her or even how you feel romantically, but explain that you just don't think sex is a good idea at this time in your life, or that it is against your religion to have sex before marriage, or you're just not ready—whatever your belief. Look serious and be serious when you say this. You don't have to sound angry, but your verbal message and body language should both be saying the same thing: "Listen to me. I'm serious!"

What should I do if my partner pressures me into having sex?

Any person who tries to get you to do something you don't feel is right is someone you should avoid being around.

If your girlfriend/boyfriend is one of these people who seems to ignore what you say and makes excuses for pressuring you, it may be time to trade up and find someone who is more sensitive to who you are and what you're about. Try communicating your feelings again. Perhaps there was some miscommunication or misunderstanding. If your partner continues with the pressure, it's clear she/he is only interested in getting what she/he wants and doesn't really care about who you are, what you're about, and what you feel.

It's difficult being your own person and doing what you know is right, but the more you stand up for yourself and defend what you believe in, the stronger you become as a person. The stronger you become as a person, the easier it is for you to defend your beliefs and do what is right for you.

When you start to feel the pressure, say no quickly, without even thinking. The sooner you say no, and the more often you say no, the easier it becomes to say no. Don't give in to the pressure and say yes just to make the other person happy; you will probably regret it. Remember about learning from other people's mistakes?

Ladies and gentlemen, you were not put here to be someone else's pleasure toy. You are an important individual with the freedom to think, feel, and believe whatever you choose. Your greatest challenge will be to understand another person's point of view without compromising yourself.

What if we are alone, and he/she is really coming on strong?

First, remember to think with your head, not your heart. You may be tempted to "just let things happen," which you might regret later on. To get out of this hot and heavy situation, you need to be ready to handle some of the pressure places and pressure lines that may be used on you. Be ready to avoid certain "hot spots," such as:

- Parking somewhere quiet.
- His/Her place (unless you know his/her parents are home).
- A friend's house when no parents are home.
- His/Her bedroom or any bedroom.
- Any private, secluded place where there are few or no people.

If your partner mentions going to any of these "hot spots" or seems to be heading toward any of these places, don't follow. Don't go along, or tell him/her (both verbally and nonverbally) that you don't want to go. You can make up an excuse why you don't want to go, or use a "put off" move.

Keep in mind that you don't need to give an excuse if you don't want to. You don't need to explain why you don't want to do something. "No" is good enough. You can also be creative and come up with your own responses or "put off" moves.

If for some reason you do find yourself alone with your boyfriend/girl-friend in a "hot spot," be prepared to hear some pressure lines:

"If you love me, you'll have sex with me/you'll prove it."
RESPONSE: "If *you* love *me*, you'll stop trying to make me do something I don't want to do." Or,
"If you love me, you'll prove it by respecting my feelings."

"If you won't have sex with me, I don't want to go out with you anymore."
RESPONSE: "If you are only with me because you want sex, I guess our relationship really means nothing to you." Or,
"I don't like being threatened and I don't want to be with some-one who makes threats when he doesn't get what he wants." Or,
"Obviously you want sex more than you want a relationship with me, and I'm not interested in anyone who doesn't care about me."

"If you won't have sex with me, I'll find someone who will."
RESPONSE: "I'm not a sex toy for you to use, and, based on your com-ment, I see you don't want me for anything except sex. I'm going to find someone who I can have a more meaningful relationship with."

"Don't be afraid, the first time is always scary."
RESPONSE: "I'm not afraid. I'm standing up for what I believe is right." Or,
"What's scary is how I will feel about myself if I let you talk me into doing something I don't want to do."

"Everybody has sex."
RESPONSE: "I don't care about everybody. I care about this body. I'm responsible for me." Or,
"Well, you are with *some*body who isn't like *every*body!"

"It's a natural part of life."
RESPONSE: "So is pregnancy, disease, and death, and I'm not ready for those things, either." Or,
"It may be natural, but it's not time, and timing is everything!"

"You want it as much as I do."

RESPONSE: "I want to stand up for what I believe in even more." Or,
         "No I don't. Aren't you listening to me?"

"We had sex before. What's the problem now?"

RESPONSE: "The problem is I did something I didn't want to do and now I
         regret it." Or,
         "I'm learning from my mistakes." Or,
         "I changed my mind. I have too much I want to do without
         risking it all again."

"Just relax and let your feelings go."

RESPONSE: "My feelings won't last nearly as long as a pregnancy, an STD,
         or AIDS." Or,
         "My feelings are telling me to go home." Or,
         "A moment of passion can change my future forever."

"Don't worry. I've got a condom."

RESPONSE: "And I've got my feelings. Don't I matter to you?"

"Don't worry. Nothing will happen."

RESPONSE: "What will happen is I'll be giving up my principles for your
         pleasure. I'm my own person." Or,
         "You can't guarantee that nothing will happen. But I can—by
         not having sex."

"Don't you want to do it at least once to see what it's like?"

RESPONSE: "That day will come when *I'm* ready, not when you're ready." Or,
         "I see what pregnancy/parenthood/STDS/AIDS is like—and I
         don't like!"

"You got me all excited now."

RESPONSE: "I don't owe you anything. If you're this easily excited, maybe
         we should just cool it for a while." Or,
         "Then I'll leave so you can go home and take a cold shower."

"Don't worry. No one will know."

RESPONSE: "I'll know." Or,

> "I'm not worried—and I don't care who knows—I care about my principles."

"I want to marry you; you know we're going to get married."
RESPONSE: "If and when that day comes, we can discuss it then." Or,
> "What does marriage later have to do with sex now?"

"I'll always love you. Let me share this with you."
RESPONSE: "If you love me, honor me; respect my feelings."

"Making love will only make our love stronger."
RESPONSE: "Sex doesn't make love." Or,
> "Sex doesn't make a relationship stronger; it complicates it."

Obviously all these responses are logical and well thought out. You may not even speak like this. The important thing to remember is to verbally and nonverbally communicate how you feel in your own way.

When you are romantically involved or love someone, it is easy to give up what you feel is right or what you believe in to make the other person happy. Sacrifice and compromise in a relationship can be a beautiful, enriching experience, especially in a committed relationship like a marriage or other long-term partnership. But sacrificing your principles, beliefs, and future for sex is a mistake. Even when sexual sacrifices are made in marriages, it is a sign of a relationship in trouble. You can sacrifice "things" like belongings, but you should never sacrifice your principles or beliefs, even in marriage.

For the sake of simplicity, if you are still being pressured into having sex, regardless of the pressure line being used, simply stand up, back away from the person, and, with a serious or angry look on your face, say, "I'm just not getting through to you. I don't want to have sex." Or say, "You seem to care more about sex than my feelings," and walk out. At the least it will give you a chance to go home, go to the bathroom, or just get out of the situation so you can think more clearly and you won't be as likely to be forced into making a mistake.

In the heat of the moment, thinking of a witty, strong response may be impossible, but if you're interested in more ways of responding to pressure lines, here are Basso's top 50 Ways to Say No to Sex. Some are serious, most are humorous, but all of them can be used if you say them with a straight face.

Basso's Top 50 Ways to Say No to Sex

1. "If you want to have sex with me, you need to speak with my father."
2. "I'm menstruating."
3. "Don't you have another boyfriend/girlfriend?"
4. "I have to go."
5. "You're not my type."
6. "I don't look good naked."
7. "It's against my religion."
8. "My back hurts."
9. "I'm having personal problems."
10. "I have a headache." (Be ready to follow up with, "I'm allergic to aspirin.")
11. "I have an STD."
12. "I really have nothing to gain from having sex with you."
13. "Are you ready to deal with anything that might happen? I'm not!"
14. "Go take a cold shower."
15. "Sex doesn't solve problems; it creates them."
16. "The only thing that needs to be turned on in here are the lights."
17. "My mother will be here in a few minutes."
18. "I have a cold."
19. "I have an upset stomach. (I think I'm going to throw up.)"
20. "We need to get a blood test first."
21. "I've got crabs."
22. "Not unless you have a recent doctor's clearance."
23. "The doctor told me not to have sex for a year."
24. "The football game is on."
25. "I would have sex with you if you were the one who got pregnant."
26. "I've got a terrible toothache."
27. "Those bean burritos I ate earlier are starting to have an effect."
28. "Is that a herpes blister?"

29. "You're too ugly."
30. "You have bad breath."
31. "Not today, I'm constipated."
32. "I love another girl/guy."
33. "You smell bad."
34. "I'm joining the priesthood/becoming a nun."
35. "I don't believe in closeness with lower life forms."
36. "Don't worry, blue is a good color on you!" (After hearing the old "blue balls" line.)
37. "I have a tampon on."
38. "I'm allergic to sex."
39. "I don't want a child, and you can't even take care of yourself."
40. "You have a booger on your face."
41. "My brother just got out of prison for killing my last boyfriend."
42. "I think I have a hernia."
43. "I'm not emotionally or mentally prepared to have sex."
44. "No, Bugs Bunny is on."
45. "Nothing you have to offer is worth taking that chance."
46. "I heard sex weakens your legs, and I have a game tomorrow night."
47. "What's going to happen if we don't do it?"
48. "I might have a heart attack."
49. "Put your hormones in park, as well as your hands."
50. "I'm a very pregnant-prone person."

What is peer pressure?

Peer pressure is when friends or people around your own age say or do things to get you to do something you may not really want to do.

An example would be a group of friends or "peers" standing around smoking cigarettes. In this case, they would be doing something that might put pressure on you to try smoking. If this same group of people said to you, "How about a cigarette? C'mon, try it. It's no big deal!" then they would be saying something to pressure you into what you may not really want to do.

Peer pressure is another part of growing up that all people face. Sometimes to try and fit in with a group of people, you may be tempted to do things you don't really want to do. You will be faced with this challenge over and over again.

An example of sexual peer pressure might be standing at a party and listening to a group of males or females talk about how they "went all the way" (had sex) with their boyfriends or girlfriends. They might then say to you, "When was the last time you had sex?" or "When are you going to have sex?" or "What's wrong with you?" This is classic peer pressure.

What does peer pressure feel like?

Peer pressure usually makes you feel uneasy, uncomfortable, or like something is wrong. You may feel worried, unhappy, angry, or confused. This is because you may know what is best for you, but your peers are gently trying to get you to do what they want you to do. You certainly want to be friendly with other people or be part of the crowd, so you're tempted to give up on what you know is best for you and do what your peers are saying or doing.

One of your greatest challenges will be dealing with peer pressure. To stand up for what you believe in when others are doing the opposite takes great strength. Some people handle peer pressure well, and others not well at all. Get into the habit of standing up for yourself. The more success you have early on, the easier it is to stay successful. Tell people how you feel early in the conversation. This will usually discourage most people from putting any pressure on you. Speak up!

If you have not been very successful in dealing with peer pressure in the past, remind yourself that this time you're a new person. If you're faced with a high-pressure situation, treat it as an opportunity to be successful. You will be what you act like. Be your own person—strong, confident, and ready to do what needs to be done. Avoid people who pressure you. Would a real friend pressure you to do something you didn't want to do? Would a real friend pressure you to do something that would be harmful? Friends come and go. The consequences of drugs, STDs, and unplanned pregnancy can stay with you for a lifetime.

Avoid high-pressure situations if you don't handle peer pressure very well. Places like parties, for example, can be fun, but if there are people there using drugs, having sex, or doing things you do not want to be a part of, you will feel better off choosing to go somewhere else. Otherwise, have a plan to be your own person.

Get help from parents and teachers if you're confused. Parents and teachers have gone through the same things you're going through now. Often, they are able to help you and support you. Just ask!

What if my friends bother me to have sex with my partner?

This has been going on for a long time and can be considered just one of the many types of peer pressure that teens experience while growing up. Like any other kind of pressure/harassment, it can make you feel uncomfortable.

One way of dealing with peer pressure effectively is to tell the person pressuring you how you feel (or to back off) as soon as he/she starts bothering you. If the pressure is starting to annoy you, simply say (using verbal language and matching body language) that you don't want to be bothered with his/her comments. Here are a few quick comments you may be able to use, to be accompanied by a serious expression on your face:
- "Hey, we're good friends, so I know you won't take this the wrong way, but. . . ."
- "Lighten up about this sex thing."
- "My business is my business, not yours."
- "Don't worry so much about what my boyfriend/girlfriend and I do. We're doing just fine."
- "You need to get a life of your own instead of poking around in mine so much."

These comments are a bit aggressive, and most experts will say to use "I" statements like, "I don't like when you ask me personal questions about my romantic life," which can be effective with some people. However, you know and I know that most teens don't speak in such rational terms. Even so, some people just don't seem to get the idea unless you spell it out for them. Sometimes a comment that is quick and to the point can be as effective as an "I" statement.

Part of the fun in going out with someone is being able to talk to your friends about the fun places you go and the fun things you do with your boyfriend/girlfriend. Whether or not you have sex with your boyfriend/girlfriend is not something that should be shared with your friends unless you and your partner agree on it. You may be tempted to share every detail about your romantic life, but this usually makes things messy. By sharing intimate moments or feelings that your partner may not want other people to know about, you may betray the trust your boyfriend/ girlfriend has in you. You might also add fuel to the fire by getting your friends all worked up about your relationship. It's usually best to keep the private things private between you and your boyfriend/girlfriend.

How can I let my boyfriend/girlfriend know I love him or her?

"Love" is a combination of many feelings that can be expressed in just about everything you do with the person you care about. Believe it or not, there are many different ways you already express your love without even realizing it. A funny note, a warm smile, listening when he/she is worried, and helping with a problem can all be part of love. In fact, most successful relationships display the love between two people in the small, seemingly insignificant things that they do together. Anything that two people do together can be done in a caring way that will communicate how you feel about one another.

There is not any one thing that proves you're in love. For example, buying an expensive gift for your partner does not prove your love. Nor does constantly calling on the phone prove it. Of course, having sex does not prove your love, either. Sex doesn't mean that two people are in love with each other. Many times people just have sex for the sake of having sex—without love.

The activity of sex can be a dangerous one. Therefore, your decision to postpone sex is a good move. You and your partner can do many other things without putting yourselves at risk or violating your principles.

Even the simplest things two people do together can be expressed with love. When this love is expressed, you both will feel it. Here are just a few of the many thousands of different ways you can express your love for your boyfriend/girlfriend:

- Say "I love you."
- Give a little hug or a big hug.
- Say "I care about you."
- Hold hands and go for a walk.
- Make a tape of his/her favorite songs/movies.
- Express your thoughts and feelings.
- Snuggle up together.
- Sit together at a public lake or park.
- Go on a picnic.
- Compliment his/her outfit, ideas, grades, athletic performance, tastes.
- Go window shopping at the mall and play with different gadgets.
- Play a video game together.
- Make your specialty lunch or dinner for him/her.
- Caress each other.
- Do homework together.
- Plan a day trip together.
- Throw a lunch or dinner party for your friends together.
- Bake something chewy, gooey, and chocolaty.
- Exercise together.
- Dance to "your song."
- Surprise him/her with a little sweet treat in his/her locker or knapsack.
- Sit or walk in the moonlight.
- Write a love poem.
- Write a really bad love poem.

- Whisper something sweet in his/her ear in front of people.
- Sing a song for him/her and record it.
- Make a list of things you like about each other.
- Hide a love note or card where only he/she will find it.
- Have your picture taken together.
- Be courteous and spend time with his/her family.
- Meet somewhere to watch a sunrise.
- Give each other secret nicknames.
- Give him/her your best picture of yourself.
- Dedicate a song on the radio to him/her.
- Share a deep secret with him/her.

You can express your feelings without giving up on your beliefs or giving in to another person. The decision to stand up for what you believe in and do the things you know are right takes courage. Many people just go along with what other people are doing or what other people want. Being an individual, being strong, means being able to resist the pressure to give up on yourself and your values. You can be your own person.

What is sexual harassment?

Sexual harassment is when someone repeatedly makes comments about your body or sexual orientation, sexual jokes, come-ons (requests for dates or sex), or other sexually related comments/actions that you do not want to hear or see. Sexual harassment is also when someone repeatedly touches you when you do not want him/her to.

Am I protected from sexual harassment at school?

Yes! You have the right to go to school without being bothered by another person's comments, touching, or repeated attempts to go on a date—that includes harassment not only from other students, but also from any adult working at that school or school system. If you are being sexually harassed at school, let the person in charge (like the principal—unless it is the principal who is committing the sexual harassment) know what is going on and that you want it stopped. If the harassment continues, you need to get help from other people like the school board members, school counselors, or even the police. It would be a good idea to let a parent, guardian, or other trusted adult know what is happening at school and allow him/her to contact the right people at the school and school board. Schools are legally responsible to make sure that you are free from being sexually harassed at school, and many schools have paid large lawsuit settlements for not protecting students' rights. You must speak up and let the school know what is happening, and if it continues, then you need to get more people involved.

Am I protected from sexual harassment at work?

Yes! Businesses also have policies in place that prohibit sexual harassment. Again, you must speak up if you are being sexually harassed and let the person in charge know what is happening. If the person in charge is the one who is sexually harassing you, then you may be wise to file a complaint at your local Equal Employment Opportunity Commission (www.eeoc.gov) and allow the commission staff to guide you in your next steps.

How can I prevent sexual harassment?

If anyone, young or old, makes comments about your body or sexual orientation, pressures you for a date you don't want, makes other sex-related comments, or puts his/her hands on you, you need to let that person know that he/she is making you feel uncomfortable. This person will likely make some kind of excuse, like he/she was only joking and didn't mean anything. Regardless of the excuse, if he/she makes another comment or touches you again after you have said that it makes you feel uncomfortable, then this constitutes sexual harassment, and your rights have been violated. You need to contact the person in charge and let him/her know what is happening. Again, it is a good idea to let your parent, guardian, or another trusted adult know what is happening so he/she can help. Once the people in charge of the school or job site have been notified of the situation, it is their legal responsibility to solve the problem and make sure that it stops. If they don't, then they may face legal problems.

Is sexual harassment my fault?

No. Nothing you say, do, or wear allows any person to continue to make comments or touch you after you told him/her to stop.

What if I want to date or have a sexual relationship with someone who is much older than me?

One major problem with sexual relationships between a young person and an adult is the difference in power. A young person is often manipulated to satisfy the sexual needs of the adult. This manipulation can come in many forms. The adult may seem or be sweet and kind, providing gifts, transportation, and financial resources, or the adult may use disapproval or anger to manipulate the young person into doing what he/she wants. The young person is unable to have equal power in the relationship and so is unable to protect herself/himself (emotionally, sexually) from being manipulated or pressured by the adult. In short, the young person is more often used as a sexual object than an equal partner in a relationship.

If you have more questions about abstinence, how to say "no" to sex, or any other sexuality related issue, you can find additional information at Youth Embassy (www.YouthEmbassy.com).

11

Drinking, Drugs, and Rape

Unfortunately, each day, many people are victimized and forced into having sex against their will. Sometimes a complete stranger will be the attacker, but most of the time, the victim knows the attacker.

There are certain things to look for that will help prevent you from being attacked and forced into having sex against your will. Read on to find out what you should look out for to protect yourself.

What is rape?

Rape is when a person is forced into having sex. A person may be raped by being physically hurt (held down, hit, or having an arm twisted) or verbally threatened (promises to hurt or do something bad to you or your family). Rape is also when a person has sex with another person who is too drunk or high on drugs to make a decision that she/he might normally make.

Although there are cases where males have been raped by females or other males, or where females have been raped by females, most rape cases involve women being raped by men. Rape is a terrible crime against a person that can cause severe psychological trauma and suffering. It is never okay to rape someone!

Should anyone be forced to have sex?

Never! It doesn't matter what a female wears, says, or does, there is never any excuse for rape. Unfortunately, some people may think "women want to be raped" or, because of what a female is wearing, "she was asking for it and got what she deserved." This is incorrect and a big mistake.

For some of you guys who might not understand, it's like driving a shiny red Corvette with a racing stripe down the side and revving up the engine at a red light. Suddenly a police officer pulls up behind you, flashes his/her, lights and gives you a speeding ticket. Is it fair to get a speeding ticket just because you drive a shiny red Corvette? Just because a female dresses a certain way doesn't mean she should be treated a certain way based on YOUR assumptions. Of course, comparing rape to a speeding ticket is like comparing a nuclear explosion to a firecracker—rape is a devastating crime.

If a female is forced to have sex when she doesn't want to, is it her fault?

No. Being forced into sex is never the victim's fault, regardless of what she says, does, or wears.

When a female says no, doesn't she really mean yes?

When a female says no, she means no. Unfortunately, if you watch too many TV shows or movies, the opposite seems true. Guys: in real life, when a female says no, stop whatever you're doing and back off, regardless of what she said or did previously. Here's an example. If you and a girl are kissing and undressing each other on her bed, and you are just about to have sex, but she says, "Wait, I've changed my mind. Stop."—guys, you stop! Although the female may have led you on, she has every right to change her mind, and you must honor her decision.

Guys, it's like if you want to go skydiving and you show up at the airport, get into the jumping gear, put on your parachute, climb into the plane, soar up to 12,000 feet, and watch the plane doors open—then you suddenly decide you'd rather not jump out of the plane after all. You have every right to change your mind and you wouldn't want anyone trying to push you out the door saying, "You said you wanted to do it, and now you're going to do it!" Would you?

How can a female avoid rape?

Most rapes are committed by someone the victim knows, but other times the rapist is a complete stranger. These are just a few things females can do to prevent a rape:

DON'T WALK ALONE, ESPECIALLY AT NIGHT. Stay with a friend or, even better, a group of friends if you are walking around after school, at the mall, at the movies, or even in your neighborhood.

WALK CONFIDENTLY, with your head up, eyes forward, and shoulders back.

STAY IN AREAS THAT HAVE PLENTY OF LIGHTS AND MANY PEOPLE.

DON'T STOP TO HELP STRANGERS WHO ARE PARKED IN CARS OR VANS. You're not being rude, you're protecting yourself. Just keep walking.

IF YOU ARE APPROACHED, SCREAM or use your personal alarm (a device that makes a loud, sharp sound), then run.

IF YOU CAN PUT UP A STRUGGLE WITHOUT GETTING SEVERELY HURT, then try to stun the attacker with mace, a finger jab or claw to the eyes, a punch to the throat, or a quick kick to the groin. If you are able to momentarily stun the attacker, don't hang around. Don't try to be a martial arts movie star and finish the job—run! Beware, as some attackers may be expecting a fight. Some attackers may become violent and are insane enough to seriously hurt or kill someone. If struggling makes the attacker crazier, then saving your life is your priority.

ALWAYS TRUST YOUR INSTINCTS OR GUT FEELINGS. If you are in an area or situation where you don't feel comfortable, get to a safe area as quickly as possible. Don't be afraid to run into a store and approach another person or the clerk and ask for help.

What is date rape or acquaintance rape?

Date rape or acquaintance rape is rape committed by someone's date or by someone the person knows. Date rape is a growing problem, because some guys think if they pay for a dinner, movie, drink, or anything, they should get sex in return. Ladies and gentlemen, it doesn't matter how much money is spent on a date, it has nothing to do with sex.

How can a female avoid date rape?

STAY SOBER. Don't drink or do drugs when you are out on a date or at a party. Alcohol and drugs slow your ability to think and make you unable to make good decisions. Drinking clouds your thinking. Beware of guys who want to buy you drinks or give you drugs. Avoid parties where alcohol is being served or drugs are being used. Even if you don't drink or use drugs, parties can get way out of hand and put you in a situation where you are not able to protect yourself. There are many cases where a female has been pulled into a room and raped during a party.

TELL YOUR DATE BEFORE HE STARTS DRINKING THAT YOU DON'T FEEL RIGHT ABOUT HIM DRINKING. If he decides to drink or use drugs anyway, call your parents, a friend, or a cab for a ride home. If he doesn't care enough to listen to your feelings when he is sober, there is a good chance he isn't going to listen to you when he is under the influence of alcohol or drugs.

GO TO PLACES WHERE THERE ARE A LOT OF PEOPLE. Avoid parking in the woods, walking near a lake or park, or going back to his place or to an empty house.

BRING ENOUGH MONEY TO PAY YOUR OWN WAY, plus a little bit extra for cab fare, in case you need it. If you pay for your own meal, movie, etc., there is less of a chance that your date will feel the need to be "repaid" at the end of the night, and you are less likely to feel that you owe him something for spending so much money on you. You are not a commodity or product; you are not something that can be purchased and used. A date is an opportunity for two people to get together, spend time with one another, find out about one another, and generally have fun. Dating is not a form of prostitution where the male pays a certain amount of money and gets sex at the end of the night. If a guy wants to spend one dollar or a million dollars on you, that is his choice. You are not obligated to provide anything in return. It is also a good idea to bring along some extra money for a cab in case you are ever in a situation where you don't feel comfortable. You want to be able to leave a situation without relying on your date for a ride home. At the very least, bring enough money for a phone call to Mom or Dad, a family member, or a friend who can come pick you up. And remember, you can always call a cab and then pay for it when you get home.

DON'T GIVE MIXED MESSAGES. Ladies, you are free to wear anything you want any way you want, and you can act any way you want (of course, with input from Mom and Dad!). However, you need to realize that some guys are easily confused and may get the wrong idea when they see you dressed a certain way or hear you say certain things. And almost all males who have had some alcohol or used a drug will become easily confused when it comes to interpreting the messages you are sending. You may be saying one thing with the way you are dressed or the way you touch someone, but guys might be thinking something entirely different. Here are a few examples:

You wear a short, tight skirt and a loose blouse that shows off some cleavage (the space between the breasts and/or part of the breasts).

> YOUR MESSAGE: I'm being fashionable and wearing something that is in style.

> MALE INTERPRETATION: She's sexy! She wants me to see her breasts because she wants to have sex with me.

You are dancing at a party by holding your partner's hips or swinging your hips back and forth toward your date, or bouncing your butt up and down and around to the beat of the music. Your date moves his groin up and down to your rhythm.

> YOUR MESSAGE: I know how to dance. Everyone dances like this because this is just how you dance to this type of music. This is great. I love dancing!

> MALE INTERPRETATION: This girl is hot! She's driving me crazy. She must be a wild woman in bed, otherwise she couldn't move like that. She must want to have sex as much as I do.

You are standing near your date, talking, and casually touch his arm or put your hand on his chest.

> YOUR MESSAGE: I was raised in a very warm, touchy family, and I casually touch all of my family and friends.

> MALE INTERPRETATION: Why does she keep touching me? She must really be interested in me. Let me start touching her and see what she does.

You are alone with your boyfriend and start kissing him on his mouth and face. You warmly put your arms around his shoulders or waist.

YOUR MESSAGE: I really care for you and would like to share some gentle kisses and caresses. This is so romantic.

MALE INTERPRETATION: She wants to go all the way. She's kissing me and touching me. She wants to have sex.

You are alone with your boyfriend, and he begins kissing you. You don't mind and even enjoy it, but suddenly his kisses become more heated and wet. You weren't really ready for this, but it's okay. Then his hands, which were around your shoulders or waist, start to move toward your butt or breasts. You don't say or do anything. Then he starts to unbutton your blouse and pants. You still don't say anything, but you do push his hands away.

YOUR MESSAGE: I'm not ready for this. Doesn't he know this? We have talked about this before, so he must know that I don't want to have sex. I guess I'll just remind him and push his hands away.

MALE INTERPRETATION: Oh, yes. I'm getting more and more hot, and she must be as well, because she is letting me feel all over her. What? She pushed my hand away. She must be playing hard to get. She really wants it, too.

Now, of course not all females will have these intentions, nor will all males think like this, but this happens enough that we can say it is common. Ladies, some general guidelines when going out on a date:

BEWARE OF WHAT YOU WEAR. Anything tight or revealing, although it may be stylish, may be misinterpreted by your date.

KNOW HOW YOUR DANCING MIGHT BE INTERPRETED. Today's popular dance moves may also suggest an interest in sex, even though that may not be what you intend it to mean. Move your body in any way that you wish, but recognize that you might be sending out messages that are not exactly what you mean to send out. You may want to save different dance moves for when you are around people you trust and who know you well.

BE CAREFUL WHERE YOU PLACE YOUR HANDS AND CASUAL TOUCHES. Some people come from backgrounds where touching may mean something different than it does to you.

IF A GUY COMES ON TO YOU AND SAYS SOMETHING THAT MAKES YOU UNCOMFORTABLE or touches you in a way that you don't want to be touched, speak up and let him know. Don't assume the guy knows what is on your mind. Be loud if you need to be, be forceful if you need to be, but do something. If you do nothing, the message you send is that it's okay for him to continue. Let me repeat, if you say nothing and do nothing, it can be interpreted as meaning "yes" or "okay, please continue." You must let your date or boyfriend know what you want and don't want, both verbally and with body language. Be loud and forceful if he doesn't understand.

SPEAK UP. Tell your date to stop if things are moving too fast. Sometimes pushing a guy away or backing away is not enough to get your message through. You may need to say "stop" or "no." Say it like you mean it—loud, serious, and with a straight face; otherwise the guy may not get the picture, especially if he has been drinking or using drugs.

How can a guy avoid hurting his date and getting himself into trouble?

Gentlemen, you are responsible for your actions regardless of the situation or your condition. It doesn't matter if you're drunk, high, don't know the law, or if you misunderstand the messages the female is sending you. You will be held accountable, so be responsible. Here are a few tips to remember when you are out with a young lady:

- Never force yourself onto a female.
- It doesn't matter how much you spend on a date, she is not your property, and she owes you nothing.
- It doesn't matter how she dresses, how she acts, or what she says, you never have an excuse to force yourself onto a female.
- Don't drink or do drugs on a date. Alcohol and drugs can give you "stinkin' thinkin'" and cause you to do something stupid that you would not normally do. Being drunk or high is not a legal defense for rape.
- Don't try to get your date drunk or high. A female who has sex under the influence of alcohol or drugs can legally prosecute you for rape.
- Whenever a female says no, it means NO!

Is it considered rape if a girl is drunk and a guy has sex with her?

Yes. When a female is drunk, she loses the ability to make decisions she would normally make, and the court judge knows this. If a couple were to go on a date, get drunk, and have sex, the female could legally charge the male with rape.

So, guys, be a gentleman. If your date has been drinking, take care of her and bring her home safely. (If you've both been drinking, find a friend who hasn't or call a taxi for transportation.) She'll respect you in the morning, and you can avoid the embarrassment of being arrested as a rapist.

Why shouldn't I drink when I go out on a date or to a party?

Drinking on a date or at a party is like driving 110 miles per hour on an icy highway. There's a good chance that pretty soon things are going to get out of control, and there's going to be one heck of a mess. When a person drinks alcohol (beer, wine coolers, wine, vodka, rum, whiskey, scotch, or any type of alcohol) or uses any other type of drug, his/her ability to make good decisions decreases. Even one drink can influence a person enough to make a bad decision about sex. Of course, there are times people drink on dates or at parties and no major catastrophes occur, but the more often you put yourself at risk, the greater the chance of a disaster. Just open the paper or watch the news and you will hear about friends, neighbors, and people in your community who have hurt someone else while under the influence. You are just like every other human being. You too can hurt someone or be hurt in many different ways while under the influence of alcohol or other drugs.

Alcohol reduces your anxiety and fear as well as your ability to think clearly. This is why so many times a male will buy drinks for a female or try to get her drunk. The female will not be able to think clearly and is more likely to be persuaded to have sex. This is an old trick that is still popular today, so ladies, beware!

Gentlemen, drinking will reduce your anxiety and fear as well as tend to make you more aggressive. Combine this "I'm invincible. I'm powerful. I'll do what I want" attitude with a desire to have sex, and you may find yourself tempted to do something you would not normally do when you have good judgment.

How can I still be cool if I don't drink?

Ladies and gentlemen, in this day and age, it is cool not to drink. A few simple ways of refusing a drink when you're asked are:

- "I'm driving."
- "Not tonight."
- "I don't feel well."
- "I'm on medication."
- "I'm leaving soon."

Then follow up your response with, "I will take a soda/juice/water if you have it." This way you have a cup in your hand and nobody else knows you're not drinking, if what other people think really matters to you.

What should I do if my date gets drunk?

If your date gets drunk and things start to get out of hand, stay where there are plenty of people around. Don't be alone with the person. If you're with friends, let someone know you're concerned and you need help or want to go home. Don't let the drunk person drive you home. Call someone else for a ride. If you are being harassed, don't be afraid to get loud or angry and let people know you're being bothered.

What is a date rape drug?

A date rape drug is a chemical that is put into a person's drink. It makes her/him unable to know what is happening or remember what has happened. The two most common date rape drugs are gamma hydroxybutyrate (GHB) and Rohypnol. Either of these two drugs can be slipped into a drink (soda or alcohol) without the person knowing. Both are difficult to detect through taste or sight, so the person will drink it without knowing what happened. Soon she/he will be weak and unable to make decisions or stop someone from taking advantage of her/him. If the person is raped, she/he will not be able to remember what happened. Some tips to remember while you are at a party include:

- Do not accept open drinks that are handed to you.
- Watch your drink being made.
- Do not leave your drink unattended. If you leave your drink to use the bathroom, ask for a new drink rather than drink the one that you left.
- Be aware of your surroundings and the people who are near you. Some date rape drugs have been used where one person distracts the female while the other drops the drug into the drink when she is not looking.

What should I do if I think that I might have been given one of these drugs?

If you taste or see something strange in your drink after you had a sip, do not drink any more. If you have a friend with you, let her/him know that you think something may have happened and that you want to leave. If you think the person you are with might have been the person who put something in your drink, locate a telephone to call the police, your parents, or someone you trust who can respond quickly and get to you.

If you think you might have been raped but don't know for sure or cannot remember, go to a rape crisis center or hospital immediately. Most rape crisis centers and hospitals are able to test for these drugs for up to three days after they have been taken.

What is gang rape?

Gang rape is when two or more people force another person to have sex. This can occur at college fraternity parties, high school parties, or when athletic teams get together at a party. Ladies, it would be a good idea to be cautious and avoid going to these types of parties altogether.

Is a husband allowed to rape his wife?

No. This is known as mate rape. A husband has no right to force himself onto his wife. A marriage license is not an ownership license. The female does not give up her rights as a human being once she becomes married. As always, when the female says no, it means no.

Is sex with a person under the age of eighteen considered rape?

In most states, the answer is yes. A female under the age of eighteen (sixteen in some states) who engages in intercourse can file charges of statutory rape. Even if the underage female agreed to sex, legally she is not considered capable of making a sound decision regarding sex, and the male could be prosecuted.

Should a family member be allowed to touch me in a sexual way?

No. When a parent, stepparent, brother, sister, aunt, uncle, or grandparent caress your genitals, touches you in an intimate or sexual way, or verbally or physically forces you to touch his/her genitals or have sex with him/her, this is called incest.

Incest is psychologically damaging and will often affect the person for the rest of his/her life if nothing is done. Many victims are afraid to let someone know, because the victim often thinks the incest is his/her fault or believes that if someone finds out, the family will break up. If you are a victim of incest, it is not your fault, and you need to let someone know what is happening. The person committing the incest needs help. This is not something that just goes away.

If you are a victim of incest or know someone who is, help is available. You can notify a school counselor or your local health and social services department, or contact Childhelp USA (www.childhelpusa.org, 1-800-422-4453). This is a free phone call. A trained professional will be able to speak with you and help put you on the path to improving the situation.

If you are ever on your own because of abuse or incest, the following numbers will put you in contact with people who can give you guidance, contact law or social service agencies in your area, provide emergency shelter, or even contact your parents for you. These numbers can help you when it seems there is nowhere else to turn: Girlstown National Hotline (1-800-448-3000), Boystown National Hotline (1-800-448-3000), National Runaway Hotline (1-800-621-4000), Angels Flight (1-800-833-2499).

If you have more questions about drinking, drugs, rape, or any other sexuality related issue, you can find additional information at Youth Embassy (www.YouthEmbassy.com).

12

Preventing Adult Sexual Contact and Harm

Sexual contact with adults means any of the following:
- Any kind of touching, talk, or activity that an adult tries to get a young person to do or say for the adult's sexual pleasure.
- An adult who tries to get a young person to describe certain sexual acts on the telephone, over the Internet, or in person.
- An adult who asks a young person to touch him/her or creates a situation where the young person can be touched.
- An adult who wants a young person to pose naked, with very little clothes on, or in a seductive (sexually arousing) way for pictures or videos.

What is wrong with sexual contact with adults?

The same thing that is wrong with a stronger person bullying a weaker person—this is an abuse of power that can cause a lot of damage to the person who is being taken advantage of. Young people have not yet developed the skills they need to avoid being manipulated and taken advantage of by an adult who is trying to satisfy his/her sexual desires. The result is that usually a young person suffers psychological trauma that can last a lifetime. These scars can cause emotional pain and make the young person look at life or future relationships in an unhealthy and harmful way. He/She might even begin taking drugs, behaving violently, or contemplating suicide as a result.

Why do adults pursue teens for sex?

There are many possible reasons why some adults want to have sexual contact with teens. People become sexually aroused by different things. Unfortunately, even though these adults know that this is very harmful to young people, they are more concerned about their own sexual desires than they are about a young person's health, life, or future.

An adult may try to get a young person to have sexual contact with him/her because the adult lacks the self-confidence to develop sexual relationships with other adults. Or such an adult believes a young person is less likely to reject him/her. Or having sex with young people makes him/her feel powerful and in control. These are just a few of the reasons why an adult might try to have sexual contact with young people.

When it comes to adult sexual contact, what usually happens is that an adult looks for ways to have a young person satisfy his/her sexual needs without anyone finding out. He/She tries to gain the young person's trust. Once the adult has the young person's trust, it becomes easier to manipulate (trick) the young person into some kind of sexual contact, even though the young person is not romantically interested in the adult. Other times, the young person is seduced (tricked) into becoming romantically interested so she/he will engage in adult sexual contact. Either of these things can happen because a young person develops the ability to feel strong emotions like love, attraction, and guilt long before she/he develops the ability to know how to manage those emotions. This makes a person vulnerable to being manipulated.

Are there certain types of adults I should look out for?

Any adult can possibly be someone who will try to take advantage of a young person. These adults come from all walks of life and have all kinds of jobs and work titles. They include business and religious leaders, counselors, teachers, principals, camp leaders, coaches, and neighbors. Never think that an adult's job title means that he/she would not take advantage of people, especially young people. Wherever adults and young people spend time together, there is a risk that an adult will pursue young people for sexual satisfaction. This puts you in a position where you must always be cautious and aware of what is happening around you.

What about the Internet and chat rooms? How do I know I am talking with someone my own age?

You don't. Adults who are looking for sexual contact with young people frequently join in youth chat rooms. They lie about who they are and try to develop a romantic or sexual relationship with a young person through the Internet. These adults will try to establish a "friendship" and gain your trust.

What should I do if the person in the chat room wants to meet me?

Generally speaking, this is a risky activity and should be avoided. If your curiosity absolutely must be satisfied, you will need to do everything you can to protect yourself.

- Assume that people you have been communicating with are not who they say they are.
- Only meet in a public place where there are many people around.
- Bring at least one friend with you (a trusted adult would be even better).
- Let your parent or guardian know what you are doing, who you are meeting, where you are going, and what time you will be back.
- Do not agree to meet this person anyplace where there aren't crowds of people.
- Do not agree to meet this person alone.
- Do not agree to go anywhere with this person after you meet, especially if it means getting in a car or traveling to a place where there are fewer people.
- Do not give out your address or home telephone number.

What should I do if the person I am communicating with on the Internet wants me to send "sexy" pictures of myself, or if he/she sends pictures of naked people to me?

This is a sign that the person you have been communicating with can be very harmful to you. If this happens, you should stop all communication with this

You have no way of knowing who you are really talking to in a chat room.

person. There is no need to say good-bye or explain yourself—just ignore and block any future messages he/she sends, and do not send any type of communication back. Contact your local police department and report what happened so that they can prevent this person from doing any harm to other young people.

How do adults get young people to have sexual contact with them?

There are many ways adults confuse, seduce, and trick young people into having sexual contact with them. They may use friendliness, humor, kindness, or understanding to gain young people's trust. They may use guilt or anger to pressure young people to engage in sexual contact. Such adults may also use gifts, compliments, money, food, or car transportation to get young people to like them or feel as though they owe them something.

Most adults ARE kind and have no interest in sexual contact with young people. The problem is that it's difficult to know whether an adult is kind and caring because he/she is interested in your well-being or because he/she wants sexual contact.

How can I tell if an adult is trying to trick me into sexual contact?

At first, you probably won't know. This adult may seem like a friendly person who would never be interested in such a thing. Again, these kinds of adults might spend a lot of time trying to get to know you and gain your trust. Then, small things might begin to happen, like he/she arranges times and places for you to be alone together, or begins making inappropriate comments (sexual comments that an adult shouldn't make to a young person) or inappropriate touches (touching that an adult shouldn't have with a young person).

What are some examples of inappropriate comments?

Some examples of inappropriate comments from an adult to a young person:
  • Compliments you on how good your body looks in your clothing.
    Example: "Your figure really shows up nice in that outfit."
  • Says how he/she would like to see you in certain kinds of clothing.
    Example: "You would look so good in those shorts/that bathing suit."
  • Asks if you have ever been sexually active before.
    Example: "Are you a virgin?"
  • Asks if you know what certain sexual topics mean.
    Example: "Do you know what masturbation is?"
  • Says that you're sexy.
  • Asks if you have a boyfriend or girlfriend.

The confusing part is that there are some adults who are qualified to ask some of these questions and need to do so to protect your health. The adult's question may have nothing to do with wanting sexual contact with you. For example, a doctor may need to know if you have been sexually active to find out where she/he needs to look for answers to a medical problem you might have. Sometimes a qualified teacher may need to find out what a class of young people knows and doesn't know so she/he can focus on topics that are most important to teach. In this case, a teacher would only ask these questions in an anonymous (no names) survey of the entire class, not in private or where a person would be forced to share private information out loud.

Also, if a parent or other family member makes comments about how you look in clothing or what you might look good in, this would have a very different meaning than if another adult made those kinds of comments.

What are some examples of inappropriate touching?

Some examples of inappropriate touching by an adult to a young person:
- Caressing any body part (even a young person's hands, shoulders, back, or legs).
- Feeling or touching any part of the genital area, breasts, or butt.
- Any type of hug or kiss that is delivered in a romantic or sexual way.
- Asking a young person to touch, caress, or massage him/her. Example: "My muscles are sore. Would you just rub right here/give me a quick massage?"
- Offering to give a young person a massage.

Again, caresses or massages from Mom or Dad are considered okay in most cases. Also, when a doctor or nurse is conducting a physical exam at a medical office, this is also okay in most cases. A good rule to use is that if you feel weird about an adult or anyone touching you in any way, then trust your feelings. Tell that person to stop and that you don't want to be touched.

What are some situations that an adult might try to create when he/she wants sexual contact with a young person?

An adult who is looking to have sexual contact with a young person will try to create a situation where he/she can be alone with that young person and not have to worry about another adult or person being around to see what he/she is doing. Beware of the following situations:
- An adult asking you to go to a place where there are no other adults or young people. Examples include a school room with the door closed, an adult's home, a hotel, his/her friend's house, a party (which nobody shows up for except you and that adult), and his/her car.
- An adult inviting you to watch movies/videos where there is nudity (naked people) or sex taking place.

- An adult wanting you to look at pictures, Web sites, or other materials where there are naked people or sexual situations.
- Receiving photos or pictures of naked people or pornographic material from anyone on the Internet.
- An adult showing any part of his/her genitals or who is not fully dressed.
- An adult taking you to a place where alcohol or drugs are being used.
- An adult buying food or gifts for you and then asking for "favors."
- An adult saying he/she wants to be your second Dad/Mom or your guardian angel, or who wants to be called Uncle or Aunt.
- An adult giving you rides home, to the mall, or to other places.
- Overnight sleepovers, camping trips, or field trips with an adult.
- Teachers and other school workers who offer to alter your grades or promise to keep you out of trouble.
- Receiving a raise or promotion at work ahead of people who have been there longer or who are more qualified.

Some of these situations are usually safe—like a teacher arranging time for a student to come after school to complete an assignment, a neighbor who agrees to keep an eye on a young person for Mom/Dad, and an adult mentor or club leader who drives young people places or goes on camping trips with a group of young people and adult chaperones. But if an adult makes any inappropriate sexual comments/touches in any of these situations, then this is a sign that there could be a problem.

Of course, your parent/guardian who drives you places, feeds you, gives you gifts, and takes you on vacations or trips is okay and not normally a problem.

What if an adult "comes on" to me or asks me to touch him/her?

If an adult asks you out or says or does things that would indicate that he/she is interested in you sexually, then you should keep the following in mind:
- What this person is saying or trying to do is wrong and dangerous.
- What this person is saying or trying to do is not your fault at all.
- If an adult begins to touch you anywhere on your body, you should move away, or at the very least be suspicious and on the alert. If you

feel uncomfortable, trust your instincts! Remove yourself from the situation immediately!

- If an adult asks you to touch his/her body, you should move away, or at the very least be suspicious and on the alert. If you feel uncomfortable, trust your instincts! Remove yourself from the situation immediately!
- You will probably feel embarrassed. This is a normal response in this type of situation. Let your parent, guardian, or other trusted adult know what happened—immediately!
- Do not meet with this adult again. Let your parent/guardian know that you are uncomfortable being with this person. Your parent/guardian should make arrangements so you do not have to be near or see this person again.
- Have your parent, guardian, or other trusted adult contact this person's boss as well as the legal authorities to investigate the situation. Chances are, if this happened to you, it may have happened or will happen to another youth just like you, except the other young person might not know how to handle it as well as you.
- Talk about what happened with a trained counselor or psychologist. Even though there may not have been any physical damage, what happened can be very scary and cause fear in the future if it isn't talked out.

What if it is a parent, guardian, or other family member who is having sexual contact with the young person?

This is called incest and will likely cause tremendous negative effects in the young person's future if he/she does not receive help from a trained psychologist. The first thing that he/she should do is locate a trusted adult outside of the family. The trusted adult should be told what is happening. In almost all cases, outside help is needed to work with the family to make sure that this doesn't happen anymore. The young person and other young people in the family need help to work through their feelings.

What should I do if I feel uncomfortable in a situation with an adult?

If you feel uncomfortable or weird in a situation with an adult because of what he/she said or did, even if you don't know why, trust your feelings and get out of the situation.

If you are not too frightened by the person, say things that will get you out of the situation. Examples are:

- "I'm starting to feel really sick. I need to leave." (Then leave!)
- "I'm starting to feel really sick. I need to call my Mom/Dad/guardian." (Then leave!)
- "I need to use the bathroom." (Then leave!)
- "I forgot my medicine in the other room/car and need to get it." (Then leave!)

You do not need to explain or make an excuse to this adult. Just get up and leave. Go to a place where there are other adults or at least other students.

If you are far away from a crowded place and cannot escape safely, then try to arrange for help to come to you. Examples include:

- "I'm going to throw up. I need to call my Mom/Dad/guardian." (Then call for help!)
- "I forgot my medication and am starting to feel sick. I need to call my Mom/Dad/guardian—fast!" (Then call for help!)
- "I need to use the bathroom." (Then call a trusted adult or 911. Explain that you are afraid and need help.)

Once you have reached safety, YOU NEED TO LET A TRUSTED ADULT KNOW WHAT YOU'RE FEELING AND WHAT HAPPENED. By then you may feel as though you overreacted or made a mistake. You may feel embarrassed or afraid, or you might think that it won't happen again and that you don't want to cause a problem. These are common feelings a young person has when she/he has been taken advantage of by an adult (or anyone)! This is a serious situation, and you will need another adult to make sure that you are kept from future harm.

What should I do if an adult has had sexual contact with me?

You will probably feel confused, embarrassed, and afraid, or you may think that what happened was your fault. (It wasn't your fault!) You may just want to forget what happened and never mention it to anyone. These are all normal reactions, but you will need to fight these feelings and get help to prevent any further harm to yourself and to others. You need to let your parent, guardian, or other trusted adult know immediately.

The adult's abuse of you is a crime, and the event may leave a psychological scar that, if untreated, may affect your future dramatically. Your parent/guardian should contact the legal authorities, make arrangements for you never to be with or see this person again, and schedule time with a trained counselor or psychologist.

I repeat: this was not your fault. You are the victim of a crime and should have professional help in working through what happened. Some things that you should do:

- Let a trusted adult know what has happened.
- Cut off all communication with the adult who had sexual contact with you.
- Find a trained counselor to talk and release feelings with.
- If sexual intercourse took place, schedule an appointment with a doctor for pregnancy and sexually transmitted disease tests.
- Remember that the adult is to blame—always. It is never the young person's fault—ever!

Some things that you should NOT do:
- Don't keep what happened a secret.
- Don't think that the abuse will not happen again.
- Don't try to protect the adult who had sexual contact with you.
- Don't keep your feelings and thoughts about what happened to yourself.
- Don't blame yourself.

If I report this, won't the person get in trouble?

Adults who perform such acts need professional help to stop themselves from taking advantage of other young people. Unless they receive this help, they will continue to harm other young people. Unfortunately, these adults won't stop or receive help unless they are forced to do so. It is up to you to do your part in making sure that this individual doesn't harm other young people. That means making sure that your parents/guardians and legal authorities are notified.

How can I prevent myself from becoming a victim of adult sexual contact?

Unfortunately, anyone can be tricked or confused by an adult—even other adults! While you shouldn't be afraid of adults, you should be aware that there are some adults who look for young people to take advantage of and have sexual contact with. You should recognize the signs of an adult trying to trick a young person into having sexual contact, including inappropriate comments, touches, and situations. Remember that most adults are not interested in having sexual contact with young people and are really interested in protecting young people from those adults who are.

There is a Web resource for adults who are struggling with feelings of wanting sexual contact with young people or who have had sexual contact with young people. The site is called Stop It Now! (www.stopitnow.com). It offers information to other adults so that they can detect whether a young person may have been a victim of adult sexual contact. You may want to share this Web site with your teachers so that they can become aware of some of the signs that young people display when they have been victims of adult sexual contact.

If you have more questions about preventing adult sexual contact and harm, or any other sexuality related issue, you can find additional information at Youth Embassy (www.YouthEmbassy.com).

13

Being Gay

Someone who is romantically or sexually attracted to a member of the same sex is said to be gay, or homosexual. (This is when a male is attracted to another male, or a when a female is attracted to another female in a romantic way.) People who are bisexual are romantically attracted to people of both sexes. Heterosexual means being sexually attracted to the opposite sex.

Why do people become gay?

People don't choose to be homosexual (gay), heterosexual (straight), or bisexual. Two main theories try to explain how and what determines a person's sexual orientation:

BIOLOGICAL THEORY: This theory suggests that genetics or some other physical difference determines a person's sexual orientation.

ENVIRONMENTAL THEORY: This theory believes the way a person is raised when he/she is very young will determine a person's sexual orientation.

Neither of these theories has been proven; however, most research favors the biological theory. Whatever the reason, it is important to remember that a person has little or no control over whether he/she is going to be gay, straight, or bisexual.

How many people are gay?

The exact number of people in the world who are homosexual is not known. Some estimate that roughly 10 percent of the world population is gay. Some people argue that the percentage is higher or lower, but either way, it is difficult to get an accurate number.

Are more people gay today than before?

Probably not. Once again, people don't have a choice of being gay or not, and homosexuality has been around since the beginning of recorded history. However, for the first time in United States history, gay people are being more open about their sexuality. For years, homosexuals feared being mistreated, picked on, called mentally ill, or even being beaten up—and unfortunately, this is still too common today. Worse yet, gay people were made to feel ashamed of who they were because of their sexual orientation, so they kept their feelings secret, which is called "being in the closet." Most American people who were gay before the late 1970s were in the closet, not letting anyone know how they felt. In the late 1970s, gay people began "coming out" and letting people know they were homosexual. Today it is a bit easier for gay people to come out and let family, friends, and society know their feelings, but it is still a difficult process.

It may seem as though there are more gay people today than ten, twenty, or thirty years ago, but it is probably because people who are homosexual are coming out now more than before. In other words, there probably are no more gay people today than there were before, but fewer are hiding their homosexuality.

Does thinking about someone of the same sex or having sex with someone of the same sex mean I'm gay?

Only you can answer this for yourself, but you should know that during the teen years, quite a bit of sexual curiosity and experimentation can take place. Having a sexual encounter—whether same-sex or opposite-sex—doesn't necessarily mean you are gay or straight. It simply means you've had a sexual encounter.

If you happen to have a sexual experience with another person of the same sex, or you find yourself thinking or dreaming about having sex with someone of the same sex, try not to label yourself. Your sexuality will continue to develop and evolve for many years. And remember, whenever you are confused or unsure of what you are feeling, try to look for support from a trusted adult or another reputable resource to help you better understand what is happening.

Can a person change his/her sexual orientation?

Once again, a person doesn't have any control over whether he/she is gay or straight. Some people say they can "change" a person who is gay, but there is no valid research to show this to be true, even though there are some organizations and groups of people that say they can! At the same time, if a person is heterosexual (straight), he/she can't be turned into someone who is gay.

What is homophobia or "gay bashing"?

Homophobia is the fear of people who are gay. Many people are afraid of talking to, working with, or being around people who are gay. "Gay bashing" is this fear expressed as hatred or even violence toward gay people.

Homophobia and gay bashing are just like other social diseases, like racism, bigotry, prejudice, and sexism. Each of these is a kind of hatred or prejudging of people because they do not fit into what some people feel is "right." Any type of prejudice is unfair. Imagine being disliked or hated because you have blue eyes when most other people have brown eyes. Imagine being cursed at or hurt because your skin is a different color than someone else's. Imagine being hated because your sexual orientation is different from someone else's. Unfortunately, there are many people who have a very difficult time understanding and accepting that not everyone in this world is a carbon copy of themselves and that not everyone lives the same way as they do.

Everyone has different tastes, likes, dislikes, and ways of being. You don't have to like what another person likes or even agree with what another person thinks or does. But you shouldn't hate someone who is different from you and who means you no harm. People who are gay are like all other human beings: some are physically strong or weak, intelligent or not so bright, funny or boring, productive or lazy, trustworthy or dishonest, pleasant or grumpy, happy or sad, cool or nerdy. Each person is special. We are all different—which makes us all the same. We live in a land where a person is free to think or feel whatever he/she chooses. You don't have to like or agree with everything a person thinks or feels, but accepting another person's right to be different and to be who he/she is allows you to enjoy that same freedom.

What are some of the problems gay people face?

One problem a gay person has is "coming out" and saying he/she is gay. A person who is homosexual may often worry about what his/her parents, family, friends, or classmates will think once they find out. Quite often the person who believes he/she is gay has no one to talk with or express his/her thoughts or feelings to. Even today, people who are gay are not very well accepted. They sometimes are not treated fairly at school, work, in social settings, or even at home. Starting a romantic relationship can also be very difficult at times.

How can you tell if someone is gay?

You can't really tell by looking at someone if he/she is gay. There are some behaviors that might make you think a person is gay, such as the way a person speaks, dresses, or gestures. These are stereotypes. But not all guys who are gay have feminine characteristics, nor do all females who are gay have masculine characteristics.

People who are gay play professional football, basketball, baseball, and every other competitive sport. People who are gay have every kind of job in the world that you can imagine, just like people who are not gay, and live in every part of the world. The only major difference between people who are homosexual and people who are heterosexual is that of sexual attraction.

Can a person turn gay by having friends who are gay?

No. Homosexuality is not contagious, and you can't become gay from being with someone else; nor can you "catch heterosexuality." Hanging around people who are gay will not make a person turn gay. Likewise, a gay person who hangs around heterosexuals will not become straight.

Will God hate me if I am gay?

There are some religious groups that believe so, and there are many other religious groups that don't believe that at all. There are many religious groups that have differing beliefs and interpretations. You are free to practice the religion you choose, but you should realize that not everyone shares those same beliefs.

Are there Web resources where I can get information if I think I might be gay?

Absolutely! You may want to start with some of these: Parents, Families and Friends of Lesbians and Gays (PFLAG) (www.pflag.org); Gay, Lesbian and Straight Education Network (GLSEN) (www.glsen.org); and Advocates for Youth (www.advocatesforyouth.org, or www.youthresource.com).

If you have more questions about being gay, or about any other sexuality related issue, you can find additional information at Youth Embassy (www.YouthEmbassy.com).

14

Dealing with Sadness and Depression

Along with all the new hormones, body changes, relationships, peer and societal pressures, and the seemingly endless life struggles, young people develop feelings that are very confusing, very intense, and very difficult to manage. In fact, in the United States, feeling sad is one of the most common emotional challenges young people experience. Often this sadness is so deep and lasts so long that it becomes something called "depression."

What is depression?

Depression is a term used to describe a person who has prolonged feelings of despair, hopelessness, and worthlessness and who may even have thoughts of committing suicide. (Suicide is when a person ends his/her life.) Although the term depression is often used to describe the normal and temporary sadness, loneliness, or blues that all people feel from time to time, depression as a mental health condition usually refers to a deep sadness that goes well beyond what is normal, and it lasts more than just a few weeks. Depression can dramatically affect a person's ability to perform in school and handle social situations and relationships.

How does a person who is depressed feel?

The symptoms of depression can be different for each person. Some of the symptoms are:

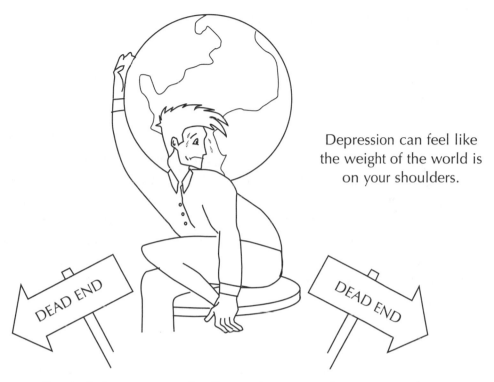

Depression can feel like the weight of the world is on your shoulders.

- Feeling sad almost every day for weeks or months at a time.
- Feeling despair, loneliness, hopelessness, worthlessness, or loss of confidence for weeks or months at a time.
- Crying or feeling like you want to cry.
- Not enjoying people and activities that used to be fun.
- Performing poorly in school.
- Indecision, lack of concentration, or forgetfulness.
- Difficulty in meeting school and home responsibilities.
- Restlessness, agitation, or anger.
- Not looking forward to anything.
- Not really caring about anything.
- Change in sleeping habits (sleeping more than ten hours per day, or having difficulty sleeping).
- Change in eating habits (eating more or less than usual).
- Lack of energy or enthusiasm, or feeling lazy all the time.
- Headaches, stomach aches.

- Being overly sensitive to comments.
- Being overly critical of yourself and others.
- Wanting to be left alone and avoiding social situations.
- Difficulty maintaining relationships with family and friends.
- Thoughts of death or suicide.

These are just a few of the many possible signs of depression. If you or someone you know (especially a family member or friend) is feeling very sad for a long period of time and experiencing three or more of the other signs on this list, chances are depression is the problem. Even if you or someone you know feels sad every once in a while but still experiences three or more of these other symptoms, it is a good idea to suspect depression and contact a trained counselor. Depression is very common and seems to become even more common among young people each year. Getting help early can make a big difference.

What is the difference between sadness and depression?

Being sad is usually temporary and comes from an event that causes emotional pain. Depression usually lasts for more than a few days, often continuing for weeks or months. A person can have depression and not know why.

How common is depression?

There are only estimates as to how common depression is in the United States. Some estimates say about 8 percent (almost one out of every ten people) experience depression at least once in their lives. Some estimates say about 17 percent (closer to one out of every five people) experience depression at least once in their lives. It is difficult to find out just how many people experience depression, so these numbers could actually be much higher.

Can a person think about suicide and not know that he/she is depressed?

Yes. A major cause of suicide is undiagnosed (not recognized) depression. Often a person can be depressed and not know about the symptoms or even realize how he/she is feeling.

What causes depression?

Some people seem to be more likely to develop and experience depression than others. If someone in your family has experienced or suffers from depression, there is a greater chance that you will as well. This means that one of the causes of depression might be genetics. But depression can also be caused by severe events (like rape, assault, personal injury), a tense home life, the death of someone you love, a divorce, physical illnesses, medications or other drugs, hormone imbalances, and other stressors.

What is stress?

Stress is anything that creates tension in a person. In fact, tension can be used as another word for stress. Anytime a person, activity, or event causes a person to feel pressure, it is considered to be stress. Stress can come from enjoyable events (birthday parties, holidays, going out with friends) or demanding events (taking tests, giving a speech). Stress also comes from people or events that are not enjoyable at all, such as someone who threatens you or acts violently.

No one can completely remove stress from her/his life. While a person can and should avoid some types of stress, like negative people and harmful situations, each day will bring activities and people that create tension. What is most important is how a person responds to stress.

How should I deal with stress?

This question always comes down to how to manage stress and relieve tension in a way that is healthy and productive rather than harmful. Since everyone experiences stress, each person must develop ways to relieve the tension caused from stress.

Many people use negative ways to relieve tension/stress. Some examples are:
- Smoking cigarettes, drinking alcohol, and using other drugs.
- Watching television. (Television for entertainment is not necessarily unhealthy, but overuse can lead to unrealistic thinking about what life should be like.)

- Shouting at family members, friends, or others.
- Overeating.
- Acting violently.

These are just a few negative ways people relieve stress. As you can see, each of these ways to relieve stress can be harmful—which can create even more stress!

Many people use healthy ways to relieve tension and stress. Some examples are:

- Going for a walk.
- Exercising.
- Taking a nap.
- Taking a bath.
- Hobbies (art, reading, crafts, playing musical instruments).
- Writing in a journal.
- Talking with a friend or family member.
- Meditation.

This list could be expanded into the hundreds. Again, each of these ways to relieve stress is positive and productive. The fact that stress happens is not nearly as important as how you choose to manage and relieve it.

How does stress affect how I look, feel, and live?

How you respond to stress will determine how you look, feel, and live. For example, if you respond to stress by eating, you will be at a higher risk for developing a weight problem or becoming obese. This will affect your heart and other parts of your body. You will have less energy. Obesity puts a person at higher risk for dangerous conditions like diabetes, heart attacks, and some types of cancer. Being obese may also affect your self-image (how you feel about the way you look). If you have a low self-image, you won't like the way you look, so you may avoid social situations, making friends, and developing romantic relationships. All of this can cause even more stress, which can cause you to eat more, making the situation worse.

Find healthy ways to relieve stress and tension.

If a person chooses to go for a thirty-minute walk each day or has some-one that she/he can talk to about the day's events (the stuff that causes stress), she/he releases the tension in a way that will not create harmful habits, dangerous physical conditions, or poor self-image.

So, the stress you experience is not nearly as important to your looks, feelings, and life as the way that you choose to respond to it.

Will depression go away by itself?

Sadness tends to come in and out of a person's life, lasting for short periods of time. Depression may last many months, and the person is likely to expe-rience it again in his/her life or it may become a life-long condition. While some people who experience depression may have it fade out, most of the time depression requires medical and emotional help to allow a person to feel better again and get back to a full, enjoyable, and productive life.

What can I do to stop being depressed?

The good news is that most people with depression can be helped with treatment and can begin to feel better soon. The bad news is that most people who are depressed never get the help they need. When depression isn't treated it can get worse, last longer, and prevent you from getting the most out of this important time in your life.

The first step to solving this problem is to realize that you might be depressed! Depression is common, especially among young people, and is not a sign of physical or mental weakness.

If you feel you might be suffering from depression, you should share your suspicions with a trusted adult who can assist you in getting help. Everyone needs help in life—and this is clearly one of the times a person can use help.

A doctor, psychologist, or trained mental health counselor will help you find out what is needed to free you from depression. Usually, talking with a psychologist over a period of time is helpful. Other times, a medication is suggested. The two together (counseling and medication) are usually very effective.

What does sadness, depression, and stress have to do with sex?

You may have noticed that some of the signs of depression are emotional pain, including feelings of hopelessness, loneliness, worthlessness, and confusion. When a young person (or adult) feels lonely, sad, and worthless, she/he may search for ways to feel better. Often, attention from another person will make her/him feel better. If this attention is coming from someone who wants sex, the depressed person can be taken advantage of. Depression and stress can affect a person's perceptions (what she/he believes is real). This can make a person vulnerable (exposed and weak) to decisions she/he would not normally make if she/he felt better and was thinking clearly.

Often, a young person who is depressed will engage in intercourse to try to receive attention or to feel wanted, needed, and worthy as a human being. Other times, sex may be used as a distraction from the emotional pain she/he is feeling. In either case, it's only a temporary relief, as usually the depressed person will begin to feel bad again, and sometimes worse. New problems may come into her/his life in the form of an unplanned or ill-planned pregnancy or a sexually transmitted disease. Sex doesn't cure depression. Sex doesn't solve problems.

Stress can also make a young person vulnerable to engaging in drug use as a way to relieve tension and problems. A person who uses drugs (alcohol, marijuana, pills, etc.) loses her/his ability to make good decisions while under the influence of these chemicals. Many pregnancies and sexually transmitted diseases occur each year as a result of people being drunk or using drugs while engaging in sexual intercourse. Many people who are raped or who rape others report being under the influence of alcohol and other drugs.

This can all be very complex and confusing. The point is that when a person is feeling strong emotions, as people do when they're depressed, she/he may be at risk for making bad decisions. It is a good idea to postpone (hold off on) major life decisions until the depression has lifted.

Whom can I contact for help with my depression?

Again, you should let a trusted adult know what you're feeling and that you want help. She/He should be able to help you find a therapist in your area. If you need help finding a therapist right away, these Web sites and telephone numbers can be a good start: the American Psychological Association (www.helping.apa.org/find.html, 1-800-964-2000) and 1-800-Therapist (www.1-800-therapist.com, or 1-800-843-7274).

How do I know if someone is suicidal?

Depression increases the risk for suicide or suicide attempts. Suicidal thoughts and comments should always be taken seriously. If someone you know displays any of the signs of depression and:
- talks about suicide,
- seems to be focused on death,
- writes letters, stories, or creates artwork about death, or
- starts giving things away,

then contact that person's parent, guardian, or another trusted adult imme-diately. Explain what you saw and heard and that you are concerned. It is better to be safe than sorry.

What should I do if I am thinking of dying or committing suicide?

If you have thoughts of dying or committing suicide, you should speak with a trusted adult right away. If a trusted adult is not in your life, contact your local suicide prevention center, the Suicide Crisis Center (www.suicidecrisiscenter.com/callchart.html), 1-800-SUICIDE (1-800-784-2433), or SuicideHotlines.com.

If you have more questions about sadness, depression, or any other sexuality related issue, you can find additional information at Youth Embassy (www.YouthEmbassy.com).

15

How to Make It through Tough Times

Throughout life, each person will experience good times and bad times. One of the problems for most young people is that they have not fully developed the skills to manage all of the situations they will face, nor do they have the perspective (experience and understanding) to realize that their tough times are temporary. Better and brighter days ARE ahead. Even more unfortunate is that many young people do not have the support they need from adults to help them manage these difficulties. Life is something like being on a sailboat in the middle of an ocean. Storms will come and frighten you and will force you to wonder whether or not you will make it through safely. As you struggle and do everything you can to survive, the storm passes and you can again enjoy the beauty of the sea as you head to your next destination. The stormy times WILL pass.

Why is my life so bad?

Maybe a bit of philosophy might be useful. One way to look at the difficulties that you are facing is to see them as tests or challenges. Each test that you struggle through makes you a stronger person. You will need to have emotional, psychological, and ethical strength to overcome the challenges that you will face as an adult.

As bad as you have it, you probably have positive things in your life that many other young people from other parts of the country and world don't have. Did you know that many young people around the world:

- Do not have clean drinking water and become sick or die simply from their water?
- Starve to death each day?
- Are bought and sold as slaves?
- Do not have homes to live in?
- Do not have access to or receive an education?
- Have little choice as to what they will do with their lives?

How bad are things going for you, really? Do you eat on a regular basis? Have clean water to drink? Clothes to wear? A home to go to? A bed to sleep in? Do you have one good friend? A trusted adult you can turn to for guidance? If you do, you are doing better than most. As rough as you have it, you probably have an opportunity to improve the situation that you are in, an opportunity to become the person you know you were meant to be. Many people do not have the chances for change that you have.

It may be helpful to direct your attention to people who have accomplished remarkable work in their lives or excelled in their fields. If you read their biographies (life stories), you will discover that almost all have faced huge challenges and have overcome great odds to become successful and make good contributions to the world. You, too, will need to face your challenges and turn them into strengths.

But my life is really bad. What should I do?

If you feel overwhelmed with sadness and hopelessness, then it is important that you speak with a trusted adult about your feelings, maybe even a trained counselor or psychologist. There will be plenty of times in life when you will not be able to handle what is happening all on your own. You will need help. Everyone needs help to face their challenges sometimes.

Am I the only one who is living in this kind of situation?

Nope. Young people all over the world struggle each day. Family violence; neighborhood violence; sexual harassment and bullying in the community,

Many young people face difficult life situations.
Persistence and determination will carry them through.

school, and home; peer pressure; harmful relationships; loss of loved ones; pressure to perform—these are just a few of the issues that young people deal with on a daily basis. This is not to overlook confusing feelings related to self-image, body image, and social acceptance—also issues that trouble young people. Unfortunately, there seem to be few trusted adults or resources young people can turn to for help and guidance.

No, you are not the first or last person to be in the situation that you are in. But you are the only person who can take steps to change your situation, and this includes getting help.

How can I survive this difficult time?

Here are a few tips to help you make it through the stormy times:

FIND A SANCTUARY. Find a safe place where you don't have to worry about being bothered and where you can relax and think.

CHANGE YOUR PERCEPTIONS. Anger, sadness, depression, and hopelessness (all strong emotions) affect a person's ability to see the many sides of a situation. Strong emotions may give a person something called "tunnel vision." This means that only one view can be seen and none of the others. Often, someone who is not emotionally involved can help you take a fresh look at the situation and come up with options and solutions. With patience, you will find a solution to every problem.

LOOK FOR THE GOOD. Everywhere, every moment, and in every situation, look for the good and positive. There are many things to be grateful for in your life—from your health to the people who care about you to the safe places where you can go. Think about what your life would be like if you didn't have good health, someone to turn to, or somewhere to go. Often, many positive things are taken for granted. By appreciating the things that you are fortunate to have, you tip the scale from despair and sadness to hope and an expectation that everything will turn out okay in time.

PUT IT IN PERSPECTIVE. Will this problem or situation really matter to you in ten years, five years, or even one year? How does this situation affect the big picture? Chances are, what you are most concerned with right now will not be remembered in the months or years to come.

DISCOVER WHO YOU ARE. You are here for a reason, a purpose. You were given certain strengths and talents. What are they? How can you develop your strengths and use them to help yourself through this situation and prepare for your future?

TRANSCEND (RISE ABOVE) YOUR ENVIRONMENT. Be who you truly are. Don't get caught up in what anyone else says, does, or thinks about you. Regardless of who may be trying to hold you back, remember who you are and what you need to do to succeed.

GET HELP. Everyone needs help. Find a trusted adult or a resource (a school, community, or national organization) that can give you the information, support, and guidance you need. Find someone you can trust and who can help you work through your problems.

TURN OFF THE TELEVISION. Television can be entertainment, but it can also cause disappointment and sadness and fuel misperceptions about life. On television, families and people's lives all seem to be perfect, or their problems can be worked out within a half hour. These portrayals are very unrealistic, and people may begin to compare their less than perfect lives with what they see on television. This causes a person to feel like her/his life is nothing special or, even worse, a nightmare. Cut back on the hours you spend in front of the television. Try to limit what you see to programs that make you feel positive. In place of TV, spend some hours each day in activities that build your strengths.

ELIMINATE THE NEGATIVE. Avoid people who make you feel bad about yourself or who only add to your problems. Turn off music or other influences that describe the negative aspects of life or negative ways to handle problems. Cigarettes, alcohol, and other drugs only complicate life and create huge problems later down the road. Avoid these things at all costs.

BE CAREFUL WHERE YOU TURN! Beware of people who suggest that you use drugs, sex, or violence or join a gang to help you solve your problems. There are those who are constantly looking for young people who are depressed, vulnerable (weak in their ability to make good decisions), or in difficult situations so that they can take advantage of them. Often these people will come across as being very nice and will try to gain your trust. Once they think they have your trust, they may fill your head with bad information or try to persuade you into drug use, sex acts, gang involvement, or other bad ideas. Be aware that not everyone who offers you a hand wants to help you.

KEEP GOING! No matter how difficult it gets or how hopeless it seems, your life will improve—as long as you keep trying.

You are your own person.
Don't let anyone take advantage of you!

What does all this have to do with sex?

When people are feeling helpless or hopeless and believe they have no chance at a good life, they become weak in their ability to think and make good decisions. When people are so vulnerable, they may place their trust and hope in someone who will take advantage of them—sometimes for sex. Someone who is vulnerable may be influenced to have sex in order to keep another person from leaving him/her. This can lead to unplanned or ill-planned pregnancy, sexually transmitted disease, and an unhealthy relationship.

To summarize, here is a note I once wrote to a student who was living in a very stressful situation. She taped it onto the inside cover of her notebook as a reminder:

> "There IS turmoil in this world.
> But there is also a great deal more love, kindness, and peace.
> As humans, we must endure life's unfairness and troubles,
> And enjoy the goodness that surrounds us.
> People do care.
> I care.
> You ARE a very special person.
> You ARE on your way to being a successful adult.
> You WILL learn to live happily throughout life, even on 'rainy days.'
> Everyone feels as you do right now, from time to time.
> Express it.
> Let it go.
> Move on.
> You have much love, much happiness, and much laughter left
>   to experience."

This young person did endure four years of a very difficult situation, graduated from high school against the odds, and now lives in peace, love, and laughter as an independent woman.

If you have more questions about how to make it through tough times or about any other sexuality related issue, you can find additional information at Youth Embassy (www.YouthEmbassy.com).

16

How to Raise Happy and Successful Parents

This chapter will be helpful for the young person who feels that her/his parents just don't understand or have too many rules, or who used to get along with her/his parents but doesn't anymore. (In this book, guardians are also considered parents.) This chapter will not be helpful to the many young people who live in a situation where a parent emotionally or physically hurts them. Of the 4,000-plus young people who have shared their lives with me, the greatest problem for many of them was a parent who abandoned them, emotionally or physically abused them, or caused tremendous psychological pain in their lives. Unfortunately, many young people grow up in situations where the adults in their lives cause more harm than good.

For young people who have parents that do a fair job at turning their love and care into positive attention, discipline, and role modeling, these parents may only be going through growing pains. Parents are human beings—just like you. They struggle to make sense out of their lives—just like you. Parents face many problems—just like you. They are not perfect—just like you. Parents will make mistakes—just like you—and parents need understanding, support, and encouragement—just like you.

This section is written to help you understand what many parents are experiencing so you can help them feel better about how they are doing as parents. Also, parents sometimes have trouble seeing your transition (change) from child to developing young adult. This section may help you get them to recognize and understand that you are ready to be treated as a young adult.

Why do my parents make my life so difficult?

Sometimes parents will purposely challenge you with additional responsibilities and higher expectations than ever before. In order to survive as an independent adult, a young person needs to learn to accept and struggle through different challenges. A parent may try to prepare you to take care of yourself when you become older. This ability isn't acquired overnight; rather, it is a skill that develops over time through practice.

Other times, parents may begin to rely on their young person to help take care of the home and other family responsibilities. This is actually very beneficial for you, even though it might not always be much fun. Responsibilities at home teach you not only how to take care of yourself, but also how to take care of a house and other people. When the time comes for you to become a parent, you will have learned about some of the responsibilities and difficulties (and joys!) that are involved in raising a family. Without this training you would have a much harder time as a parent, because you wouldn't be prepared.

Of course, sometimes parents will ask you to do things for their own convenience, or they will ask for conduct that just doesn't make any sense at all! Believe it or not, this is also beneficial to you, even if it isn't enjoyable, because when you become an adult, you will regularly be asked to do things at your job and in life that don't appear to make any sense. Being able to deal with that aggravation in a healthy way will become a valuable skill.

Why are my parents so unfair?

Sometimes parents are unfair because they have not yet "transitioned." For so many years when you were little, your parents needed to keep a close eye on you to keep you from certain dangers. Although you are older now, they haven't yet realized that your needs have changed—as have the dangers—and that how they interact with you also needs to change. Remember, parents are human, and letting go of habits and certain ways of doing things is difficult. Sometimes you just need to sit your parents down gently but firmly and let

Mutual understanding and communication
are key to raising successful parents!

them know what is going on in your life—what you're thinking and feeling and what kind of support you need—in order to help them make the transition. Sometimes it takes repeated sit-downs for people to get the message, including parents! Understanding, patience, and repetition usually win out in time.

Being treated "unfairly" is a valuable part of your personal growth, because when you become an independent adult, you will discover that, unfortunately, other people may treat you unfairly quite often.

My parents won't let me date yet or have any fun. What can I do?

Different parents have different rules on when is the best time to start dating. Each year, many teens become pregnant, catch sexually transmitted diseases, or experience violence or manipulation by people they become involved with. When you care about someone, you worry about the dangers he/she may face and try to keep him/her from harm as best you can.

One way to help parents feel more secure about letting you date is to show them through your words and actions that you are responsible, you are becoming more mature, and you know what a risky situation is and how to avoid/manage it. This all takes time to do, however. Start by finishing chores, homework, and other assignments on time without having to be asked. (I know. You're sitting there thinking that your parents paid me to say this!) Also, start talking more to Mom or Dad about different topics. Let them learn about you through your thoughts and feelings on different subjects, especially about romance, relationships, and sex. Don't be afraid to state your case for wanting to go out on a date with someone.

Sometimes starting with "group outings" is a good first step. This way the person you want to be with can meet you and a group of friends at the movies, mall, or another public area, and your parents will become more confident about your going on solo dates after a while. This is usually a good idea for you as well, because it takes some of the pressure off of having to be alone with someone and think of things to say. Having friends around lets you be with your date while giving you a safety net of other people who can keep things interesting.

If this approach fails, keep being responsible and trustworthy and honor your parents' wishes. Chalk it up to one of those frustrating situations in life that will eventually be over, and then you can enjoy all the freedom you're looking for.

How can I get my parents to trust me?

One of the first things my students learn is not to respect or trust me or any other adult just because of a title or job position. (We are all courteous to one another, however!) Respect and trust must be earned, not assumed or given based on a title or job position. Many people simply do not deserve respect or trust. A person should earn your respect and trust by being honest and fair through all that they say and do (mostly what they do). In the case of my students and me, they come to respect and trust me because I earn it—I am honest, I always do what I say I am going to do, I treat each person fairly, and I am a positive role model. I trust and respect my students because they earn it. They learn that they never have to lie to me about anything and that I will accept them regardless of what they think or say or the mistakes they may make.

What's the point in all of this? If you want your parent (or anyone else) to trust you, then you must be trustWORTHY. That means being honest all the time—even when no one is watching. It means suffering the consequences of mistakes that you make, and telling the truth about the errors rather than trying to hide them.

Here are a few ways that you can earn trust:

- If you say you are going to be at a certain place, make sure that you are there.
- If you say you are going to be with a certain person, be with that person.
- If you say you are going to be somewhere at a certain time, then be there on time.
- If you make a mistake, admit it before someone asks you about it.
- If you don't complete a chore or assignment, let the person you were doing it for know before he/she asks you about it.
- Always tell the truth. Once you lie, it becomes easier to lie again and again; once you get caught in a lie, another person may not trust you again.

To summarize, always follow this simple Basso saying and you will begin to earn people's trust: "Say what you mean, mean what you say, and do what you say you're going to do."

With most parents, the more that they can trust you, the more they feel confident in you, and the more activities they will feel comfortable allowing you to engage in. Most important, being honest leads to personal integrity—which leads to feeling good about yourself—which leads to confidence—which leads to being happy—which leads to people finding you attractive. (People are always attracted to other people who are confident and happy!)

Why has my relationship with my parents changed?

All relationships change—sometimes for the better, sometimes for the worse. Usually long-term relationships (like between parents and their daughters/sons) alter because the people change.

You have changed quite a bit since you first arrived at your parents' house. You were this needy, little child who had to have everything done for her/him, and now you are a very different person. You are now more of an adult than you are a baby. You are more independent, need more privacy, have your own thoughts and ideas, and are experiencing new feelings. You have new interests and priorities. Impressing and spending time with friends may now be more important to you than spending time with your parents and family. You are looking for autonomy (being your own person). These are only some of the major changes a young person may experience. For these reasons alone, you may see your parents in a very different way than you used to.

The other side of the story includes your parents. They, too, are growing and changing. Some parents may think that because your body is bigger than it used to be, resembling an adult's more than a child's, you don't need the same amount of affection, positive attention, and support that you did when you were younger. So you may feel a bit abandoned and alone, as if your parents don't care anymore.

Some parents may be so used to taking care of you as a child, making all of your decisions, and trying to protect you from every little possible danger that they have not realized that you are in a very different stage of development and need more freedom to make your own decisions. If they don't adjust, you may feel as though they are trying to control your life and that they don't trust you.

And as you grow older, your role in the family will change from being a playful child to having responsibilities for the home and family. This new role will shift the relationship as well.

These changes will be happening all at the same time, so it is very normal for your relationship with your parents to alter. Your relationship with your parents will continue to develop throughout your life as you and they grow older.

A few things that will help you to have a good relationship with your parents, now and for many years to come, are these:

BE GENTLE. Try not to be too hard on or critical of your parents, even if they are being hard on or critical of you!

REMEMBER THAT YOUR PARENTS ARE ONLY HUMAN. They are not perfect, and they need understanding, patience, and support.

DON'T HAVE A DISCUSSION WHEN YOU OR YOUR PARENTS ARE ANGRY. Try to forgive things your parents may say when they are angry. Apologize for things that you might say when you are angry.

ACCEPT THAT PEOPLE HAVE DIFFERING VIEWS AND IDEAS. Share your views, but don't argue over who is right or expect to change what your parents believe.

REMEMBER THAT ARGUMENTS AND BAD TIMES ARE TEMPORARY and will fade in memory. Your parents' love will be forever.

LET YOUR PARENTS KNOW THAT YOU LOVE THEM and that you appreciate everything they do for you.

How can I better understand my parents?

Again, try to remember that parents are human beings with very difficult lives. They may have jobs, many responsibilities, and many pressures that create stress in their lives. Think about putting yourself in Mom or Dad's life for a while and worrying about some of the things that she/he may be anxious about: Will I have a job in the future? How will I pay the home loan, rent, telephone, electricity, food, car, gas, television, clothes, insurance, or medical bills this month? Am I being a good wife/husband? Are my children safe? Am I being a good parent? Will we save enough money to live on when we become older? These are just a few issues that may race through parents' minds each day.

Next time you see your parents, give them a hug!

Next time you see your parents, give them a hug. Next time they yell or are unreasonable, remember what they are going through and give them a hug later when they have cooled down.

How can I help my parents to become successful?

Simple—your success is their success. By being someone who is honest and able to overcome challenges, you fulfill the most common wish of most parents. They want to raise a young person into an adult who will be happy, independent, honest, and productive.

Now notice I said "simple" and not "easy." Achieving this does not happen overnight. It takes years of work, facing challenges, making and learning from mistakes, and continually disciplining yourself to do the things that need to be done, regardless of whether you enjoy them or not. Ideally, your parents will give you opportunities to learn by giving you appropriate challenges and equally appropriate support to help you meet those challenges.

Throughout this learning and preparation, you should remember that you will need help, and that parents are not mind readers. To help your parents help you, sit down with them every once in a while and let them know what you are thinking, what you are feeling, and where you need help. They need to know what is going on before they can begin to understand and offer guidance.

What if none of this really applies to my parents?

If you live in a situation where a parent or guardian is emotionally, physically, or sexually abusive, has abandoned you, is violent/allows violence to occur in your family, or does not provide you with the love and support that you need, there are things that you should know:

YOU ARE NOT CRAZY. The title of "parent" or "guardian" is a legal term given to an adult who is responsible for taking care of a young person. The title of "parent" or "guardian" does not mean an adult necessarily has the knowledge, insight, or skill to take care of and raise a young person.

YOU ARE NOT ALONE. Parents and families shown on television are not the reality for much of America. Unfortunately, many young people are in living situations that are emotionally or physically harmful.

YOU NEED TO GET HELP. You need to find a trusted adult, preferably a trained counselor or psychologist, whom you can talk to on a regular basis in order to relieve some of the emotions that are building up inside of you.

YOU NEED TO FIND A WAY TO SURVIVE. This means finding useful activities and places where you can de-stress and spend as little time in the harmful environment as possible. These include:

- Athletics (sports after school, jogging, exercise, or weight training).
- The library (a safe, quiet environment where you can exercise your mind by writing in a journal, reading stories, or completing homework).
- Art (an after-school class to paint, make pottery, learn carpentry, or practice photography).
- Trade skills (an after-school class to learn and practice computers, auto mechanics, cooking/culinary skills, or electronics).

PAY ATTENTION TO WARNING SIGNS! If you are becoming overwhelmed by the situation, you may experience one or more of the following:

- Thinking about or actually using tobacco, alcohol, or other drugs.
- Thinking about dying.
- Feeling alone, depressed, or hopeless (see the chapter on Dealing with Sadness and Depression).
- Arguing a lot or getting into fights.
- Breaking things, destroying property, or committing crimes.
- A decline in school grades.
- Inflicting pain on yourself.
- A willingness to do anything your girlfriend/boyfriend wants because you are afraid of losing her/him.

If you are experiencing any of these, then chances are you're very vulnerable to putting yourself in danger. Try to locate a trusted adult who can help you deal with your situation.

TRANSCEND. Your current situation is not how your life will always be. Discover what your personal strengths and talents are, and develop them each day. Prepare for your future life. Realize and remind yourself each day that through your hard work, persistence, and determination, you will make it out of the situation you are in. Soon you will be free to live the life you were meant to live, as the person you really are.

If you have more questions about how to raise happy and successful parents, or about any other sexuality related issue, you can find additional information at Youth Embassy (www.YouthEmbassy.com).

17

How to Be Your Best

Being your best is one of those things that is easy to say but difficult to do. Being your best does not mean just trying. Being your best means taking everything you are as a person—all of your special talents and skills, weaknesses, limitations, and conditions—and using them to your full capacity and advantage. Being your best means striving to reach your full potential. It is this struggle that builds you as a human being, that makes you stronger and better able to overcome the many challenges you will face throughout your life.

Being your best does not mean being THE best. You will always be better at something than someone else, and there will always be someone better than you at something. Competition and contests can be useful when they motivate you to strive for your personal best. Use competition as an opportunity to put the hard work and skills that you have practiced to the test— YOUR test. This means performing better than you have ever performed before, or performing to the best of your ability given your current situation. The ability to reach your potential is far more valuable and lasting than any award or recognition. Reaching your full potential is what makes you a winner and a success in your life, not trophies. The only person you ever need to compete against is YOU.

So then how do I reach my full potential?

Whew! That is an entire book in itself! Here are just a few of the basics that you need to focus on each day:

NUTRITION. The fuel you put into your body will determine how you feel, grow, recuperate, and perform. Yes, good food does make a huge difference. Try eating well for a month and see for yourself! Breakfast, lunch, dinner, snacks—all are necessary for peak performance. Limit the high-fat, fried, greasy, and high-sugar foods to just a once-a-week or -month occasion. Make fresh fruits, vegetables, whole-grain cereals, and protein foods (especially fish and beans, but also lean meats) a habit in your daily fuel regimen.

EXERCISE. Physical exercise strengthens your bones and muscles, including your heart. Reading and doing mental work strengthen and exercise your brain (another essential organ!). The stronger your body is, the more you are able to do, and the better you are able to perform. The better your performance, the closer you move toward reaching your potential. The good news about exercise (both physical and mental) is that it doesn't matter how strong you are right now. If you just challenge yourself appropriately each day (not too hard, but by small improvements over time) you will become stronger and better.

SLEEP. Most young people do not get enough sleep. When you sleep, essential hormones are produced that allow you to grow and become stronger. All the exercise in the world will not make you stronger if you are not getting enough sleep. Muscles become stronger not during exercise but during sleep. Sleep also allows you to focus better during the day. Yes, turn off the television, hang up the phone, and make sure that you invest your time wisely by getting at least eight hours of sleep each night!

SOCIAL HEALTH. If you have at least one good friend in this world, you're doing very, very well! Try to maintain a solid friendship with someone you can share ideas and feelings with and who makes you feel comfortable being yourself. To stretch yourself, try to start a conversation with someone you don't know at least once per week. If you're shy, try to find easy ways to meet people, such as through activities you enjoy.

SPIRITUAL HEALTH. This doesn't necessarily mean organized religion, although religion can be a path to spiritual discipline. Spiritual health means strengthening your spirit—the life energy within you. Some of the best ways are by being honest, treating people fairly, and helping people when they need it. A strong spirit will invigorate (energize) you and give you strength not only to do the right thing, but to do things to the best of your ability.

STRESS MANAGEMENT. Find healthy ways to get rid of the stress in your life. Writing in a journal, exercising, walking, making art, practicing a skill or hobby—all relieve the built-up tension in your body, allowing you to think clearly and focus on the things you need to do to be your best.

BALANCE. Nothing done in excess is healthy. Balance school work with hobbies, vigorous exercise with relaxation, chores with fun time, friends with family. When you do anything to excess it means that other important areas in your life suffer and weaken, and your overall ability to perform will decrease.

PRACTICE! Practice the skills you want to improve over and over again. Perfect your talents, reduce your weaknesses and limitations, and be persistent. No one ever became their best without dedicated and consistent practice. Just ask Tiger Woods about how often he practices!

These seven lifestyle areas combined with PRACTICE create synergy. Synergy is when things combine to make a stronger, more powerful result than they would separately. For example, exercising to lose weight may help a person drop a few pounds. Paying attention to nutrition to lose weight may help a person lose a few pounds. Exercise joined with good nutrition bring far greater results! Exercise and nutrition are said to be synergistic.

Practice alone may bring you positive results. When connected with improvements in the other lifestyle areas, however, your performance will reach new heights that you would not be able to attain through practice alone.

What if I'm not good at anything?

Ah, you may not believe this, but every person is good at something. Each person is born with strengths, special skills, or talents. Unfortunately, many people will never take the time to discover what their strengths are, let alone develop them.

In the United States and other parts of the world, young people are given about sixteen years or so to discover and develop their special talents. Use the teen years to become involved in as many school subjects as you can. Try to become involved in as many extracurricular activities as you can. You might find that you enjoy these activities because you have a special talent for them. Look into music, drama, art, mechanics, culinary (cooking) skills, camping, clubs, sports, games (like chess), design, creative writing, journalism, health, volunteering—the list goes on and on! Try many of them to see where your talents and interests might be.

You have at least one talent that is strong and that can be used to your advantage, but it is up to you to discover it!

Many things that I don't do well are holding me back. What should I do?

Everyone has areas that they struggle with. It is up to you to recognize and acknowledge those area you need to improve. Find someone to help you become stronger in those areas. Almost all weaknesses can be improved through determination, persistence, and time.

Should I try to improve what I am not good at?

Absolutely! But don't let what you can't do interfere with what you can do. Try to improve on your weaknesses, but spend time building your strengths as well.

Everyone must learn what their
personal strengths are and use them
each day to become their very best.

How can I develop my personal strengths?

PRACTICE. Set a realistic goal and do something every day to reach it. Focus, persistence, and small improvements over time will bring you closer to your goal.

How do I set a goal that I can reach?

Some might say, "If you can dream it, you can be it." Well, that's not entirely true. In fact, this philosophy can sometimes hold you back. For example, a young student I knew was 5 feet, 6 inches tall as a senior in high school. She knew that no matter how hard and long she trained and practiced, she would never be able to dunk a basketball. Height is a physical limitation that can be made up for with leaping ability, but even her full potential in that area would not allow her to get above the hoop. So rather than waste valuable time trying to make her dream come true of slamming a basketball home, she set more realistic goals: being quick (which was one of her personal strengths), hitting 80 percent of her jump shots, and being able to control the ball and setup plays with precision. Through long hours of practice and a balanced life off the court, she was able to achieve all of that. She reached her full potential in basketball by setting more realistic goals for herself based on her strengths and her limitation (her height). Not only did she enjoy reaching her potential, she felt good about her goal and being able to say, "I played my best."

It is good to dream. Dreams are the fuel for determination and achievement. However, only dreams that are turned into action will create extraordinary results. If you have a dream, set a realistic goal that uses your strengths and recognizes your weaknesses. Write down the steps you will take to reach that goal.

What does all this have to do with sex?

Sometimes, young people (adults, too) don't realize who they really are, what talents they possess, or how to use those talents to perform to the best of their abilities. They think that they are worthless, can't do anything well, and will never amount to anything. When people feel worthless, they may become vulnerable (not strong enough to make good decisions or protect

Being your best means exercising your body AND your mind.

themselves from abusive people). When they are vulnerable, they may be easily manipulated (tricked) into having sex or doing other things they wouldn't do if they were feeling better and stronger. When people feel worthless, they tend not to value their health or life and may engage in unsafe sexual intercourse.

Some young people who feel this way engage in unprotected sex because they simply don't care what happens to them. They feel that since they don't seem to do anything well, they don't have any value and their lives will be a failure—so why care what happens?

This outlook simply isn't true. Having worked with thousands of young people who have felt exactly this way, I've found that those who are able to discover their individual talents and strengths are then able to acknowledge their worth, becoming confident in themselves and their ability to create a promising future. Once young people discover how to succeed based on who they are and what special talents they have, they pay more attention to their health and life. When you know you have a chance at a good future and you feel confident in your abilities, you tend not to take any risks that could threaten everything that you are working toward.

You have a jewel within you. Find it, polish it, and use it to make yourself a success. Only YOU can.

If you have more questions about how to be your best, or about any other sexuality related issue, you can find additional information at Youth Embassy (www.YouthEmbassy.com).

18

For Parents, Educators, and Other Adults

Sex, sex, sex! It's all around us. Like it or not, approve or disapprove, every day we are inundated with messages and information that may confuse us. Nonetheless, these messages shape our thoughts, attitudes, and behaviors.

Turn on any television set and you'll find talk shows, sitcoms, and soap operas focusing on any number of sexual topics with a sensationalistic view that is more destructive than constructive. Movie theaters, videos, the Internet, and cable premium channels bring us explicit scenes of intercourse between men and women, women and women, men and men. They show us bondage, sadomasochism, male dominance, female submission, and violent intercourse. These scenes either consciously or subconsciously mold our views and thoughts regarding sexuality. (Please don't think your young person hasn't been exposed to this.)

Travel down any roadside, open any magazine, or watch any commercial and you will see products advertised by bubbly, bouncing babes in bikinis, body suits, and lingerie, while carefree, fun-loving, not-an-ounce-of-body-fat studs show us what kind of man is acceptable and how men should behave. Those of us who don't fit can transform into one of these babes or studs by purchasing the advertised a product.

How about music? Turn on your stereo and listen to the words of today's musicians. Along with the catchy beats and melodies, you may discover messages like "give up that sex and let's do it again and again because

I'll make you feel good all night long, ooh baby baby, ooh baby baby, ooh baby baby." And this is only the beginning.

What's that, you say? I'm exaggerating, and you don't allow your young person to go to movies, watch television, open magazines, use the Internet, listen to the stereo, or look at billboards? Well, that's not all. Let's go to school, shall we?

The latest fashions can include guys' pants several sizes larger than what fits around the waist, leaving the pants hanging around mid-butt to expose those not-so-chic boxers or cotton briefs. (I'm not making this up.) The young ladies may wear see-through blouses and skirts, revealing body suits, lace underwear, or push-up bras. Mini-miniskirts make it nearly impossible for young females to sit without drawing the attention of a small posse of young males. Of course, fashions vary, so some of this can be discounted. But discussions about sex, as well as peer pressure to engage in sex, are inevitable. Unfortunately, the information discussed among teens is not much different from the myths and downright dangerous beliefs that have been passed on for decades.

What's a teen to do? Hours each day, for weeks, months, and years, young people are glued to the television and stereo, watching and listening to their idols scream and whisper messages like these:
- Sex is good.
- The more sexually experienced you are, the more accepted you will be.
- The cool guys are studs. Promiscuity is in.
- Fun and popular girls have sex.
- Girls want to have sex, even when they say no.
- Sex is an all-night fantasy filled with simultaneous, earth-shattering multiple orgasms.
- Only the physically beautiful people really enjoy life.
- You don't need birth control or condoms because only other people get pregnant, STDs, or AIDS.
- Sex makes you a respected adult.

Of course, you could argue that these interpretations are not 100 percent true. Yes, some programs, music, and advertisements do not promote these messages. But turn on your television or stereo or open a magazine and ask yourself if these statements are far off the mark. You could probably add a few things to this list yourself.

Before you start thinking that an eighty-year-old prude is really making a big deal out of nothing (incidentally, I am neither a prude nor close to eighty), let me alert you to another problem. The statement, "Kids know more about sex than we do!" once started out as a joke, but unfortunately this opinion is now accepted as fact. Another version goes, "Okay son, it's time we talk about sex." "Sure, Dad! What do you want to know?" Although funny, this is far from the truth. Of the thousands of fourteen-, fifteen-, and sixteen-year-old students whom I have instructed over the years, only 10 percent even knew the basics of sex. Of that 10 percent, most were females. Males usually talk a good game because they are expected to, but in reality, most young males don't have a clue.

This presents us with an enormous challenge. As we all know, puberty is a wondrous, beautiful, agonizing, and terrifying time in one's life. Just remember this time in your own life! Physically, mentally, and socially, teens are changing from children to young adults. Hormones are rampant. (Once again, think back.) Body parts are changing all the time. Feelings toward guys and girls are also changing, as is the desire to be socially accepted. Let's not forget the curiosity and endless questions.

Guess where today's youth are getting their sexual information? That's right! Television, movies, music, advertising, fashion, and word of mouth are the direct information lines to the young. Young people tend to believe anything if it comes from a friend's mouth, television, radio, or magazine. As you might guess, our young people are getting the wrong information and are developing dangerous attitudes and behaviors.

How do I know this? I have been fortunate enough to spend eight to ten hours a day with young people during class, after class, before school, and after school. I have been blessed because my students and I develop a special relationship that parents might only dream of having with their teens. My students bestow on me the confidence and acceptance of a friend and the respect befitting a mentor. In return, I give them unopinionated, nonjudgmental, accurate information. Through honesty, trust, and openness, my students have allowed me into their hearts, their minds, and their worlds.

Each year when I teach health and lifestyle management (which includes human growth, development, and sexuality education), my free period and after-school time tend to be the busiest times of the day. Students, past and present, know that they are welcome in my class and are important and special people. My real contribution is made one-on-one or with small groups of friends after class. Because of this I am often inundated with questions and problems my students have never expressed before. On average each year, a hundred-plus teen females will ask to speak with me personally and privately about possible pregnancies, sexual intercourse, peer pressure, birth control, menstruation, abortion, breast and gynecological exams, relationships, and physical concerns such as the strange appearance of lumps, aches, pains, and a host of other maladies.

Young guys also keep me busy with questions and concerns about their bodies. Gaining weight, acne, how to talk to girls, what is sex, and the strange appearances of lumps, fluids, and the like are the most common topics.

Sadly, a number of students have come to me and broken the silence around incestuous abuse.

Most young people can't go to just anybody and ask questions about sexuality. There are a number of criteria young people usually have that will determine whether or not they share their thoughts and questions with you. Sometimes a young person will ask a basic, nonthreatening question to test you. But for a teen to want to express his or her true feelings, the listener will usually need to:

BE AN AUTHORITY ON THE TOPIC. If you are a bit rusty (most people are), obtain a few college textbooks or even easier-to-read books (such as this one) that provide accurate and factual information. Don't always believe what you read in magazines or newspapers; they can be erroneous.

Also, if you're asked a question and are not sure of the answer, say that you're not sure but that you will find the answer and get back to your young person. Young people know when you're bluffing. If they discover that you made something up or gave them false information, you will lose credibility and the ability to communicate with that person.

BE NONJUDGMENTAL. No one likes being judged, preached to, or told what to do. Regardless of whether you think a young person is making the biggest mistake of his or her life, do not insist that the teen is wrong and you are right. If you do, you may never have another opportunity for discussion again.

BE UNOPINIONATED. (Primarily for school educators.) This is difficult to do. In class, students will often beg for my slant on an issue. As tempting as it would be to oblige them, it would be doing them a great disservice and would detract from the educational experience. Young people are bright. Give them the correct information and both sides of the story, and let them form their own opinions. They are almost always good ones.

BE GENUINE. Young people know when someone is "just doing their job," is being phony, or really wants to be doing something else. Show love, respect, and thorough enjoyment at being with the young people in your life. Every comment, movement, gesture, and facial expression should breathe the message that you care. Almost always, I have found that young people will reciprocate. If you don't have a genuine passion to be there for a young person, he or she will know it.

BE APPROACHABLE. An easygoing smile-on-the-face, see-me-if-you-want-to attitude generally puts young people in the driver's seat. There is no pressure to talk if they do not want to. Many times young people will come by to chit-chat about other things a dozen times or so before they feel comfortable enough to talk about what's really on their mind or in their heart.

BE A ROLE MODEL. Nothing turns away a young person more quickly than a do-as-I-say-not-as-I-do person. If you want to be respected, be respectable. If you want to be admired, be admirable. If you want to be trusted, be trust-worthy. If you want young people to talk with you, talk WITH them, not TO them. Be someone a young person can look up to. Don't assume anything from a young person because of your age or position. Earn it!

If your young person does decide to share his or her thoughts, feelings, or questions with you, here are some tips on how not to destroy the experience in under two seconds:

- Don't laugh. Regardless of how humorous or ridiculous he or she sounds or how nervous you may be, do not laugh at your young person.
- Don't overreact. Don't make a big deal out of a question, comment, or feeling. Be cool. Don't praise young people or tell them how proud you are of them for coming to you. This makes some young people feel

awkward and may create undue stress, which will shut down the communication. Regardless of how thrilled you are, just act like, "Hey, no big deal. Anytime."

- Don't put them down. Nobody enjoys looking like an idiot for not knowing something. Don't be surprised if your young person is confused about something you think everyone knows about. Every question is a good one. Treat it as such.

- Be serious, but not overly so. A concerned look on your face with an occasional accepting smile and nod of the head helps show a young person that what he or she is saying to you is important. If you think a little humor (not at his or her expense) will ease some tension, a funny comment may do wonders.

- Give short, to-the-point answers. Young people don't want to know everything at once, they just want the answers to their questions when they arise. Resist the temptation to show your depth of knowledge by providing long dissertations exploring the history and all other facets of the topic, which include your revered opinion and arguments. Don't make them sorry for asking. If they want to know more, they'll ask.

- Don't tell stories about when you were their age. Unless they ask, don't tell! They came to you to talk about their lives, not yours. You may say that you had similar feelings, but don't go into your history unless they ask.

- Never belittle another person's feelings. If a young person says that he or she is in love, then this is true. Their feelings are very real and very intense. Don't ever say, "Oh, it's just . . ." and then downplay a young person's feelings for any reason. Remember that what a young person feels is very real, powerful, and often confusing.

- Relax. Your relaxed body language will often set the tone for the experience. If you're confident and calm, it will often help put the young person at ease.

Of course, there are other criteria that can affect communication with young people. For now, these suggestions should give you an idea of how to develop an open line of communication regarding sexuality.

These are not tactics to be used to find out the hidden secrets that lie within. As tactics, they would be crass and ineffective. If you are naturally the kind of person who displays these characteristics, you are a good candidate for being accepted by a young person.

You might be saying to yourself, "This guy doesn't have to make the house rules, worry each time my kid goes out the door, or try to keep my young person out of trouble. Let's see him be nonjudgmental and unopinionated when his daughter comes home at 1:00 A.M." Well, you're right, to a point. I don't have the same responsibilities to the same degree that you do. Believe me when I say that I have nothing but appreciation for the headaches and difficulties that parents experience trying to raise young people. If your family survives with few major catastrophes and your young people develop into well-adjusted adults, then congratulations on a job well done!

This is not a book that professes "the tried and tested right way" to raise young people. This is a guide for young people to get the answers to the questions they want, when they want them. This book is offered to encourage healthy views and feelings about sexuality. The characteristics mentioned above often work to open the lines of communication between young and old. If these characteristics just don't fit into your personality, they don't have to. It would be worse to not admit this and put on some half-hearted charade because a book mentioned it. Nobody would believe you anyway.

These approaches are not guaranteed to encourage young people to talk with you about sexuality. Every person, young and old, will respond differently.

If you find it uncomfortable to discuss sexual topics with your teen, this does not make you any less effective a parent. Think back to your younger days or consider your feelings today. Did you feel comfortable talking about sexual topics with your parents? Can you today? I couldn't then, and today I still cringe when either one of my parents brings up a topic related to sex. But you love your parents and agree that, although they weren't perfect, they did a decent job of getting you through it all. Your young people will also feel the same way, at the very least.

Perhaps you have a teen who means everything to you, but you don't seem able to speak comfortably with him or her. You're not quite sure what kind of information, education, or personal bias is being given to your young person. You worry that your teen is getting the wrong information from friends or subconsciously falling prey to the repeated messages of our media. What do you do?

In this book, I present accurate, up-to-date information on the sexuality topics most often on the minds of today's youth. If you flip through the pages, you'll notice that the book is written largely in question-and-answer format. The questions throughout this book are the ones that are most often asked of me each semester. Certainly the topic of sexuality could be expanded to include many things that aren't mentioned in this book or that are on the minds of many adults. Once again, this book has been written for young people and their interests, not for older people. *The Underground Guide to Teenage Sexuality* answers the sometimes tough questions on the minds of teens today.

I make no differentiation between good or bad other than when it comes to the values of equity, responsibility, health, and honesty. On occasion I describe what is frequently being practiced by a majority or minority of people in the United States. Whether a belief or practice is expressed by a majority or minority, readers should not interpret them as right or wrong, good or bad.

I am hoping that parents and guardians will step in where I cannot and provide our youth with helpful guidelines regarding morals. Neither in my classes nor in this book would it be appropriate for me to influence a young person with my moral beliefs. Parents/guardians should be the primary source of morals for their teens. I simply won't discuss my personal morals, because what I believe may not be congruent with what parents want.

Ethics (not morals) can and should be taught and modeled by all adults. I try to model ethics in my interactions with young people. Ethical behavior based on honesty, personal integrity, and personal responsibility serves as the foundation for successful living and decision making. I do believe that ethics and attitudes about sexuality should be taught in the home. I also know that this does not always happen. In these days of scandal, corruption, and special interest groups influencing the law of the land, a crisis of ethics exists in all walks of life. The next generation will live differently only if today's adults show personal responsibility, honesty, and equity to our young people.

In an anonymous survey I give my students (this is not required, yet 100 percent of my students respond), 70 percent of my fourteen-, fifteen-, and sixteen-year-old students come from single-parent homes. Less than 30 percent of my students received sexuality information from their parents/ guardians. Of those students who received some of their sexuality information from their guardians, most couldn't remember much of what was discussed. And 90 percent of my students didn't know the basics about anatomy or menstruation.

The fact is, teens rarely talk with their parents about sex. If your teen does, that's wonderful! Your situation is certainly in the minority.

Here are just a few of the possible reasons (not in any particular order) why it is difficult for parents and teens to talk about sex:

TEEN EMBARRASSMENT. In the United States, the topic of sexuality is somewhat taboo. When teens don't know what is socially acceptable, they are going to reserve their questions for people who they feel will not judge them. Teens often wonder if they are "normal." For example, if you were to have recurring dreams (or nightmares) about being caressed and fondled by your mother, and these dreams stimulated you, how secure would you feel in talking to someone about this? Even now as an older person, would you talk to Mom about it? Dad? Family? Friends? Imagine what you might be thinking. I hope you're starting to get the picture about how young people feel and how difficult it is to approach adults, especially parents, about anything sexual.

PARENTAL REACTION. Parents sometimes need to discipline or even punish young people while growing up. For this reason, teens often fear that they will be punished for asking certain questions or having certain thoughts or feelings. Young people will often tell me, "If my Mom ever knew what I was thinking—forget about it!" Whether the teen is correct about how Mom/Dad will respond makes no difference. The young person's perception of what will happen is very real—and reason enough to keep quiet.

Other reservations that teens have about talking to parents about sex are:

• "Parents don't listen." Sometimes we are so quick to talk or share our own knowledge and experiences that we open our mouths instead of our ears. Teens want someone to listen to them. Don't we all?

- "Parents just try to force their opinions on you." This is so tempting to do because your opinion is the right opinion, the best opinion, and everyone should be entitled to your opinion. (I hope you're laughing.) Sometimes we are guilty of having our mouths open instead of our minds. This is a major mistake. Give a young person the facts, and you will be surprised at what develops. Certainly you want your young person to grow up to be a thinking, caring individual who can make wise decisions for himself/herself. This doesn't happen magically. Careful thinking should start in the home. Nobody likes being force-fed someone else's ideas and opinions.
- "They wouldn't understand." If you think back to your younger years, you'll recall that your music, clothes, street language, and environment were different from your parents'. You may have felt that Mom and Dad were out of touch with the world. Guess what? Your teen feels the same way. To a certain point, he or she is right. It is a whole new world. Although parents may not fully understand twenty-first century life, basic feelings and questions concerning love, security, and acceptance tend to stay the same. This means that teens today have the same feelings as their parents did; it is just a different time and place. Teens have a tough time understanding this.
- "Parents don't feel comfortable talking about this." Unless you discuss topics of sexuality openly and frequently, you may feel a bit squeamish talking. I feel comfortable discussing these issues with young people because I have spent thousands of hours doing so. Yet I notice when I am out with friends or older people, when a topic about sexuality comes up and I go into my usual spiel, these grown people tend to squirm, perspire, lose eye contact, and generally become nervous. At this point, I have to remind myself of where I am and tone it down a bit. It's normal to feel uncomfortable bringing up these topics.
- "Parents are too nosy." Teens are becoming more autonomous and require more privacy than they did as young children. Sometimes a teen may ask a single question and want a short answer, but Mom or Dad turns it into an Oprah episode, verbally probing the teen for more intimate thoughts, feelings, and opinions. It is usually best to allow

teens to share what they want with you, when they want. Please don't give them the third degree and destroy any future communication.

FEELINGS OF INADEQUACY. Teens often feel that everyone else knows something they don't. Rather than be ridiculed for not knowing, teens would prefer not to ask questions that might alert someone to their perceived inadequacy.

DESIRE FOR INDEPENDENCE. Teens need to feel that they are in control of their lives. Teens begin to want freedom from the rules, from "child treatment," and from constraints their parents have used to direct their lives thus far. In regard to talking to parents about sex, a teen will often show independence and equality with a parent by purposely avoiding such questions. Asking questions about sexuality means the teen does not know something Mom or Dad knows. This makes the parent superior and in control. It may sound illogical, but whether these feelings are correct or not makes no difference. They are real!

MIXED MESSAGES FROM MOM AND DAD. "Not until you're married!" "When you meet someone special and fall in love." "Don't worry. You'll know when it is the right time." These are typical words of wisdom from parents to teens.

"Not until you're married" is usually clear-cut, until the teen discovers that Mom or Dad didn't follow that rule, or Mom or Dad can't give reasons for waiting until marriage. There is also a major glitch in this recommendation for the gay youth.

"When you meet someone special and fall in love" is a tough one. Teens fall in and out of love frequently. Does this mean that when two people are in love, sex is a way of expressing true love? A parent might come back with "That's just puppy love or infatuation." So what is the difference between love and infatuation? Guess what? You lose! Sure, you can find all kinds of people who can tell you the differences between love and infatuation. You might be able to come up with a few goodies yourself, but when you are in love or infatuated, you experience the same emotions. Both bring very strong and very real feelings of passion. (If you would like to know how I deal with this situation, read the chapter "Love, Love, Love!")

"Don't worry. You'll know when it is the right time" is a beauty. A teen will not know for sure when it is the right time any more than an older person will. The teen will either follow his or her emotions or listen to someone else say when it is the right time.

To be fair, teen wariness is not the only source of poor communication about sexuality. Parental perceptions and feelings also play an important role. The role of parenting can be a 24-hours-per-day, 365-days-per-year, heartbreaking, acid-in-your-stomach, pain-in-your-forehead, tremor-in-your-hands, hair-losing, life-shortening, thankless, "What did I ever do to deserve this" adventure. Yet most would agree that it is one of the most gratifying undertakings in life. One thing is for certain: as special and as wonderful as parents are, we are human, complete with unique personalities, hang-ups, quirks, and the need to be self-actualized individuals.

Parents have the full-time job of raising a young person to be a responsible, self-sufficient, well-adjusted adult. Most parents today also have another full-time job, which is their means of supporting their first full-time job. But there is a problem here. Guess which job comes with job training, guidelines for correct and superior performance, frequent reviews, positive feedback and support from coworkers, gratitude for good service, promotions, and something tangible to bank at the end of the week for a job well done? It's not parenting. Yet most would agree that parenting is much more difficult than the forty-, fifty-, or sixty-hour-per-week career at the office.

Parents don't get a training manual with easy steps to nurture another person. Even after centuries of parenting, there is still no concrete, works-100-percent-of-the-time formula for success. There are so many things to be responsible for that the topic of sexuality may not be a high priority when food, shelter, and clothing are daily concerns. Nor is the topic of sexuality an easy one to bring up to young people whom you may not see as often as you would like. Here are a few of the problems parents may have:

PARENTAL DISCOMFORT. Parents may not be comfortable discussing sex with young people, or any other people for that matter. How parents were raised and how their parents dealt with sexuality may influence how comfortable parents feel in discussing sexuality.

Many times parents might not be comfortable because they don't quite remember how everything works. Sometimes it is difficult for parents to say "I don't know." Rather than take a chance of being in that situation, parents may choose to stay quiet. Sometimes parents may feel that if they get stumped on a question they will somehow be admitting that they are not the all-knowing, all-powerful wonder machines that their teens know and love.

Most parents, when they get involved in speaking with their teen about sexuality, do a decent job of explaining what happens to the body during puberty, childbirth, and menstruation. The actual act of intercourse and contraception are often sensitive issues for older people to explain, but most of the time, both parents and teens muddle through without any serious embarrassment.

The tough ones for most parents are the "why?" questions, detailed questions, and questions using today's street lingo. It may have been many years since a parent received information on sexuality—if any at all was taught. There is no shame in not remembering all or any of the details. In fact, if a person had to try and explain history, geometry, or chemistry to someone, he or she probably couldn't do it unless he or she works directly with the topic each day. Parents certainly don't want their teens to know that they don't remember something this important.

THINKING TEENS ALREADY KNOW ABOUT SEXUALITY. Parents may tell this to themselves to avoid the subject, and they may honestly believe it. Remember that nine times out of ten, young people don't know much of anything about sexuality. Often they have questions.

ASSUMING THEY'LL PICK IT UP IN SCHOOL. While this is true in most schools, to rely on the school system and teachers to do a superior job is a mistake. In all fairness, I should say I have observed many sexuality education classes that have had outstanding instructors who have done a beautiful job and certainly are a credit to the profession. If I were to make an assumption, I would say the sexuality education that most teens receive is fair to good, and, at the very least, better than nothing at all, which is what many teens get at home. While some parent/teen relationships are not conducive to open communication about sexuality, no one should be blamed. Still, the topic of sexuality is an important one and critical in the development of a young person.

A fifteen-minute talk on the birds and the bees at home does not constitute significant education. Nor does one day or one week in school studying the male and female reproductive systems count as very much. It is like going to a car dealership where the dealer says, "Yes, folks, this here is a red Toyota—it has four wheels, four doors, brakes, a steering wheel, and a stereo," and walks away. You will probably want to know more about the car than just the parts. How does it work? How does it handle? What's the gas mileage? What kind of care does it require? How long should it last?

Sexuality education also requires more than just the identification of parts. Each person's sexuality is an evolutionary process constructed of biological urges, emotions, self-awareness, factual knowledge, morals, family values, societal norms and taboos, cultural influences, self-worth and self-esteem, and the ability to communicate—to name just a few of the many components. How can any one source, be it a parent, guardian, or school, provide complete sexual preparation for a young person? Ideally, a combination is best.

Most schools attempt to provide the factual knowledge a young person needs, while leaving the moral preparation and enrichment to the home. Schools are not able to provide, nor do they attempt to give, what parents provide. To rely solely on schools to deliver the entire package would be short-sighted. Young people need the synergy of both parents and schools to increase their chances of success.

Sexual intercourse can be a beautiful, exciting, loving, and sharing experience. It is a primal urge that swells within us and is a necessity for human survival. However, as wonderful as intercourse and intimacy can be, with them come potential consequences that can alter one's life negatively or even destroy it. This book attempts to explain the many facets of the topic. This information was not written to replace the parent's and school's roles in sexuality education, but to supplement and complement them.

If this book can increase sexuality knowledge and awareness while displacing street myths and anxiety in teens, then my efforts have been worthwhile. Ideally, this book will create emotional awareness that will help prepare a young person to meet the challenges of the intense feelings and situations that he or she will experience.

Although the pressures of our media and culture exert a strong force in the decision-making process of our young people, their knowledge, emotional awareness, understanding, and confidence can empower them to make sound choices in their lives. I hope that this book will help provide teens with these necessary tools.

Bibliography

"Abortion Clinics under Siege." *Contemporary Sexuality,* AASECT Newsletter 27, no. 11 (November 1993): 4.

"AIDS without H.I.V." *Contemporary Sexuality,* AASECT Newsletter 26, no. 9 (September 1992): 7.

"American Youth at Risk." *Contemporary Sexuality,* AASECT Newsletter 25, no. 10 (October 1991): 1–2.

"Barriers to Better Condom 'Killing People': Regulatory, Political Hurdles to Development." *Contraceptive Technology Update* 16, no. 1 (January 1995): 1–6.

Barth, Richard, et al. "Preventing Adolescent Pregnancy with Social and Cognitive Skills." *Journal of Adolescent Research* 7, no. 2 (April 1992): 208–232.

Brody, J. "Guidelines for Parents of Teen-agers Who Are, or Are About to Be, Sexually Active." *New York Times.* 30 April 1986. Personal Health Column.

Carabasi, J., W. Greene, and F. Bernt. "Preliminary Findings from the Survey About AIDS for Seventh and Eighth Graders (SASEG)." *AIDS Education and Prevention* 4, no. 3 (Fall 1992): 240–250.

Cassell, C. *Straight from the Heart.* N.Y.: Simon and Schuster, 1988.

Cullins, V. "The Adolescent's First Gynecologic Examination." *Medical Aspects of Human Sexuality* (November 1991): 56–59.

"Depo-Provera Approved." *Contemporary Sexuality,* AASECT Newsletter 26, no. 12 (December 1992): 8.

Eisen, M., et al. "Evaluating the Impact of a Theory Based Sexuality and Contraceptive Education Program." *Family Planning Perspectives* (November/December 1990): 261–271.

"Female Condom Approved." *Contemporary Sexuality,* AASECT Newsletter 27, no. 6 (June 1993): 11.

Gale, J. *A Parent's Guide to Teenage Sexuality.* N.Y.: Henry Holt and Company, 1989.

Gale, J. *A Young Man's Guide to Sex.* Los Angeles: The Body Press, 1988.

Gale, J., and J. Voss. *A Young Woman's Guide to Sex.* Los Angeles: The Body Press, 1986.

"Genetic Link Found for Male Homosexuality." *Contemporary Sexuality,* AASECT Newsletter 27, no. 9 (September 1993): 9.

Glenn, H., and J. Nelson. *Raising Self-Reliant Children in a Self-Indulgent World.* Rocklin, Calif.: Prima Publishing and Communications, 1989.

Haas, Kurt, and Adelaide Haas. *Understanding Sexuality.* Third Edition. Mosby, 1993.

Hatcher, Robert A., et al. *Contraceptive Technology.* Sixteenth Revised Edition. Irvington Publishers Inc., 1994.

Jacobson, B., S. Aldana, and T. Beaty. "Adolescent Sexual Behavior and Associated Variables." *Journal of Health Education* (January/February 1994): 10–12.

Kieren, D., and J. Morse. "Preparation Factors and Menstrual Attitudes of Pre- and Post Menarcheal Girls." *Journal of Sex Education and Therapy* 18, no. 3 (Fall 1992): 155–174.

King, B., and P. Anderson. "A Failure of H.I.V Education: Sex Can Be More Important Than a Long Life." *Journal of Health Education* (January/February 1994): 13–18.

Levy, S., et al. "Young Adolescent Attitudes toward Sex and Substance Use: Implications for AIDS Prevention." *AIDS Education and Prevention* 5, no. 4 (Winter 1993): 340–351.

Madaras, L. *The What's Happening to My Body? Book for Boys.* N.Y.: New Market Press, 1988.

Madaras, L. *The What's Happening to My Body? Book for Girls.* N.Y.: New Market Press, 1988.

Masters, W., and V. Johnson. *Human Sexual Response.* N.Y.: Bantam Books, 1986.

Masters, W., V. Johnson, and R. Kolodny. *Human Sexuality.* N.Y.: HarperCollins, 1992.

"New Condom." *Contemporary Sexuality,* AASECT Newsletter 27, no. 10 (October 1993): 4.

"One in Four" (Americans will contract an STD in his/her lifetime). *Contemporary Sexuality,* AASECT Newsletter 27, no. 5 (May 1993): 1.

Profet, M. "A New View of Menstruation." *Contemporary Sexuality,* AASECT Newsletter 27, no. 11 (November 1993): 4.

"Risking the Future: Adolescent Sexuality, Pregnancy, and Childbearing." *National Research Council, National Academy of Sciences* 1 (1987): 141–323.

Rosenthal, T., et al. "Teenage Pregnancy: Dating and Sexual Attitudes." *Journal of Sex Education and Therapy* 18, no. 4 (Winter 1992): 264–276.

Rosenthal, T., et al. "Teenage Pregnancy: Predicting the Adolescent at Risk." *Journal of Sex Education and Therapy* 18, no. 4 (Winter 1992): 277–285.

Rosenthal, T., D. Muram, E. Tolley, and J. McAlpine. "Teenage Pregnancy: A Small Comparison Group of Known Mothers." *Journal of Sex Education and Therapy* 19, no. 4 (Winter 1993): 246–250.

"RU 486 Used as Morning After Pill." *Contemporary Sexuality,* AASECT Newsletter 26, no. 11 (November 1992): 6–7.

"School Clinics to Offer Norplant." *Contemporary Sexuality,* AASECT Newsletter 27, no. 1 (January 1993): 7.

"Sexual Harassment Is Rampant in School Hallways." *Contemporary Sexuality,* AASECT Newsletter 27, no. 7 (July 1993): 7.

Sly, D., et al. "Young Children's Awareness, Knowledge, and Beliefs about AIDS: Observations from a Pretest." *AIDS Education and Prevention* 4, no. 3 (Fall 1992): 227–239.

Soper, D. "The Female Condom." *Medical Aspects of Human Sexuality* 26, no. 1 (January 1992): 14.

"Study of Lesbian Twins Points to Genetic Basis for Sexual Orientation." *Contemporary Sexuality,* AASECT Newsletter 27, no. 5 (May 1993): 7.

"Tablets End Injections for Abortion Pill." *Contemporary Sexuality,* AASECT Newsletter 27, no. 7 (July 1993): 7.

Tannahill, R. *Sex in History.* Scarborough House, 1992.

Taylor, M., et al. "Effects of Contraceptive Education on Adolescent Male Contraceptive Behavior and Attitudes." *Journal of Health Education* (April/May 1989): 12–17.

"Teenage Girls Have More Sex Partners." *Contemporary Sexuality,* AASECT Newsletter 27, no. 2 (February 1993): 7.

"Teenage Sexual and Reproductive Behavior." *Facts in Brief.* The Alan Guttmacher Institute, 1993.

"The Truth about Latex Condoms." *SEICUS Report* 22, no. 1 (October/November 1993): 17–19.

"Ulcer Drug Used for Abortions in Brazil." *Contemporary Sexuality,* AASECT Newsletter 27, no. 7 (July 1993): 6.

U.S. Congress, Office of Technology Assessment. "Adolescent Health, Volume II: Background and the Effectiveness of Selected Prevention and Treatment Services." Washington, D.C: U.S Government Printing Office, November 1991: 333-427.

"Will Your Clients Want the Plastic Condom?" *Contraceptive Technology Update* 16, no. 1 (January 1995): 6–9.

"With Proper Diet and Exercise, You Can Take Control of PMS!" *Contraceptive Technology Update Supplement* 16, no. 1 (January 1995).

Yates, A., and W. Wolman. "Aphrodisiacs—Myth and Reality." *Medical Aspects of Human Sexuality* (December 1991): 58–64.

Zabin, Laurie, et al. "Evaluation of a Pregnancy Prevention Program for Urban Teenagers." *Family Planning Perspectives* (May/June 1986): 119–126.

Index